THE ART OF LOVE

*

OVID

PUBLIUS OVIDIUS NASO

Translated by
CHARLES D. YOUNG
Together with the ELEGIES
translated by
CHRISTOPHER MARLOWE

*

Horace Liveright Inc., New York

MADE IN THE UNITED STATES OF AMERICA

CONTENTS

Introduction _____ vii

The Art of Love

    Book One _____ 15

    Book Two _____ 43

    Book Three _____ 69

Love's Remedy _____ 97

The Art of Beauty _____ 125

The Loves

    Book One _____ 133

    Book Two _____ 161

    Book Three _____ 191

Ovid's Elegies

    Book One _____ 225

    Book Two _____ 257

    Book Three _____ 289

Publius Ovidius Naso was born at Sulmo, a town of the Paeligni, on March 20th, in the year 43 B. C. His family had been of equestrian rank for several generations, and Ovid studied rhetoric with a view of obtaining some public post. In company with his brother, he visited Rome and Athens; but much to the chagrin of his father, Ovid showed strong inclinations towards poesy. The elder Naso viewed an artistic career as a proverbially precarious one, and he exercised considerable suasion to make the poet into a barrister. After the death of his brother, which occurred when Ovid was only nineteen, his father seems to have relented somewhat, and Ovid was permitted to devote himself to his muse. He did in fact declaim with considerable applause in the forum and he recalls in some of his poems his apprenticeship at law. But more frequently he refers to the beauty and lush verdure of his native Sulmo, whose fertile fields were the background of his childhood.

His poetic compositions were sophisticated and dexterously put together, and earned for him a justly high reputation. He was a man of society and partook with considerable delight in the elegant delights of the capital. His books bear ample testimony that he was well acquainted with the cunning subterfuges of the polite world, and in many instances he proves himself a master not only of the art of loving but of living as well. It is due to some fashionable intrigue, the exact nature of which is subject to many conjectures, that the gregarious and pleasure-loving poet was eventually banished to Tomi, an obscure town in what constitutes present day Bulgaria. His banishment did not entail a loss of property or citizenship but his sufferings in the distant hamlet on the Black Sea have been recorded in the *Epistulae ex Ponto* and the *Tristia,* two poems in the nature of laments which he composed during his exile.

The most common assumption for the cause of his banishment has been the somewhat lascivious nature of his Love Books, whose corrupting influence seems to have been feared by Augustus. But Ovid himself implies that there were other reasons, and indeed it appears implausible that he should have been punished so rigorously years after his works had been written and disseminated. Among the most likely explanations is the one which credits him with having involved himself with Julia, the profligate daughter of Augustus, and of having fallen the eventual victim of her rancor. Judging the poet's character by his own testimony, it seems feasible that he knew a good many polite secrets of the court, and he may have merited his doleful exile by some whimsicality disconcerting to Caesar.

Ovid was married three times and divorced twice. His third wife was a member of one of the oldest and most distinguished families of Rome, and a certain relationship of esteem and affection seems to have existed between himself and his spouse until the very end. One daughter was the sole fruit of their union. The poet languished at Tomi without returning to his beloved Rome, and died there in the year 18 A. D., at the age of sixty-one.

His literary activity lasting over a period of forty years is generally divided into three groups: the love poems, consisting of the *Loves,* the *Heroines,* the *Art of Beauty,* the *Art of Love,* and *Love's Remedy;* the *Fasti* and the *Metamorphoses;* the *Tristia* and *Epistulae ex Ponto.*

With this new translation such liberties have been taken as seemed consonant with a perfect understanding for some of the more obscure allusions of the poet. A rendering in prose is of necessity less circumscribed, and the translator has in no case abridged or transmogrified the original. This represents to the best of our knowledge the first complete translation by an American into prose, and if the work thus humbly and reverently submitted to the reader is not entirely without merit, we too may say, "Ovid was our master."

CHARLES D. YOUNG.

New York, 1930.

THE ART OF LOVE

BOOK ONE

I F art and cunning are required for the sailing of ships, for the steering of swift chariots, it will become you well to listen to me and guide yourself by my advice on Love. Tiphys was a sailor of the good ship Argo and safely he steered his fragile bark. It is my desire to be another Tiphys adroitly piloting your Love boat. Automedon was a daring skillful charioteer whose capable manipulation controlled the fiery, willful steeds. I shall aspire to be known as the Automedon of Love, appointed to this task especially by Venus. Frequently, Love is unruly, but being a boy, gentle influences can be brought to bear upon his rude tempers. Chiron softened the robust nature of his pupil Achilles by the subtle and pacific strains of music. This mighty warrior, before whose fearful prowess great armies were destined to tremble, who frequently struck terror and amazement into the hearts of his own soldiers, was ever gentle and polite when he heard his tutor's voice, and held out to him on many occasions those hands that crushed the mighty Hector.

Chiron was the teacher of Achilles; I am the teacher of Love: dangerous pupils both and both of them born of the gods. But as the fiery horse eventually consents to bear the bit and the ferocious bull submits beneath the yoke, so Love shall learn to bow beneath my curbing hand. This will be no easy, casual task. Well do I know that I shall become a target for his arrows, and that the flames from his torch are likely to sear my locks. These wounds shall not deter me from my purpose. They will make my vengeance more complete and his conquest more secure.

I do not rely upon the help of Clio nor the whispered advice and consolation of Apollo. No bird has secretly imparted important news of stratagems. Naught have I to guide me but my own experience and wisdom. I am no shepherd tending to his herds in the vales of Ascra but a man who truly knows the things he sings.

The love of which I sing does not trespass on the laws. I shall not lead you into shame or treachery. Listen attentively, you who are novices at this game, and it shall go well with you.

First, remember to choose carefully the woman you will set your heart upon; second, you must secure her submission; third, you must perpetuate her attachment to you. This is my entire syllabus and text.

Needless to emphasize, it will take effort to find the woman of your fancy; no passing zephyr will casually deposit her in your lap. You must use your head. The hunter spreads his net for stag and boar, the fowler studies well the habits of his prey, and carefully the fisher baits his hook. You, too, aspiring to a lasting love, study carefully the haunts and promenades of your potential paramour. No great hardships will impose themselves upon you: there are no seas to be crossed and no battles to be fought.

Perseus fetched his bride from torrid Indian climes

and Paris sought his precious frail in Sparta. You need not deviate so far in search of beauty, which well abounds in all the streets of Rome. Numberless as the stars in the high heavens, as the grapes in Methymna, as the corn on Gargarus, and as the fish in the sea, are the ravishing faces in Rome. If you prefer the ungainly grace of green young striplings, or crave the lush flamboyant charms of fullbodied maturity, or have a weakness for something between these two extremes, you need not be troubled by a lack of choice to glut your appetite. Stroll any evening in the shade of Pompey's portico when the summer sun is just about to set, or pass the wall embossed with foreign marbles, and surely your greedy eyes will have their fill. Also, you will be well repaid if you visit the colonnade which is called the portico of Livia, upon whose walls you will see the Danaides, conspiring the death of their doomed cousins. You must not miss the festival of Adonis nor the weekly celebrations of the Syrian Jews. Mingle freely with the crowds at public gatherings, even if the occasion be a matter of law in the forum, for all places are equally propitious for Love. At the stone basin near the shrine of Venus, where the Appian water flows, many a lawyer has been trapped in Love's snare. Frequently, he who with great circumspection defends his client, makes but a poor attorney for himself; and great orators are at a loss for words in such a pass. There he stands, the great advocate, caught in a snare that will not yield to argument or persuasion, and from the nearby temple there sometimes seems to echo the triumphant laughter of Venus. But the most auspicious place for your researches is undoubtedly the theater. How many women you will find here, for the fancy of a moment, for the entertainment of a night or the love of a lifetime. Like ants that march in legions upon their predatory quest, like bees bearing sweet burdens in swarms from flower to flower, gay throngs of women crowd the theaters, ostensibly to see the play. Sometimes it is difficult to choose in this bewildering galaxy of gay frocks and faces. Surely this is the last place where virtue grows luxuriant.

Romulus set a pleasant precedent for public amours when he beguiled the Sabine ladies to become the paramours of his bachelor army. The theater in those rugged days was bare of curtains and marble pilasters. The stage was innocent of the red of liquid saffron and its only adornment was branches from the woods of Palatine. The audience sat upon unyielding turf and lacked our subtle refinements.

Each Roman, once settled in his place, cast about for some comely dame to rest his gaze upon. While the actors, in untutored mimicry, stamped about, and the spectators were noisily applauding, their chief shouted a warning signal, and all the men arose. Like eagles falling on their prey, each man swooped down upon his choice, whose frightened cries set the very earth atremble. As the young lamb paralyzed with fear stands shivering at the approach of the unrelenting wolf, the Sabine women cowered before the band of warriors. Some swooned, some shrieked, some shuddered and some wept; one group stood silent, stupefied with fright; some tried to run and some prepared to fight. But the doughty Romans, undeterred by any qualm of pity, carried them all off, sweet victims for their bed. Some one or two, fiercely fighting to free themselves from the embraces of their rude seducers, would hear this whispered in their ears: "Be not in dread of me, my fair one, for I shall be to you whate'er your father has been, when he and your dear mother were in bed."

Our Romulus knew well how to reward an army. No soldiers in our day have had such luck, for if they had, each citizen of Rome would join the ranks. But ever since those days the theater has seemed a fitting trap for every sort of loveliness.

Remember, also, the arena, where well matched steeds strain for the palm of glory. How favorable is this crowded place for Love! Here it is unnecessary to signal by mysterious signs or practice any sort of doubtful mimicry. Sit close beside your loved one; the stalls are narrow, so she cannot prevent that you accidentally brush against her; the closeness of the place makes her acquiescence utterly unnecessary. There is one thing you must keep steadily in mind: sitting beside her will avail you little unless you know how to start a conversation. Begin, let us say, with the usual banalities reserved for such occasions. A horse has entered the arena, this is your chance to ask the name of its owner. Whichever color she favors in the races becomes automatically your own. When the solemn procession of the gods and goddesses passes your stall, arise and give a cheer for Venus. You must manage poorly indeed if you cannot espy some disfiguring speck of dust upon her bosom. Flick it off with a delicate gesture and an appropriate disclaimer for her gratitude. But if the dust will somehow fail to settle and you descry no blemish, flick it off nevertheless; for any pretext to serve her must be dragged in by the hair if necessary. If the train of her garments drags in the dust, lift it up and caution her. You might by chance be permitted a fleeting glimpse at her leg. Be careful who sits behind you; let no rough knee be digging in her shoulder blades. These seemingly trifles have a cumulative value. Many a conquest has been made by the careful arrangement of a cushion, or the adroit management of a fan. A stool produced at the right moment has achieved miracles. Don't doubt that the circus and the forum are ideal places for the commencement of a love affair. Love comes here for many a trial of strength and many an innocent bystander is wounded. Many a man has asked a fair one for a glimpse of her racing card, has bet his money on the horse of her choice and has been struck by an arrow before he knew who won the race.

Why, it happened only recently, when Caesar produced his famous sea maneuver showing the Persian and Athenian ships in action. Of all the thousands that foregathered in our city to view the spectacle, how many, think you, remained untouched by a foreign flame carried in some woman's eyes?

And even now, Caesar prepares to conquer all the world. He will subjugate the arrogant Parthians and plant our flags in many alien lands. The Crassi in their graves shall be avenged. Do not fear, in counting out his years, how much too young he is for this great task, for he is a man whose prowess belies time. The infant Hercules strangled two serpents in his cradle, proving himself a worthy son of Jove. Genius forever trespasses upon the limits set by common expectation and rises unexpectedly to such tasks as would baffle meager minds. Thus did Bacchus, suffused with youthful fire, subdue the whole of dusky India. An aura of great promise lies about your brow, Caesar, and with the courage inherited from your sire, you will conquer and subdue our foes. It will be fitting that you conquer in honor of the name you bear. Now you are a prince of youths; erelong you will be prince of the elders as well. Being a brother, it behooves you to avenge your brothers; being a son, you must defend your father's rights. You are armed by your father, your country's father, in this unequal fray against a foeman who undutifully seized a scepter from the hand of his own parent. Your sacred sword is bound to triumph against a perjured Parthian foe. Your arms shall smite him, and to the wealth of Latium, you will add the glory and the riches of the Orient. O father Caesar, father Mars, one a god, the other soon to be, guide him successfully in all his wars! My keen prophetic eye discerns the future well, and I can clearly see that you will conquer. And I shall sing your praises in verses consecrated to your fame. Grant that my poem be deserving of the victories it celebrates. I will chant of the cowardly Parthian fleeing from Roman courage, and of your brave legions calmly facing the arrows of your enemies.

The day is not too distant when, robed in unheard of splendor and drawn by four white horses, you will enter this city. Leading the train before you there shall pass your vanquished enemies, each of them burdened with chains which will prevent them from seeking safety in flight as they have been successful in doing once before. The hearts of all assembled to behold your glory shall be overflowing with happiness.

And you, my pupil, as the cavalcade is passing, perchance you will be standing near some fair and curious damsel who is likely to inquire the name of this and that now conquered rebel king, what country or what mountain he originates from. Then answer civilly her questions and render an account of birthplaces and extractions. Elucidate the meaning of the emblems, standards, weapons, garb and gait, and tell what rivers cross each country, and any other matter pertinent to the occasion. Speak confidently, like a man of parts who is well acquainted with these mundane matters. If you know naught about these things, speak confidently none the less. "That one with his crown of reeds is Euphrates; the other old one, with blue hair, is Tigris; those people are Armenians; and there's a Persian—that's the place where Danae's son was born. Those people over yonder come from the vales of Achaemenes, and that group on the other side are captured generals." And if you really know their names, then mention them; and if you don't, invent them.

Other auspicious places that furnish ready access to a woman's favor are dinners and large festivals. Remember that besides the food the wine is frequently a lover's best assistant. When cupid's wings are drenched with wine, he oft grows drowsy and will not stir. But once he's roused, he shakes off the superfluous moisture, sprinkling those around him, and strange is the behavior of those upon whom the dew of Bacchus is thus sprinkled. The pauper fancies that he is rich, bellows at caution and carelessly throws his limbs about. The wrinkled brow unfurls and the calloused heart softens. Truth wells suddenly upon the lips that practise craft and cunning. Love and wine go well together, feeding fuel to the fire, clouding the critical faculties and making all things seem what they are not. If you truly want to know the why and wherefore of her lips, by all means see her then by daylight and when you are sober. It was thus, beneath a radiant sky, that Paris said to Venus: "You are far lovelier than your two rivals."

The sable mantle of the night covers a multitude of blemishes; in fact, there are no ugly women in the night time. If you examine rare cloths and precious jewels, you choose the sunlight. Let it be thus with women.

It is difficult to make a list of places where the woman hunt can be carried on favorably, for these places are as numerous as the sands in the sea. I suggest Baiae, famed for its hot sulphur springs, with white sails gleaming on the horizon. Many a bather, who has gone there for a cure, comes away saying, "Those precious baths are not so healthy as I thought." Not far outside Rome, there is the temple of Diana, beneath whose trees many a youth and maiden have fought a battle of Love. The chaste Diana has frequently avenged herself for these trespasses—and will frequently avenge herself in the future.

I have been content thus far to advise you where and how to seek your love. Now I am prepared to tell you the means of captivating and holding her. I will insist that this is the most difficult and important of all my teachings. So harken to me, lovers of every land and clime, for I am ready to redeem my promises.

Before all else, make up your mind that there is no woman alive who cannot be won, and then decide quite definitely that you are the man to win her. Only, you must be careful to prepare the soil. It is more likely that the birds would stop singing in the spring, the grasshopper sit sullen and silent in the summer or the hare pursue the hound, than a woman overlook the ardent wooing of a young lover. You may believe she does not want you. You are mistaken. Deep within her heart she wants to yield. Man is naturally a very poor dissembler. Woman, just as naturally, is the very born actress and artificer. If we all should decide not to make advances to women, soon enough the lot of them would be beneath our feet. Out in the dew-drenched meadow the love-sick heifer lows and languishes for the bull and the mare whinnies at sight of the stallion. With us Love is less obvious and passion less unbridled; we keep within the bounds of decorum. For instance, there was Byblis who conceived an incestuous affection for her brother, and hung herself to neutralize her shame. There was a certain Myrrha who had a more than filial affection for her father and now her crime is covered by bark: she has become a tree, and her tender tears exhale a delicate perfume that recalls to us her tragic story.

In the shady valleys of Ida there roamed in majestic aloofness a white bull of unparalleled beauty. Between his horns there was a single black spot and this merely emphasized the exquisite pallor of his coat. And as he passed, the love-sick heifers of Gnossus and Cydonia longed for his caresses. But more than all these, more than the youngest and most frolicsome among the cows, Pasiphae, the queen, loved him with a great and fierce passion. And Crete, rich and powerful though she be, aye, and a great liar to boot, has never dared to deny it. The love-sick Pasiphae bruised her delicate hands to tear fresh leaves and young branches from her garden, and gathered grass and sweet blades of all sorts for the white bull. Over the hills and dales her longing gaze pursued him. She disdained her spouse, and would have given all the fair lot of Minos could she have been born a member of the herd, with horns upon her brow. Despairingly, she gazed at her soft ringlets in the mirror which gave back but the reflection of a woman. Her adulterous dreams centered around the snowy quadruped —and great was the shame of the king. At night she fled his lawful embraces and pursued her paramour through forest and dell, like a mad Bacchante, tormented by her restless spirit. Fierce jealousy would rack her at sight of some fair heifer and she wondered how the ungainly brute found favor in his sight. Her rage would prompt her to decapitate the hapless beast or else she would banish it to bear the yoke. Many an innocent and soft-eyed cow was served an offering upon the altar of the gods, and afterwards the queen would gruesomely bury her fingers in the steaming entrails of her expired rival. She would dream of being Europa or Io, because the one was borne away on the back of a bull, while the other had been a heifer. And when her lust had grown too powerful, she threw all caution to the winds and had some cunning artisan construct a cow of maple wood, all hollowed out inside. Therein the queen did then secrete herself, and the king of the herd performed with her the culminating act of love. The offspring of this union, part bull, part man, betrayed her gruesome lechery, and the world had proof of her great shame.

There was another girl in Crete who, unable to forego her passion for Thyestes, compelled Phoebus to halt his steeds and to drive his chariot back into the night. The daughter of Nisus stole a lock from her father's hair and is the victim now of ever-ravening dogs. The son of Atreus came safely out of battlefield and ocean to perish beneath the dagger of his wife. There, too, is Medea, hands stained by the blood of her children, and Phoenix, weeping from sightless sockets.

These are a few examples of woman's uncontrollable passion. It is ten times fiercer than ours and full of madness. So be of good faith and you cannot fail. Not one in ten thousand will offer resistance. But whether she grants or withholds her favors she will be flattered that you asked her for them. And even if she repulses you definitely, you have run no risks,—and besides, why should she refuse? One does not struggle against new pleasures. We always envy other people and think their crops are better than ours.

The best thing to do is to make friends with her maid. She can be very helpful. Find out how her mistress treats her, whether she is in her confidence, and discover, if possible, some secret sordidness or dissipation. This is very important: you must win the maid. Once this is accomplished, all else will be easy. Let her keep you posted about what is the most favorable time for her mistress to be persuaded and when your solicitations will have a fair chance of success. When, due to some fortuitous set of circumstances, she is feeling particularly gay and sprightly, and her heart is a-flutter like summer butterflies, it is then that Love can climb gently but deeply into the folds of her consciousness. When Ilion was drowned in sorrow, her warriors staved off the Greeks, but when she rejoiced and danced and made merry, she received within her walls the treacherously freighted horse that proved her undoing. Another time

26

THE ART OF LOVE

auspicious for attack is when your fair one has been troubled by the insults of some rival. Permit her to use you as a means of revenge. Tell the maid that, in the morning, when she dresses the hair of your charmer, she suggest tactfully and deftly that you be the means of paying him out in his own coin. Let her report some tittle-tattle regarding your bravery, your riches, or your bearing, and let her press your suit without delay, for woman's anger lasts but a little while and you must use the time.

As to the maid herself, if she prove sprightly and a likely wench, is it advisable to win her first? A difficult and treacherous position! At times it goads their zeal; at times it quite defeats your purpose. She might promote your case to serve you and your mistress; also, she might want to keep you for herself. You will have to try and see what happens. My advice to you is: *don't.* Stick close to me and I promise I'll lead you safely through and bring you to the right road and success. If, however, you are so completely fetched by the charms of the baggage that you can't resist her pretty ways, then win the mistress first and afterwards devote yourself to gain the maid. But don't be satisfied merely to play around. You have got to see it through right to the end or else you're lost; for if the girl herself is involved deeply enough she won't tattle about you. The bird with clipped wings will not soar high. The time to talk to fish is when they are on the hook. So take my advice and don't rest until you have conquered all and made her a companion in your treachery. For then she will tell you all about your mistress. Remember to be careful.

There is a strange conception abroad that the change
of seasons is a matter of concern solely to farmers and
fishermen. That's a mistake. There is a time to sow and
a time to sail and certainly a time to start up with a girl.
Nine-tenths of success depends on the choice of the
proper moment. Be careful of her birthday; beware the
Ides of March. Don't start when there are specially big
shows at the circus. Ah, how you will be washed ashore
then, clinging to a spar, and howling for aid! The best
time to begin, as I see it, would be on the anniversary of
the day when Roman blood was spilt into the waters of
the Allia, or on Saturday, when the Syrian Jews will do
no work. But chiefly, you must remember not to dare
go near her on her birthday, or any other day when she
will expect a present from you. It will be useless for you
to sigh or pretend; you will have to buy her something.
They all know how to exploit a guileless lover. Some
unexpected wretch of a pedlar is bound to turn up at
the right moment and she is sure to find, since shopping
is a malady of hers, the very thing she has been looking
for for months. It will be useless to insist that what
she wants is so much garbage; she will insist that she
has longed for it and wanted it since she was knee-high.
It will be purposeless to admit that you have no money
with you; you will merely be asked to make out a check,
and you will curse the day you learned how to write. Re-
member there is a birthday every year; in fact, there will
be a birthday every time she wants something special
from you. Ever so often she will come around and tell
you she lost something; her eyes will be red with weep-
ing, and when you will ask what's wrong, she will blub-
ber out that one of her favorite earrings has disappeared.

Ah, what a game it is, my friend! They will ask you to lend them money. What your chances are to get it back I will not trouble to elucidate. If I had ten mouths and ten tongues, I could not begin to tell you all the tricks that they are up to.

In the beginning, I would suggest that you write her a letter. Tell her you are wild about her; throw in a few compliments; if necessary, plead with her. Achilles was moved by the supplications of Priam; even the gods give way to the voice of entreaty. Above everything else, promise, promise, promise. Promises cost you nothing. You're a millionaire in promises. You can do wonders if Hope is carefully fostered. She's, of course, a deceitful goddess, but an uncommonly useful one. After you have given her something, she may throw you over. She will have had her show-down. It is infinitely better to make her think that you are about to give her something any minute now. But don't. Everyone knows the farmer who keeps on manuring his barren field in the vain hope that it will some day produce a crop, and the gambler who keeps throwing away his money in the hope of recouping his losses. I think the greatest problem that confronts a man and takes the most awful sort of skill is to make a woman love him without giving her a present. If you are successful in doing this, she will keep on being good to you so as not to lose all the balance of the favors she has already cast away upon you. So when you send your letter, remember to make it full of sweetness and promise. It should pave a roadway straight to her heart. A few scratches on an apple led young Cydippe astray and after she looked at them for a while she discovered that her own words had ensnared her.

Another thing, my fellow citizens, acquaint your-selves thoroughly in the fine arts but not merely to be the mouthpiece of some trembling protégé. The mob, the judges and those great people, the senators, are not the only ones that can be stirred by eloquence. Be care-ful: don't show your hand: don't be too eager. If you have great powers of speech, bide your time, and don't be too oratorical. Don't write to your mistress as though you were addressing a citizen's meeting. A letter either too witty or too glib may turn her against you. Be charm-ing but simple, as if you were talking to her. If your letter comes back unopened, don't worry; start all over again. The worst sort of bull can be made to bear the yoke and the most ructious colt can be taught to pull a chariot. Even iron is worn through by continuous fric-tion, and the plough makes naught of the hardness of the soil. Water wears away the hardness of the rocks; and if you are persistent and take your time, you can conquer even Penelope. Troy stood a long siege but it had to give in at last. If she has read your letter and hasn't answered, what of it? Write her another, and keep her reading. Some day she may answer; every-thing has its appointed time. She may write you to stop writing. In reality, she'll be trembling lest you obey her command. You go right on and nothing can stop you from having your heart's desire.

If you see her passing on a litter, go near her and talk at random in ambiguous terms as if you feared some one might overhear you. If she lounges through one of the arcades, join her. If she goes to the theater, dressed in the pink of style, make it your business to be there. Ad-mire her bare shoulders, let your eyes speak un-

ashamedly, let your gestures be supplicating. Applaud
the actor who takes the girl's part; applaud even more
when the lover appears on the stage. Pattern your
movements upon hers: sit when she's sitting, stand
when she's standing. Never mind the time; you have
other things to think of.

Under no circumstances have your hair curled, or
powder yourself. Such nonsense befits the effeminate
priests, who sing their Phrygian chants to the glory of
Cybele. Dress simply, for you are a man. Theseus won
Ariadne without worrying about his curls. Phaedra went
wild about Hippolytus who was anything but a fop.
Wash yourself, get tanned, wear clean clothes, take the
tartar from your teeth, and don't galumph about in shoes
that are three sizes too large for you. Don't neglect your
hair; and keep your beard reasonably trimmed. Cut
your nails and file them. Cut the hair from your nostrils
and see that your breath is not objectionable. In any case,
don't stagger around smelling to high heaven. Leave
the more subtle toilet refinements to females and
pederasts.

Ariadne, beating her breast, shattered the night with
woeful cries on the lonely shores of Naxos. Barely clad,
her fair hair tossed by the wind, she cried wildly for the
unfaithful Theseus, while the tears ran in torrents down
her cheeks. "What will become of me, what will be my
fate?" cried the unhappy maiden as she fell upon the
sands. Suddenly there came a sound of strange and eery
music; the beat of drums and cymbals came to her fright-
ened ears. The Maenads, with tangled hair, and swift-
footed Satyrs—the band that generally leads the proces-
sion of the vine-god—appeared upon the scene. Fat old

Silenus, barely able to keep his seat upon a staggering ass, pursues the Maenads, who evade him with mockery and laughter. Beating his long-eared beast with a huge staff, the unskillful rider only succeeds in tumbling from his steed. The air is filled with laughter and shouting of the Satyrs.

A lofty chariot appears upon the scene; the golden reins are held by the vine-bedecked Bacchus; a team of tigers draws the vehicle. The frightened Ariadne thrice attempts to flee but thrice she fails. "Fear not," says Bacchus, "I shall prove a lover far more faithful, tender and devoted than Theseus. Daughter of Minos, you will be my bride. Henceforth, your dwelling shall be in the sky; you are destined to be a new star, whose steadfastness will be a guide to sailors."

Then, leaping from his chariot lest the tigers should affright her, he clasped the fainting, unresisting maiden to his breast and bore her away. It is the privilege of gods to do as they will and there is no one to gainsay them. Loudly the nymphs cried "Hymenaee," and "Evoe" the satyrs cried, as Bacchus to his sacred bed now escorted his bride.

If by chance you attend a feast and some charming woman shares your couch, whisper a prayer to the god whose mysteries are celebrated at night, that the wine may not too deeply affect your brain. This is the time when you may easily discourse with your mistress in symbolic terms, the meaning of which will be obvious to her. A drop of wine upon your finger will enable you to draw strange devices on the table, wherein she can discern some proof of your affection. Let your looks bear out the message of these hieroglyphs; the language of the eyes can be uncommonly persuasive. When she has sipped from out her cup, then quickly seize her goblet and drink becomingly from the same spot that her lips have abandoned but a moment before. If she touches any food upon the common platter, lose no time in picking it for your own plate; and as you reach for it, your hand may softly brush hers.

Be polite to her husband. It is to your advantage that he be friends with you. If you play at dice and by chance you win the crown, disclaim the honor for his benefit. Take off your laurel wreath and place it smilingly upon his head. Dismiss all notions regarding his inferiority. See that he is invariably served before you; say nothing to him that might be unpleasant. You must strive to gain his friendship. Be careful, for you may go too far and overstep the boundaries of what serves your purpose best.

These are the limits that I would observe in drinking. If you imbibe too freely, you will befog your brain and your gait will be unsteady. Too much wine may make you quarrelsome and easy to take offense. Eurytion drank too much and died of it. Remember his sad fate. The food and wine are useful if they fill you with a modest and infectious gaiety. If you think you have a voice, sing; if your limbs are graceful, dance; in other words, move heaven and earth to make a pleasant impression. Drunkenness is always repulsive; but it may serve you to simulate a state of fierce inebriety. It may give you an opportunity to stammer out some cunning falsehoods which from a drunkard would be undoubtedly believed. Pretend to have great difficulty in pronouncing your words, so that in case your statements

33

have a slightly risky color, you will be excused for having imbibed too freely. Drink a toast to your mistress and a toast to the man who shares her bed. It is your privilege to curse him under your breath. When everyone rises from the table, you can look for an excuse to get close to her. If the opportunity offers, rub your foot against hers.

Let us say you have succeeded in getting hold of her and are free to talk in unrestrained terms. At this point, abandon all rustic modesty: fortune and Venus favor the doughty. I can no longer advise you what to say. Say anything at all in the beginning. The words will come fast enough by themselves after a while. Play the fierce lover; stake everything on the moment. Tell her how you longed for her. Don't worry, she will believe you. They all think themselves attractive in certain ways inimitably their own. The plainest thinks herself possessed of certain curious qualities and charms. It often happens that the hypocrite pretending to a passion that he does not feel eventually falls in love quite earnestly. Ah, my dear charmers, be indulgent with the false lover's airs, for shortly, without noticing, he may be in love in very earnest.

With flattery you are free to steal into any heart, even as the river imperceptibly trespasses upon the gently sloping shore. Sing paeans of praise to her face, her hair, her figure and her limbs. No woman is so cold, no girl so young and green, that she takes not pleasure in her looks. Remember, Juno and Minerva blushed when they failed to carry off the prize of loveliness within the woods of Ida. The prancing steed in the chariot race proudly displays his waving mane. Be bold in your praises and forward in your promises; they all love promises. You are free to swear by all the gods. Don't worry, for Jove looks down upon all lovers' treacheries and smiles benignly. He hands them to Aeolus as a plaything for the winds. He often swore to Juno he'd be faithful—and he always broke his vows. Let his brave example give you courage.

It is well for us that there are gods and we all should cherish them. Their altars should be filled with offerings, for the gods are omnipresent. Observe the dicta of religion with nicety, and disdain all fraud and subterfuge. You are free to practise deceit only upon women, but in all other matters let your word be your bond. In short, you are free to deceive deceivers. You may utilize the snares and traps of their own conniving.

When Egypt suffered from a drought that lasted nine continuous years, Thrasius came to Busiris and said, "Jove will be appeased and send you rain if you will shed a stranger's blood upon his altar." Then said the good Busiris, "You shall be the first victim offered to the god and we shall be indebted to you for the needful rain from heaven." Phalaris caused the fearful Perillus to be roasted within a brazen bull which he had made, and the cunning craftsman was the first to put his own handiwork to the test. Both these penalties were fair, for it seems no more than right that the contrivers of death should perish by their own devices. And as woman sets the fair example of willful treachery of every sort, it well becomes her to be served with treachery.

There is also the matter of tears: a very useful resource upon occasion. If you have quarreled, let her see you weep. Quite likely you will be unable to squeeze out anything when the occasion requires, for they don't always flow when you want them to. Have the presence of mind to poke a finger in your eye. Kisses are another matter of importance. She may refuse to be kissed; don't mind her in the least. She may struggle and cry out; do you persist nevertheless. Don't injure her or treat her brutally; be reasonably severe. And once you've kissed her, you can take the rest for granted, for if after that you don't succeed, you are not deserving of what you have already gained. Some women like force and struggle merely to be overcome. They like being hurt; they like to have the feeling of having been robbed of favors they would not consent to give. When they come out successful from a struggle, they may try to look pleased but they are furious at heart. Phoebe was raped and her sister Elaira likewise; they loved their ravishers nevertheless.

Here is an old story, but one that stills bears re-telling, of Achilles and the maid of Scyros. Venus had rewarded Paris for the homage he had paid her beauty at the foot of Mount Ida. As a result, a new daughter-in-law has come home to Priam, and, within the walls of Ilion, fair Helen dwells. The Greeks have joined the injured husband and are preparing to punish the affront. Meanwhile, Achilles, the descendant of Aeacus, was busying himself with a distaff, disguised in woman's clothing. What a task for a hero! What had he to do with work baskets. His arm was made to bear a shield; his hand to hold a javelin to lay great Hector low. Once Achilles and the princess shared the same bed chamber, and the fierce attack she suffered swiftly revealed the sex of her companion. We may believe she yielded to superior force; we know for certain that she was not angry that the force was superior. "Stay yet a-while," she said when he was eager to be gone, "stay yet a-while with me." And what is the proper term to describe adequately his violence, now that Deidamia retained with pleading tones her wild seducer near her bed?

Admittedly, it ill becomes a woman to make the first advances. Nevertheless, it is her privilege to yield with grace when once her lover has taken the initiative. Don't be too confident and trust in your good looks. It is not likely that she will fall around your neck unless you ask her. She is only waiting to be asked and it is fitting for you to do so. Jove loved many women in the olden times, yet none came to him unaccosted. It may be you strike one who will disdain your suit, for there are some females who like only what is beyond them. Pretend to be her friend, for friendship's just as good a road to Love as any other, and I have often seen it serve as such.

A sailor who looks ill and pale can hardly be a sailor. The salty spray, the burning sun, should give him rugged features. The farmer, working out of doors, should sport a well-tanned skin. It is the duty and privilege of lovers to look pale; it is the symptom of their malady. Your pallor will cause anxiety to your mistress and make her solicitous for your well-being. Daphnis was pale with love for the Naiad who ignored him; Orion, haunting the woods for Lyrice, was pale with anguish. Try to be thin if you can manage it, for this is another unfailing sign of deep affection. Sleepless nights will readily reduce your weight. Be not ashamed to wear a hood as if in mourning, for Pity is a helpmate not to be despised in matters such as these.

I hardly dare to frame my next admonition. At any rate, let you remember how closely vice and virtue are allied in matters of romance. Place no reliance upon friendship. Your exuberant description of the charms of your mistress may readily incite your dearest friend straightway to seek your couch. You may object to this that the grandson of Actor never betrayed Achilles and that Phaedra never sinned with Pirithous; that Pylades loved Hermione chastely as did Phoebus love Pallas. Quite reasonably, you could mention the love of Castor and Pollux for their sister Helen.

Just one more thing I would like to add and that is: Women are creatures of varying moods. Each mood requires special caution and attention; no two of them are quite alike. One piece of soil is good for grapes; another excellent for olives; a third especially suitable for corn. A truly adroit lover will know how to suit his actions and his words to the need of the moment. Remember Proteus, who sometimes is a graceful wave, sometimes a lion, then a tree, and frequently, a tottering, vicious boar. Not all fish can be caught in the same manner; for some are speared; some are most readily captured with hooks; while others require the casting of a cunning net. The different methods of your pursuit should be conditioned by the people you are dealing with. Consider carefully the age of your mistress, for an old hind knows well the snares of the hunter, while the young doe will be frightened by too lavish a display of skill. And thus it sometimes happens that some cautious charmer fails to respond to a man of society but falls readily into the arms of some worthless rascal.

There is still a good deal more of advice that I have to offer but let us at this point heave anchor and give ourselves a spell of ease.

BOOK TWO

SING high the praises to the gods, for you have snared your quarry and she is yours. Put the fragrant laurel upon your brow and turn your back on Hesiod and Homer, for obviously Ovid is the man for you. Remember Paris racing home from Sparta and Pelops bearing Hippodamia away: so, you too, with task but half completed, are now ready for a premature celebration. You are too hasty by far, for your slender craft is on the open sea, and the harbor of your destination far off indeed. It is not enough that my songs have brought a mistress to your arms. My skill has served you well; my art has told you how to get her. It now remains for me to show you how to hold her. It is a glorious thing to gain a conquest; it is more glorious still to perpetuate your success. So far you may have had but luck; now you must exercise craft. O Cytherea! forsake me not, and you, my Muse, protect me, for ambitious is my task. I set out to pinion the wings of a fickle child who wanders up and down the world and hardly anything can stay his willful flights.

Minos was determined to retain Daedalus within his gates, the cunning Daedalus who had imprisoned the Minotaur in the labyrinth—that same Minotaur, half-man, half-bull, whose erring mother had crawled into the heifer made of maple wood. And Daedalus wept sorely and pleaded with the king to permit him to return to his home, but Minos was adamant and deaf to his entreaties. Seeing himself baffled, Daedalus looked about him and saw that Minos had all power over land and sea and that it was futile to attempt escape by these means. "There is but one way to achieve my purpose: I will have to cleave the air, I and my child Icarus. Far be it from me to attempt the heights of heaven and may Jove forgive the ambitiousness of my plan, but so eager am I to return to my native country that if it were required of me to cross the somber Styx, I would not be afraid to do so."

Out of his need and anxiety was born a splendid plan. He gathered feathers and bound them cleverly together with wax and wool and fashioned thus by artifice two pair of wings. His son, delighted with the prospect of rising in the air like any bird, cried out with joy. Said Daedalus, "By means of this my handiwork, we shall fly safely back to our country. Take heed, however, not to fly too near the virgin of Tegea, or come too close to Orion. In all things follow me, for I shall be your guide. Attempt naught of your own, for if we soar too near the sun, the wax may melt, and our wings should fail us; nor come too close to the surface of the ocean, for the moisture of the sea would drag you down. The middle way is ours; and guard you well the winds that they may bear you up and spare your strength." Thus spoke the crafty Daedalus; then fitted wings upon the shoulders of his son and taught him how to use them, as the mother bird instructs her feeble fledgelings. When once the boy had mastered

44

all the strokes, his father likewise donned a pair of wings; then kissed his offspring, while the tears ran down his face. Their flight began from a little hill, from whence they launched themselves with an invocation upon their lips. Frequently the old man gazed back at his child, and a strange exuberance filled both their hearts at their unexpected success.

The land lies spread below them, like a toy, and they see people going to their tasks like dwarfs out of a fairy tale. Already they have left Samos; passed Noxus, Paros, and Delos sacred to Apollo. They have seen Lebinthos, and Calymna, when suddenly young Icarus, grown playful in his airy sporting, decides to steer a different course and rises higher. The fiery sun has loosened the feathers, which now fall one by one into the sea beneath. The frightened, panic-stricken boy waves his arms—to no avail. Looking down, he beholds the dark and treacherous sea; he cries out for his father, once, and once only. Then the waters entomb him and his voice. And Daedalus, a father no longer, shatters the air with frantic cries, "Icarus, Icarus!" when from aloft he beholds the scattered wings upon the surface of the ocean.

The sea was destined to bear the name of the unhappy youth.

And thus failed Minos in restraining the flight of a common mortal, while I attempt to capture and to dictate to a winged god. Place no faith in magic spells, or secret incantations, for if they had any value, surely Medea would have held the son of Aeson, and Circe would surely have retained the love of Ulysses. Philtres and potions may make you ill but have otherwise no value; in fact, they have been known to drive people insane, so I advise you to avoid such dangerous experiments. If you wish to be loved, make yourself worthy: that is the best way to proceed. It is not enough to be equipped with a handsome face and figure. Why, if you were handsome as Nireus, of whose beauty Homer sings; nay, if you were Hylas, snatched away by the Naiads, you could not hold your mistress unless you had accomplishments of the mind as well. Beauty is skin deep; each passing day robs you of some of it; and the longer it endures, the more surely it will pass. When a rose falls to pieces, nothing is left but a stick with thorns, and the lilies and the violets do not bloom forever. Be reconciled to the fact that your face will be a web of wrinkles and your hair turn white. While there is time, equip yourself with such accomplishments as shall defy time; those are the only ones that will lead you consolingly to your grave. Study life; become accomplished in the treasure-troves of the Latins and Greeks. Ulysses was not handsome. He was eloquent, and goddesses were frenzied with love for him. How poor Calypso trembled when she saw him preparing for departure and how she warned him that it was a bad time for setting sail. A thousand times, perhaps, she asked him to re-tell the siege of Troy; each time he told it in a new form. One day, while standing on the seashore, she asked again to hear the story of the fall. Ulysses broke a twig which chanced to grow nearby and drew a plan upon the sands. "This would be Troy," said he, "and this would be my camp out in the plain. This place was stained with the blood of Dolon, who tried to steal the horses of Achilles in the night. Here are the tents of Rhesus, King of Thrace; here I returned with the horses that had been stolen from him." And as Ulysses talked

46

to fair Calypso, a wave came from the sea and overlapped the plan; and with one gentle scoop, abolished Troy and Rhesus, camp and horses, all together. "See," said the nymph, "what famous names this little water washed away, and still you hope the waves will be kinder to you, when once you shall set sail upon them."

To return to our subject: whoever you may be, don't trust too much in beauty. Endeavor to equip yourself with something more enduring than mere comeliness of body. Great things can be accomplished with the possession of ingratiating manners, for women are fond of sweet, gentle ways, and they dislike uncouth behavior. The hawk and wolf are rarely popular: they are too gruesomely aggressive. The swallow and the dove enjoy man's confidence, for they are famous as quiet and pacific creatures. Well-modulated voices and kind words are the very food of Love. Quarrels will estrange lover and mistress, husband and wife. Fighting is the dowry with which married folk begin to set up house-keeping. Let your mistress hear only pleasant things. You have met in her bed through no machination of law. Your only law is Love. Approach her with sweet caresses and dainty sentiments, so that she may be cheerful whenever you approach her.

Let it be understood that these my maxims are not coined to aid the idle rich. It is not to them that I am eager to impart the art of Love. A man who can freely lavish gifts has certainly no need of any lesson I can teach him. He has talents in abundance if he can say: "Would you like to have this? I shall be glad to get it for you." I am the poet of the poor, for I am poor myself, and, so being, have been in love. Lacking the gifts that riches can bestow, I gave my poetry. It is the poor man's duty to be very circumspect and cautious, for it ill behooves him to use high language or to behave in a rude manner. It is his privilege to endure what no wealthy rival would suffer. In a fit of ill-temper, I once tousled the hair of my mistress. It was an evil day for me. It robbed me of many pleasures. She insisted that I tore her dress, though I am sure that that was not the case. Need I remark that I was compelled to purchase her a new one? My friend, surpass your master in caution, for if you don't, you will fare poorly. If you must fight, join the war against the Parthians, but live in peace with your woman. Be playful and considerate, so that you may excite her love.

If your mistress is preoccupied, don't be impatient. In a short while she will change her mind and be good to you. Bend the bough gently or it will break. Gliding with the stream, you will eventually get to the other side, but if you struggle against the current, you are very likely to drown. The fierce Numidian lion can be subdued with patience, and tigers are tamed by persistence. Atalanta of Nonacris was fierce and adamant, but even she succumbed to a lover's assiduities. Quite frequently, Milanion would fall upon the ground and weep in despair over the rudeness of his mistress. He was strong and courageous, knowing well how to wield the spear, but the wounds he bore were made by darts most cleverly devised.

You need not climb the forest heights of Menelaus weighted with nets and arrows or bare your breast to the weapons of your enemies. My advice is simple to follow and you will be successful in the end. Obey her in whatever she bids you and remember to side with her in all matters of discussion. Be cheerful in her joy and weep with her sorrow; in short, become the mirror of her moods. If you play games with her, have the discretion to let her win. No matter what the pastimes, see that you are less skillful than she is. This is a most important matter.

When you escort her about, be careful to shade her from the sun, and free a passage for her through the crowd. Be always ready to fetch a chair and to assist her toilette, and though you yourself be well-nigh perishing with cold, you will do well to warm her hands within your bosom. It is no disgrace to hold her mirror for her. Console yourself that even the mighty Hercules who performed so many feats of daring and of strength, learned how to spin coarse wool to obey his mistress. And if so great a hero, who gained a seat in the Olympian realms, did not consider such a task beneath him, then you can well afford to swallow your vanity. If you have an appointment with your mistress in the forum, come early and wait patiently. If suddenly she changes the place of your rendezvous, don't argue but leave everything and run. If she has been out late at a banquet or a theatre, and she sends for a slave to see her home, offer your services. If you are out of town on business and she unexpectedly sends for you, don't delay for a moment. Lacking a vehicle, you must walk. Nothing must hinder you, neither storm, nor tempest, nor snow, nor any other thing on heaven or earth. Love is like a battle and weak-kneed simpletons had better stay at home. A man engaged in such an arduous campaign must be prepared for long and weary marches, cruel sufferings, hunger, toil and pain. Apollo did not disdain to tend the herds of Admetus, so it does not befit you to blush beneath your hardships. Above all things, forget your foolish pride. If the common, simple means of gaining access to your mistress are denied you, and her gates are closed in your face, you are free to climb upon her roof and enter her house through the chimney. She must be of stone not to appreciate the dangers you have passed for her sake; it will be a further token of your affection. Leander swam the Hellespont to prove his love. You will do well to win the confidence of all, even her humblest servants. Bring them some trifling gifts you can afford, and when the festival of Juno Caprotina approaches, don't fail to give a handsome gift to her maid. Be on good footing with all the members of the servants' quarters and count among your friends the slave who sleeps upon the doorstep of your mistress.

But don't be extravagant with the gifts that you offer your love; let them be more tasteful than expensive. For instance, when the trees are bent beneath their load of ripened treasures, then send a basket full of fruit to show you think of her. You might imply that they are a little harvest you have personally gathered at your country place. What matter if you have purchased them in Rome? Remember that chestnuts and grapes were beloved by Amaryllis and ignore the fact that the modern Amaryllis is much less enamored of chestnuts. Or you may, upon another occasion, send her a brace of thrushes or pigeons. You might object that such a policy is generally pursued by the expectant heirs of some wealthy, childless dowager. Forget your qualms.

I don't advise you to send poetry. Play safe and venture only on substantial gifts. The most ill-mannered boor, if he is wealthy, has a fair chance to be successful. Remember, you are living in the golden age, for gold will buy you anything you wish. It will purchase Love, esteem and any honors you may set your heart upon. Blind Homer, if he now approached escorted by the nine Muses, could hardly find a willing listener, if once his poverty were well established. But don't be cynical, for there are some cultured women. They are very rare, most of them being content to appear cultured. If you do send poetry, praise them. If you write badly, learn to declaim your verses so effectively that none would notice their weak structure. The best you can hope for is that if they are perfectly written and perfectly recited, they will be considered as a very, very trifling present.

Now, let us assume that you have convinced your mistress that you wish to be in her service. It might chance that you have decided to free one of your slaves —a simple matter. First of all, ask the servant to see your mistress for the purpose of petitioning you for his freedom. If now you let the slave go free, she will think you have done it all for her sake. It costs you nothing and will please her enormously. Quite likely she will feel she can twist you round her finger. There is no harm in letting her think so; there is no surer method of obtaining what you want. Be careful to notice what she wears. If you find her wrapped in Tyrian purple, tell her that nothing becomes her so well; if she is all decked out in cloth of gold, tell her her charms surpass the brilliance of the metal. When it is cold, and you find her wrapped in furs, assure her that you wish for a perpetual winter. If she wears a flimsy shift, tell her that her charms might cause a conflagration and you hope she isn't catching cold. If she parts her hair in the middle of her forehead, insist that you have never seen her looking fairer. If she has it curled and fuzzy, tell her it is the only kind of hair you fancy. When she sings or dances, fall into proper ecstasies of delight and regret that the performance was so soon ended. When you find yourself in bed with her, pay the proper obeisance to the source of all your bliss, and assure her that you think yourself in heaven. Aye, and if she is a very Medusa, you can make her docile with the proper words. Remember that your mimicry must be consistent with your statements, for if hypocrisy is once discovered, it will be rough sailing ever afterwards.

The autumn is a strange season, when the bursting grape and colorful foliage seem to belie the treacherous, nipping cold that steals out from the woods at eventide. It is a dangerous season, and may your mistress be careful of her health. But let us say that she grows languorous and ill. Now, then, is the time for you to show your mettle. Be not discouraged by the peevish, multitudinous demands upon your patience. Render whatever service is required and let her see you weep with worry for her welfare. Tell her you've had a dream filled with a hopeful prophecy. Produce a grandam with withered hands, who, with ointments and herbs, will sweeten and purify the sick chamber. Don't forget sulphur or the eggs of atonement. These kindnesses, item by item, she will treasure in her heart, and many a worthwhile legacy has been bequeathed for such like simple acts of charity. But be cautious, my friend, and don't show too much anxiety. Don't be a busy-

body; don't fuss too much; above all else, don't pre-
scribe some diet; and in heaven's name, don't bring her
ill-tasting medicines to drink. Such things you'd better
leave to your rival.

The wind which sails your bark when you first leave
the harbor is not the wind that you require on the open
sea. Love is frail at birth, but it grows stronger with
age if it is properly fed. The roaring bull that frightens
you today was the tender calf you stroked not long ago.
The tree beneath whose foliage you seek a grateful shade
was once a slender sapling. The little rivulet runs on
and gathers force and eventually becomes a roaring tor-
rent. Let your mistress become accustomed to you and
your curious ways, for the most potent thing in life is
habit. Be with her on all occasions until you notice
that she is used to you and needs your presence. At this
point you can absent yourself for a while, for the soil
that is given rest renders with interest the eventual seed
that you will sow. Remember how the shrewd Ulysses
tortured his Penelope and how Phyllis longed for the ab-
sent Demaphoon. At any rate, play safe—don't stay
away too long. Time has a way of curing every an-
guish, and while you are gone, another may take your
place. Menelaus left fair Helen to her own devices and
she found consolation in the arms of her guest. What
a fool he was to depart leaving his wife at home with a
stranger! No innocent dove was ever more calmly de-
livered to the tender mercies of a buzzard. He has
nothing to complain of: he merely proved a most ac-
commodating husband.

A boar, when cornered by the huntsman, a fright-
ened lioness beside a litter of cubs, a viper that an in-

nocent traveler has accidentally trod upon are all less
dangerous than a woman who finds her husband in
another woman's bed. Her fury knows no bounds and
she will fling anything that comes to hand. She will
dash at her rival like a Maenad driven mad by the
Aonian god. Medea murdered her children for the
misdeeds of Jason. If you are cautious, you will be care-
ful to avoid all scenes of jealousy and fury.

Don't fear that I shall suddenly begin to preach a
set of morals and insist that you pay homage to one mis-
tress only: nothing could be more absurd. But keep
your liaisons from becoming notorious and manage your
affairs with discretion. Don't brag of your good luck
and don't make a gift to some woman that another
woman can easily recognize as having originated with
you. Make your appointments at divers times and places,
and when you write, read carefully what you have writ-
ten, for many women read between the lines such news
and promises as you have never intended.

Venus retaliates when she is wounded and pays back
blow for blow. When Atrides was faithful to his wife,
she was loyal to him. When she learned that Chryses
had come to beg that his daughter be restored, her sus-
picions were aroused. She learned of the abduction that
pierced the heart of Briseis, and understood the reasons
why the war continued to drag on. Her vengeance was
a swift and sure one, for from that day on she made free
of her heart and bed.

If in spite of all your caution your secret peccadilloes
are discovered, remember to deny emphatically all your
guilt. Don't look sheepish and don't gush—these are
sure signs of a guilty conscience. Stake everything upon

your cunning and audacity, for it is a matter of your peace which is at stake. You must show unusual prowess in your amorous dalliance, to convince her that her suspicions are unfounded. If this is difficult for you, some fool is likely to advise you to take some noxious drugs, like thistle seeds steeped in old wine. This is pure nonsense. The goddess who dwells on Mount Eryx disdains such violent means. Nevertheless, white onions from Megara, mixed with eggs and a dash of honey from Hymettus, might prove beneficial.

But why get side-tracked into this nonsensical medical discussion? All this is none of my affair. A moment ago I cautioned you to be discreet about your love affairs. It may serve you just as well to blazon them abroad. Notice how the sailor slips the ropes through the rings; how well he takes advantage of the changing breeze: all winds are welcome to his cunning hand. Your mistress may be the sort of woman who needs the apprehension of suspecting that she has a rival. A surfeit of happiness renders certain people irresponsible. A small flame must be nursed carefully or grey ashes will smother its feeble light; but if you add a little sulphur, rapidly, fresh flames are kindled. Many a heart grown torpid in its dull routine of safety requires the sting of jealousy. If your mistress is of that sort, then bring new fire into her heart, or let the pallor of uneasiness cover her cheeks. Happy is the lover whose mistress squirms in agony when she hears he is unfaithful! To think that his mistress is raving and tearing her hair, that she pounces upon him and digs her nails into his face, that she drowns him in a flood of tears, while he is certain all the time that she cannot live without him—what happiness for a lover! But when her rage has reached its point of greatest frenzy, hasten to pacify her; press her tear-stained face close to your breast, and ratify your concord on her bed. It is the cradle of forgiveness; and let it cheer you to know that I envy you then.

In the beginning there was naught but Chaos; then, gradually, the heavens rose and the seas retreated to their fitting place. The woods and mountains became populated with birds and insects and all wild and living things, while fish cut invisible paths through the waters. In those distant days, brute man walked cautiously across the hills, and brawn was his only resource. He lived in the semi-darkness of the forest, nourished himself on the roots and grasses, slept upon the leaves that were dry and brittle; and he lived in ignorance of his fellow men. Later he discovered the soft lights of Love, and tender passions joined him to some female on a single bed. They had no tutor for the task of Love, nor did they need one. The gentle Venus filled her office by subtle, devious ways. The bird and the fish have their mates and the hind follows the stag. The snake finds another snake, the dog seeks the bitch, and the ewe and the heifer rejoice in the caresses of ram and bull. The goat and the mare anticipate the coming of their mates; and you may be cheered by knowing that you too possess within you a capital remedy for all the grievances and angers of your mistress. You possess a medicine more potent than the juices of Machaon, and so long as you possess this balm, you need not fear that you will fail to gain her pardon.

Quite suddenly, in the midst of chanting my poem, I had a vision. Apollo appeared to me as in a dream, bearing a lyre in his hand, while a wreath of laurel encircled his brow. In a prophetic voice he urged me to lead my disciples into his temple. He pointed above the gates to that famous inscription: "Man, know thyself."

"This maxim," he said, "is especially applicable to all lovers, for only he who truly knows himself, will have the chance to utilize fully all his potentialities. If he is handsome and has a fair skin, let him lie uncovered in his bed. If he is a good talker, let him recite. If he has a sweet voice, by all means let him sing; and if the wine suffuses him with gentle gaiety, then let him drink. But whatever he be, athlete or orator, don't let him interrupt a conversation just to declaim his verses."

Phoebus is right and we will all do well to obey him, for naught but wisdom has ever issued from his divine lips. But let us return to my discourse. Whoever patterns his endeavors upon the precepts of my art will surely attain his heart's desire. Not every seed cast in the furrow bears its fruit. Not always are winds propitious to a vessel's course. Little pleasure, much pain,— such is the lot of lovers. Their sorrows are numerous as the hares on Athos, as the bees on Hybla, as the shells upon the seashore and as the olives on the tree of Pallas. Love's arrows have been steeped in gall.

Sometimes you will be informed that your mistress has gone out, when you yourself have seen her through her window. Don't make a fuss; deny the certainty of your own knowledge and pretend she is not at home. Another time she has promised to receive you in the night; when you arrive at her gates, they are closed against you.

Lie down upon the moist, cold ground, and compose yourself to wait. While lying thus, some surly rascal of a servant may perchance insult you. Be patient and be courteous, not only to him, but to the doorstep and to the door as well. Ere you depart, remove the roses from your brow and leave them on the threshold.

A sensible man will never make himself obnoxious and he will take stock of the unreasonableness of all womankind. He will put up with their strange whims and mind them not at all. If they kick him, he will bide his time, and eventually kiss their feet.

But these are all trifles; let us turn our attention to more important matters. I am about to discourse of dangerous enterprises, but let us be of good cheer, for nothing worthwhile can be accomplished which is not somehow fraught with daring. What I propose is not easily attained.

If you are conscious of a dangerous rival, submit to his existence without murmur, for only then have you an opportunity to make a conquest. You may believe me that this is not the prophecy of a mere frail mortal. There is an oracular precision about my prognostication. It represents the very pinnacle of wisdom that I can offer you. If your mistress shows by various signs that she has a secret understanding with your rival, submit to it quietly. If she writes to him, don't try to intercept her letters. Let her do as she pleases. Many a clever husband practises this indulgence, and you will do well to follow suit.

I frankly confess that I, myself, have been quite unable to live up to this sensible precept. If I noticed any such duplicity on the part of my beloved, I should not be able to control my jealous fury. One day I observed how she exchanged a tender kiss with her husband, and I simply stormed with fury. Love is concocted of strange promptings and emotions. A cleverer man would take such matters casually, and my inability to be reasonable on such occasions has frequently been the cause of my undoing. The proper course is to ignore the whole matter. Permit her to hide her infidelities, lest by making her confess, you teach her to become more adroit at her duplicity. Avoid catching her unawares in the arms of another man, for once discovered, they shall love each other more ardently. You will merely bind them more closely by their common shame.

The story is well known, how Vulcan, by a clever ruse, surprised Venus in the arms of Mars. Many and many a time, fair Venus had dealt harshly with her husband's failings; had imitated his awkward gait, and laughed at his toil-worn, scaly hands. And for the special amusement of Mars she mimicked Vulcan's clumsy maneuverings. In the beginning, they were most careful to conceal their affair and were most secretive and tactful; but the sun, whose ever-wakeful eye nothing can quite escape, revealed to Vulcan the treachery of his spouse. How badly the sun managed, when he could have obtained any favors from the goddess as the price of his silence!

Meanwhile, old Vulcan set about to trap the unwary lovers. He pretended to set out upon a pressing journey to Lemnos. The lovers, feeling safe during his absence, sought out their favorite trysting place, and naked like young Cupid himself, they fell into a net that Vulcan had cunningly prepared for their capture. No sooner had the treacherous coils enfolded them, than Vulcan roused the whole of high Olympus to gaze upon the imprisoned wrongdoers. Their plight was a sorry one and it was made less easy by the jeering comments of the spectators. Yielding at last to the prayers of Neptune, Vulcan set the captives free. Mars hied himself to Thrace and Venus went off to Paphos.

And what did the righteous Vulcan gain thereby? That while formerly they had hidden their amours beneath careful subterfuges, they now quite openly and freely indulged their passion. The proper payment for a prying fool! It is quite likely that even now he regrets the circumspection of his jealousy.

Forego all traps. I do forbid them to you, and the great Venus, herself once caught in one of them, forbids you the use of all such childish tricks. Don't prepare cunning snares to catch your rival. These are devices only fit for lawful husbands, whose sacred rights are hallowed by fire and water.

And as for me, I must again insist I only chant of pleasures which the law permits.

It shows a great lack of judgment to divulge to the common mob the mysteries of Ceres or to blab about the rites of Samothrace. The pointless babbling about things that should be kept secret is a grave trespass upon common decency. Tantalus is punished justly for his indiscretion, and it serves him right that the fruits hanging above his head shall ever more be out of reach; and right it serves him, too, that standing as he does with water all around him, his throat is parched with thirst. Cytherea forbids above all things that her mysteries should be revealed. No talkative knaves should ap-

proach her altars. The sacred emblems of her worship
are not hidden in mystic caskets; no noisy cymbals are
beaten at her celebrations. She opens the gates of her
temple to all on the condition that all keep silent about
her mysteries. Venus never appears without her veil,
and with modest hand covers her charms. The beasts of
burden and all wild things abandon themselves to the act
of love in any public place, and frequently it causes em-
barrassment to young girls. But we seek out the hidden
places for our dalliance. We close the gates, bar the
doors, and cover with a fitting vestment the secret places
of our body. Perhaps we do not seek complete dark-
ness, but surely we cherish a certain dimness. When
men and women roamed the earth without protection
against sun and wind and rain, and the oak fed and
sheltered them, they sought the caves and darkened for-
ests for the pleasures of Love. They were uncouth and
yet some inward modesty persuaded them to search for
the solitudes of nature for their amorous devotions. Now-
adays, it is something of a fashion to prate of our noctur-
nal callisthenics, and it almost seems that we would pay
to have the whole world know our secret vices. It has
become usual with certain fops to stop and talk famil-
iarly with any girl, as if to imply that she's another casual
mistress. And there are some who fabricate such tales,
which, if they were true, they would be the first to dis-
avow. To hear their prating one would think that the
woman who resisted them has not been born. Their
specialty is to tarnish faultless reputations. These silly
tattlers will invade the greatest privacy and boast of con-
quests that were perpetrated in their dreams. But let
us be modest and speak sparingly of our real affairs and

let us hide our precious secrets beneath covers of impenetrable silence.

Don't discuss with your mistress, even playfully, any of her defects. This is a very profitable axiom to remember. Perseus did not complain that Andromeda had a swarthy skin. The whole of Troy considered Andromache too tall and only Hector believed her of average height. Learn to accustom yourself to the things you don't like. After a while you won't mind them so much. Remember it is only a matter of habit. Love is a frail creature that is easily crushed by trifles. The newly grafted twig can be disturbed by even a slight breeze. In due time, after it has grown strong, it will not mind the blowing of a gale; it will become a sturdy branch richly endowing the alien tree with fruit. Time will accustom you to anything, and even serious physical blemishes that once disturbed you will eventually disappear before your accustomed gaze. Your nostrils are offended by the rutting smell that is emanated by a herd of bulls; eventually you can learn to bear it without discomfort.

Furthermore, miracles can be worked by the proper use of adjectives. If a woman's skin is darker than Illyrian pitch, call her a brunette. If she is red-headed, comment upon her resemblance to Minerva. If she is just skin and bones, and seems to have one foot in the grave, sing praises to her graceful figure. If she is short, tell her how light she is. If she is squat, you can interpret it as an agreeable plumpness. To every defect there is a next-door neighbor that, properly appraised, becomes a quality. It is foolish to demand her age; nor date her birth by asking who was consul at the time. Leave that to the Censor, especially if she is no longer young. Don't be discouraged that she has to pull out her grey hairs, for that age, and even older age than that, can still bestow many pleasures.   To you, these are but fields in need of sowing, so that the harvest may be rich for you some day.   Labor while you are young and in the prime of your strength, for soon enough a tottering old age will creep upon you.   Cleave the water with your valiant oar, or the ground with your ploughshare; wield the battle-ax and the deadly spear; or devote yourself to the service and care of women.   This, too, is a sort of military service in which rich trophies may be won. And don't forget that women getting on in years have knowledge apt and curious in many matters denied to youth and inexperience.   Cleverly they know how to repair the ravages of time and sometimes do conceal their rightful age quite cunningly.   They are well versed in all the mysteries and attitudes of Love, and thereby are able to enhance your pleasure.   Being old hands at the game, they can grant you a great many voluptuous liberties. Their appetites do not need to be provoked by wearisome titillations and they will share their pleasures with you equally.   It is painful to be involved in such embraces in which only one side truly consumates; that is one of the reasons I have but little pleasure in boys. How hateful is the woman who gives herself out of a sense of duty, who is cold and unresponsive, and who at the height of your excitement, calculates upon her sewing.   Dutiful embraces repel me, for nothing can be more pleasing to the ear of a lover than the trembling voice of the beloved when she whispers ecstatically of her joy.   What can compare to my happiness when my fair one pleads with me to prolong her rapture? Naught can be sweeter than my beloved, inebriate with ecstasy, holding me at arm's length and pleading with swimming eyes that I slacken my pace.

Such accomplishments one does not readily discover in young virgins. It is the woman over thirty-five who is more likely to be familiar with the intricacies of a real affair. You are welcome to drink the new raw wine that sets your teeth on edge. As for myself, give me the full-scented, rich vintage that dates back to one of our elder consuls. It takes years to equip a tree with sufficient foliage to grant you pleasant shelter, and fields but lately reaped will hurt the naked foot.

You might reasonably ask: would I prefer Hermione to Helen? Let it suffice that if you would enjoy the fruits of Love in their full and ripe maturity, my suggestions are worth pondering, and your reward may prove deserving of the effort.

But our two lovers have now happily contrived to meet in bed and I will stay my Muse before their door. No further advice is required as to what they are to say to one another, nor will their hands lie idle. Their trembling fingers will unerringly seek out the secret, familiar places where Love is wont to dwell.

Bold Hector was valiant and bore himself skillfully in Love's battles with Andromache, and Achilles was a hero as he lay beside his fair captive on a soft couch. Briseis did not fear caresses from the hands that had but lately shed the Trojan blood. Her voluptuous pleasures were undoubtedly increased by the knowledge that these victorious limbs had exerted themselves on the gory fields of battle.

If you will listen to me you will not be too hasty in attaining the culmination of your happiness. Learn by skillful maneuvering to reach your climax by degrees. When you are safely ensconced in the sanctuary of bliss, let no timid fear arrest your hand. You will be richly rewarded by the love-light trembling in her eyes, even as the rays of the sun fitfully dance upon the waves. Then will follow gentle murmurs, moans and sighs, laden with ecstasy that will sting and lash desire. But now you must be very careful and remember that cramming too much sail upon your masts, your pace may be too swift for your mistress. Be careful, too, lest she outstrip you on her way to the waiting harbor. The very height of achievement is to ride on the crest of a high wave of pleasure and to arrive at the haven simultaneously with her. Let this be your rule on all occasions unless fear of discovery may cause you to grab what you can. Sometimes there is danger in delay, in which case you are to pay no heed to caution but lean well forward and ride to victory, regardless of consequences.

My task is well-nigh done, and now you have your chance to show your gratitude. Wreathe my brow with fragrant myrtle leaves and present me with the palm of victory. Podalirius was famed for his skill in curing maladies, Pyrrhus for courage, Nestor for his counsel, Calchas for his shrewdness, Achilles for daring, Automedon as a charioteer: so am I worthy to be known among lovers as the best of poets. I have supplied you arms as Vulcan did to Achilles; and when you have successfully conquered your Amazon with the sword I have sharpened for your use, inscribe upon your trophies with a flourish: *"OVID WAS MY MASTER"*

BOOK THREE

HAVING supplied the Greeks with weapons against the Amazons, there remains for me the task of supplying you, Penthesilea, with the proper tools of war against the Greeks. You and all your handmaidens are free to command the resources of my cunning, and let the victory go to the side favored by that winged and willful urchin whose playground is the world. Surely it were unfair to leave you defenselessly to face a foe so marvellously equipped. Victory for man would be disgraceful under such unequal conditions.

Mayhap some man may rise at this point and say: "How thoughtful of our master Ovid to replenish the snake with poison." It is hardly reasonable to condemn the entire sex for the faults of a few of its members. Let each be judged by the merits of her own case and the failings of her person. Alcides had just cause to complain of Helen, and his elder brother was with equal justice chagrined by Clytemnestra, her sister; and through the misdeeds of Eriphyle, the daughter of Talaos, Amphiaraus had to descend to the underworld. Nevertheless, it is also true that Penelope remained chaste and faithful to her husband who was absent from his fire-side for twenty years; and Laodamia died long before her time in order to join her husband in his grave. Alcestis sacrificed her life to redeem her husband from the tomb, and the daughter of Iphis jumped upon her husband's funeral pyre. Virtue has ever been pictured as a woman, and it is fitting that she should favor her own sex. My advice, however, is not addressed to pure, superior souls. My bark is used to carry lighter freight and thus do I address myself to ladies that seek sure means of making themselves beloved.

Women are extremely foolhardy in these matters which cause them much more damage than men, for it is ever the male who is the deceiver. In re-scanning the pages of history, we discover that very few women have been treacherous. Medea was cast off by the faithless Jason, who took another woman to his breast without a thought for the disconsolate mother of his children. The story of Ariadne abandoned by Theseus upon a lonely island must be familiar to all of you.

Remember Phyllis coming down nine times to the seashore while the woods in grief over her loss shed their foliage. Recall Dido's guest who left as his only heritage a sword that served to bring her death.

A little reflection reveals at once the cause of all the mischief: they lacked the knowledge how to love. Much planning is required, much cunning and much art, to make Love last; and all of you are destined to repeat such errors, unless you listen to these instructions, which I give you at the bidding of Cytherea. She came into my presence and spoke thus: "What manner of man are you to have brought sore distress on all defenseless women? Two of your poems have you devoted to instructing men, and you have taught them how to arm themselves with all propriety for Love's battles. And now, do these frail creatures that never did you harm, request your aid. Knowing you as well as I do, it seems but reasonable that you will be kind to my protégées and that you mean to serve them." And having finished, fair Cytherea took a few leaves from the wreath that crowned her head and gave them to me. Suddenly I felt imbued with a benign flame, and a heavy burden seemed lifted from my heart.

And thus, inspired by Venus, I admonish you to heed me and my counsel insofar as it does not violate modesty and the law. It will be of infinite help if you consider the unavoidable approach of old age and that the days of your youth are limited. The stream returns not to its source and the opportunities for your happiness pass beyond recall down the ever-moving river of time. The soil, barren and withered, that now lies at my feet, was once abloom with violets; this thorny bush was weighted by the sweet burden of roses.

Reject Love today, if you will, but it behooves you to remember that an indefinite future of loneliness in a solitary bed is awaiting you. Don't count too certainly upon the love-sick swains that will come with noisy poundings at your door, in fierce rivalry, when once old age has overtaken you. The roses are not likely to be strewn upon your doorstep then. When once the color fades from out your cheek, the gruesome wrinkles come to take their place. It will avail you little to swear that you were born white-haired; only the snake, when he sloughs off his skin, or the stag, when he renews his horns, renews his youth and vigor also. But time gives nothing for the things it takes from us, and it is wiser to pluck the rose than to leave it wither on the stem purposeless and forlorn. The drain of childbirth will affect your bodies as harvests too frequently gathered affect the earth. So Phoebe did well to love Endymion, and Dawn did well to carry off Cephalus. Venus mourns Adonis to this very hour, and it is fitting that you follow in the footsteps of these goddesses.

If men betray you, your loss is little, as long as you are unbereft of charms. It matters naught that thousands have enjoyed them—your beauty will be unimpaired. Iron and stone can be worn out and corroded, but the part of you required for Love defies both wear and friction. The torch does not diminish by giving light to another torch, nor the ocean lose if we drain from it but a bucket. If you object that a woman ought not thus make free with herself, we can pertinently ask: "Why not?" Surely she loses nothing but a bit of moisture replaced easily enough. But this is just the merest beginning. My sails are hardly spread. Once out upon the open surface of the sea, a wind more powerful will be required to waft me on.

First of all, let us consider your attire. A carefully tended vine yields an ample, bounteous crop, and the corn grows high and sturdy in the fields well tilled. Beauty can be bestowed by the gods only; but few have this gift laid within their cradle. The greatest part of your appearance is determined by your dress and the care with which it is draped. This considered, you need not fear to face comparison with the goddesses of Ida. Remember that in olden times females were not so careful of their appearance as they might have been; but in those days men also were less concerned with the nicety of their toilette. Andromache wore a coarse shift, and this was fitting, for she was the wife of a warrior. Ajax, attired in the skins of oxen, could hardly expect to approach his wife if she were less ruggedly clad. Our ancestors were rough and simple people. Rome, on the other hand, is full of gold and riches, brought from those parts of the world that she has conquered. The Capitol is nothing like it used to be, and the palace of the Senate, well worthy of encompassing that dignified assembly, was once a simple shack, in the days when Tatius was king. Those splendid buildings situated on the Palatine in honor of Apollo were once but fields where teams of oxen ploughed the ground. Let whoever will rave of the good old days; I am content to live right now. I am not interested in the gold we drag from the bowels of the earth, nor am I amazed to see the mountains disappearing as we drag the marble to build these glorious edifices, nor am I impressed with the precious dyes that we import from distant lands. The only thing I am concerned with is that the rough, ungracious ways of our forefathers have been displaced by subtle and elaborate manners that add to the enjoyment of life.

It is unnecessary for you to weigh down your ears with pearls dragged from the seas by dark-skinned Indian divers. Disdain the garments heavily wrought in gold, for this wealth, so ostentatiously displayed, will repel a sensible man. Fastidiousness, more than anything, should be your aim. Comb your hair carefully, for there are many ways of doing even so simple a thing as that. By trial you will discover the style most suited to your peculiar personality. Consult your mirror.

If your face is long, part your hair in the middle as did Laodamia. If your face is round, comb a knot on top of your head and expose your ears. It will become one woman to wear her hair loose, like Apollo with the lyre; another to have it tied up in back, like Diana at the hunt; a third can have loose ringlets; a fourth can comb it closely to her temples. There are women who like to wear tortoise shell; others who comb their hair high up on their heads—but there are as many methods of combing as there are bees on Hybla and acorns on an oak tree. Besides, you are free to invent new fashions altogether. Some women appear best when their hair falls in a studied carelessness, as if it had been neglected for days, when as a matter of fact it has been done a few minutes ago. Great art is draped with indifference. This was the case with Iole, when Hercules first espied her in the conquered city, and Ariadne when, forsaken on her island, Bacchus suddenly appeared and bore her away amid the cries of the Satyrs.

Think how great your advantage is. Kind nature has left you many loopholes to repair the ravages of time. All men do sooner or later grow bald. Like the leaves that the frosty winds bear down in winter, the storm of years carries off our hair. You are free to dye it any color you wish, and the new color may be more becoming to you than the one you were born with. You can wear a wig of hair that has sprouted on another's head and pass unblushingly before Hercules and the whole band of virgins.

As for clothing, spare me those gilt embroideries dyed purple; I am satisfied with cheaper colors. It is unnecessary to display all of your riches on your body.

The glorious azure sky, cloudless and calm, displays a color truly exquisite. Phryxus and Helle were saved by a ram who was pure yellow. There is a green whose tint imitates the water; it would become a nymph. Aurora drapes herself in saffron when first she yokes her steeds before her chariot. The myrtle of Paphos has an exquisite shade; and the amethyst, the rose, the Tracian stork, the chestnut, the almond and wax all have beautiful and becoming colors. There are as many kinds and colors of cloth as there are flowers when winter has gone and the vernal carpet is spread over the landscape. Make your selection with care, for not all colors will be equally becoming to you. If you are pale, wear black, as did Briseis when she was carried off. If you are a brunette, wear white, like Andromeda when she came to Seriphos.

Be careful that your armpits don't exude an unpleasant odor and that your legs are free from unsightly hair. Needless to say, I am not addressing myself to vulgar, low-born Caucasian women, so it is unnecessary to point out to you that you must wash your mouth carefully every morning and scrub your teeth. Whiten your skin with wax and redden your cheeks so that they bloom with a color nature has denied you. Widen the space between eyebrow and eyelash, and cover carefully the footprints of the years. Increase the luster of your eyes with saffron. I have written how to assist beauty in another work which I advise you to consult and study with the utmost care. It contains advice well worth taking.

When your lover calls, do not let him see your dressing table covered with waters, salves and lotions, and all other aids that your appearance may require. Let no one suspect that your beauty is achieved with effort, for no one could help feeling uneasy, wondering that perchance the bloom of your cheeks may fall in your lap. Avoid ill-smelling ointments from Greece and the oil extracted from sheepskin. Don't clean your teeth while some visitor is calling, nor rub yourself with the fat of deer. Many things are disgusting in the process although their culmination well justifies it. The greatest masterpieces of the sculptor were once but shapeless clods of marble. A ring of gold was once a lump of metal. The cloth of your tunic was once on the back of an ill-smelling sheep. And that exquisite figure of Venus was once a block of stone.

Let your maid say you are still sleeping if you are not finished dressing, and complete your toilette before we are permitted to see you. It is unnecessary for us to be privy to your beauty secrets; there are a great many other things we had better be kept in ignorance of. Many of your doings might turn a delicate stomach and repel a sensitive nose. The glorious trappings of a theater are only giltwood; therefore, the audience is not permitted to clamber up and examine them. Do all your repairing in the solitude of your boudoir. You might comb your hair before us—it is pleasant to see it fall in charming waves upon your back—but don't indulge in too many artifices while doing it. And don't make your maid tremble with fear; for it is detestable to think that you pinch her in a fit of temper, or throw things at her when you are out of sorts. It leads one to suspect that she sometimes moistens your recalcitrant tresses with tears. If you are getting bald, you may discount the above advice.

Coming in upon my mistress unexpectedly one day, her excitement was such that she hastily put on her wig all awry. Let us hope that such things only happen to our enemies and that such disgrace is reserved for the women of the Parthians. A crippled animal, a barren field, a tree bereft of foliage, and a hairless head are all equally odious to behold. My advice is not to Semele, not to Leda, nor to her who was borne away on the back of an enamored bull, nor to Helen, whom Menelaus justly sought and Paris justly kept. My advice is to the beautiful and to the plain, and in the nature of things, the latter are in the majority.

The fair ones of my audience are less likely to heed or need my advice, for they are already well endowed with gifts that can dispense with artifice. When the sea is untroubled, the mariner seeks his ease; but when the tempest rages, he is ever alert and zealous on the lookout. The face without a single blemish is rare, and you will do well to know your faults and to conceal them adequately. Study the shortcomings of your figure and behave accordingly. If you are short, by all means sit down, lest some chance visitor may think you are sitting already. If you are quite dwarfed, cover your feet and lie down. If you are pathetically frail, wear dresses made of thick wool and place a cape about your shoulders. If your complexion is sallow, put red upon your cheeks; if you are swarthy, smear bleach upon your face. If your foot is awkward, wear a becoming shoe; if your legs are thin, don't show your calves in public; if you are round-shouldered, pad out your back; if your bust is too full, put on a tight brassiere; if you have ugly hands, don't gesticulate when you talk; if your breath is malodorous, don't come too close to your lover, particularly when your stomach is empty; if your teeth are in bad condition, smile with your mouth closed. When you laugh, don't open your mouth too wide lest you show your gums; see that you have two small dimples and don't raise your upper lip too high. Don't be too boisterous and guffaw all over the place: let your laughter be charming and infectious. Don't screw your face into a ferocious grimace as if you were crying, and don't bray like an ass approaching his stable.

It is important that you learn to weep in an attractive manner, and with a little effort you ought to be able to do so at will. If you think that lisping certain letters will enhance your charm, then by all means lisp. A defect can be made into a virtue by an adroit female. Learn how to walk bearing your body gracefully; it is very important how you carry yourself, and it will do much to attract or repel strangers. One woman walks undulating her body gently from the hips, and her drapes sway gracefully around her limbs. Another woman careens into a crowd with enormous ungainly steps, like a peasant woman from Umbria. Above all else, have a sense of proportion about these things. While one woman will emulate the crudeness of a country wench, another will stagger about with so much affectation, that it is hard to tell which is the more ludicrous. If your skin has a fine texture and is unblemished, show your shoulders and the upper part of your left arm. This fashion is so tempting that I can hardly pass a charming female thus accoutered without wanting to cover her exposed flesh with kisses.

Ulysses poured wax into the ears of his sailors and had himself bound to the mast for fear of succumbing to the song of the Sirens, so much afraid was he of the wondrous and enchanting music of these monsters. You should learn to sing, for music is soothing and a lovely thing. The sweetness of a voice can overcome any physical defects. Remember the songs you hear at the theater and study the sensuous airs of the East. Learn how to play the lute and the harp. Orpheus, playing upon his lyre, enchanted rocks and wild beasts and all the uncouth things of nature, even Acheron and the triple-headed Cerberus. Amphion lifted up his voice, and stones rose from the ground and ranged themselves as walls. When Arion played his lyre, the fish upon their myriad errands paused and listened in enchantment. Learn how to play the psaltery with both hands, for it is an instrument especially auspicious for Love's dalliance. Study by heart Callimachus and Philetas and Anacreon. Remember Sappho, whose verses are quite apropos, and the poet who sings of the crafty Geta. Memorize the verses of Propertius. Don't overlook my own favorite, Tibullus—and Gallus—and recall the epic about the golden fleece by Varro. And how about the fugitive Aeneas and the beginnings of our glorious Rome? Perchance, then, you will remember your humble servant and my name may not be forgotten. You might read the lines wherein your master gives instructions to both sexes; or haply you will select certain passages from the *Loves* and read them aloud in a sweetly modulated voice; or if the occasion be of another sort, you may read one of the letters from his *Heroines,* a literary device of which he was the inventor. My prayers are uplifted to Phoebus, Bacchus, and to the Muses.

Nor must you neglect the dance. When the festive board is decked, and the wine-cup passes freely, it is fitting that your arms sway rhythmically to the music. We are charmed to see beautiful dancing at the theater; it is an art well worth cultivating. Learn also how to cast the die gracefully and throw the numbers with skill and how to calculate them rapidly. Learn how to play chess thoughtfully and with caution. Remember, one piece against two is going to lose, and the queen that has deserted the king leaves her spouse in serious straits. Play ball airily and guard your movements. There are many games; one particularly divided into as many parts as there are months in the year; and it is fitting that a woman should know how to play all these and more besides, for it is frequently during games that Love is born. It is not enough to know the moves; you must guard yourself, for sometimes in the heat of competition, forgetting all else but the game in hand, unexpectedly your true nature stands revealed. Your love of gain, your rage at the success of another, your vanity, and all the other shameful vices carefully hidden at other times, are likely to crop out. In their train follow quarrels and jeers and vain expostulations; fierce words are exchanged and sides are taken, while profuse swearing shocks the ears of the gods. Sometimes there is suspicion that the pieces have been tampered with, and the scene becomes bathed in tears. This is hardly a rôle for a woman who aims to please. The games I indicated are fitted for your limited skill and strength. Men can exercise their sportive spirits with spears and horses; but these rugged contests are not for you, nor is it yours to plunge into the Tiber

for a swim.   It is better for you to walk in the colonnade
of Pompey, or to promenade near the temple of Apollo,
whose brow is decked with laurel and who, at Actium,
overwhelmed the Egyptian fleet and sent it scurrying be-
neath the waves.   Ply your delicate footsteps to the altars
where gifts are offered to the sacred cow of Memphis,
and go to the theaters to display your charms.   Don't
forget the circus, smelling of freshly spilt blood, and seek
a place near the goal round which the chariots careen.
  A thing unknown is hardly a temptation.   What
no one sees can hardly be desired.   Your beauty avails
nothing if the world is unaware of it.   If your voice be
sweeter than Thamyras', who could approve your songs
if none had heard them?   Had not Apelles realized for
us his image of Venus, we should not know her.   A poet
looks for fame—that is the crown of success.   In days
gone by poets were patronized by kings, and Ennius, a
simple Calabrian, was honored by being buried next to
the great Scipio himself.   But nowadays, a poet is held
slightly better than a mere idler, and his contemplation
of the Muse considered but a waste of time.   But their
hunger for fame is undiminished.   The great Homer
would to this day be an obscure village scribbler if his
immortal *Iliad* had never seen the light of day.   Danae
would have remained unknown if she had remained in
her tower.   You will do well to practise the gregarious
life and go in for hectic social doings.   A cloistered ex-
istence will perpetuate you in a state of dull celibacy.
The wolf casts his eye over many a likely sheep before he
selects his prey; the eagle surveys a whole flock before
he picks his meal.   A fair female has therefore good rea-
son to show herself in public.   In a crowd there is al-

ways likelihood of finding a kindred soul, and you had
better show yourself properly accoutered, bearing your
most pleasing smile and most pleasing manner. It is
best to have your hook well baited for the fish may bite
when you least expect it. Sometimes the dogs roam the
woods vainly all day and suddenly a stag lurches from
the brush when it is least expected. Think of the dark
hours that unexpectedly ended for Andromeda, chained
to her rock. You may even find a new husband while
you are burying an old one, for some women look most
attractive while they are grief-stricken and bathed in
tears.

Beware of men who are inclined to be dandies and
are forever fussing about their appearance. The man
who will perish with grief merely because his hair is
slightly ruffled will say to you pleasantries he has often
practised on other women. Such men are flighty and
unreliable. Avoid men who are more feminine than
you are and who are followed by a bigger concourse of
lovers. Be warned by the fate of Troy; old Priam cer-
tainly had the right idea. There are certain men who
pretend to be enamored but in reality seek to fleece the
gullible female who is taken in by them. Don't trust
their perfumed airs, their foppish behavior and their
jeweled carcass. They are full of high-flown aesthetic
talk which merely serves as a cloak for their predatory
and rapacious characters. You may be at a loss for your
patrimony after one of these dandies has finished with
you. It will avail you little to seek tardy retribution in
a courtroom. And even Venus and the goddesses whose
temples adorn the Appian Way seem helpless to inter-
vene. Some of these gentry come to you with reputa-

tions so fly-blown that you really have only yourself to blame for being taken in by them.

It is your privilege to profit by the misfortunes visited upon your sisters. Avoid the cajoleries of a Theseus, who has already told many a fruitful lie. Demophoon, who carried on the infamous tradition of Theseus, violated all his vows to Phyllis. Repay the lover who comes laden with glittering promises in his own coin; the ones who bring you gifts deserve that you treat them fairly. If you don't treat a munificent suitor honestly by giving him his money's worth, you are sufficiently wretched to put out the sacred flame of the Vesta, or of absconding with the treasures from the temple of Inachus. But I think I am saying more in my enthusiasm than I originally intended.

When your maid has permitted herself to be persuaded by your lover into bringing you his note, read it carefully for such hidden meanings as might tend to give you a clue to his true sentiments. Scan each word cautiously for unexpected implications and don't fall all over yourself in haste to answer him. Suspense, if not too prolonged, acts as a commendable titillation. Don't gush and make too many concessions if he's a youngster; on the other hand, don't be too severe with him. Let your answer be non-committal, and refuse in such a manner that his hopes shall continue to flourish. Couch your reply in simple terms and don't go in for stylistic tricks. Frequently, a well written letter acts as the required impetus to an undecided heart, while a crude and carelessly written epistle may undo the advantages of your appearance. All of you who wish to enjoy the stolen fruits of Love, remember, in the process of cuckolding your husbands, you will do well to entrust your mail to faithful carriers. Write nothing incriminating to a young and inexperienced lover, for you are likely to regret your lack of caution. Remember that you are placing into his hands the wherewithal to frighten and dominate you for the rest of your days. You must be afraid, always, that he will take advantage of you and deceive you, and so it is fitting that you practise deceit on your own account. Learn to write in a manner utterly dissimilar to your usual script and be careful to write only on new waxed tablets, for sometimes the previous letter can still be deciphered. Address your lover always as if you were writing to a female friend, and take care that you invariably use a feminine pronoun.

But let us get on to more important matters. It is the privilege of beasts to rage about furiously, and it is the duty of man to control himself. A fit of ire swells the veins on your forehead; an ugly, hectic flush suffuses your face, and your eyes pop out of your head when you glare furiously. Pallas abandoned flute playing when she discovered that it distorted her face. If you could see yourself in a mirror when you have lost your temper and your hair flies wildly about and your visage is covered by an unsightly grimace, you would have difficulty in recognizing yourself. Avoid, whenever you can, to look haughty, for, you may believe me, it will serve your purpose far better to show a pleasant and engaging smile. It is not by words only that men are repelled; a disdainful glance is sometimes sufficient to give an index of a shrewish nature. Meet every gaze frankly and have a sparkle of recognition towards all eyes that seem to greet you. It is important that you remember these seemingly trifling preambles. Men do not generally favor women of somber countenance, in spite of Ajax and his Tecmessa. Gay hearts require jovial company; and as for myself, I could readily dispense with Andromache and Tecmessa. Nor is it likely that their husbands saw aught in them but mothers for their children and found the pleasant outlets for their lighter moments among spirits less truculently gloomy.

You will have to marshal and command your forces in almost military fashion. A general puts one officer in command of his artillery, another, of his infantry; a third has the cavalry in his keeping. It is your business to appraise the situation in a similar fashion: seek to have your lovers play such parts as are most advantageous to you. If you have a friend who is an eloquent attorney, let him plead your cases; another who is rich shall buy you the things your heart desires. Let the doctor advise you gratuitously, and the judge appraise your case and its merits in advance. We poets can give you little besides our verses; but then, we have always been the greatest lovers and spread far and wide the reputations of our mistresses. Who would know of Nemesis or Cynthia or Lycoris, unless the poet had spread their fame abroad? And even now, the whole world wants to know the incomparable Corinna whose charms I always chant. Consider that poetry is a refined and subtle art, and its practitioners reck not the common glories, riches and success, that well content the ordinary herd. Our Muse requires solitude and thought, and our simplicity makes us a facile target for Love's burning shafts. We are most easily deceived, for our mode of life is most unworldly and our attitude is always altruistic. Do, therefore, favor the poets in your kind considerations, for they are inspired by the gods and they traffic with the heavens. It would be more than mercenary to demand gifts or cash from such as we.

Don't permit your new lover to find you avaricious. You may frighten him by showing your hand too early. A young colt must gradually be taught his paces; you can do what you will after he bears the harness peacefully. Your snares must vary with the ages of your prospective paramours. If he is young, you must condition him in such a fashion that you will become the dominant influence in his life. Keep all other women away from him, for you can share nothing in Love's domain. No silly, democratic principles apply here.

With an older man, you must use different methods. He is more cautious and slow-moving; but on the other hand, he will permit you transgressions that no young lover would endure. He is not likely to break down your door in fierce and impetuous frenzy; he will not maul you up or scratch you because of fury or affection; and he is not likely to tear his own hair or yours. All this will do very well for a novice at the game; but all these furies and tantrums would ill become a man with some experience in life.

An older man will overlook a good deal in your conduct, for his affection is a small burning but lasting flame, like a moist log of wood in your fireplace. The young man will burn more brightly and intensely; but it doesn't last very long. The preliminaries past, there is no need for you to give yourself completely for awhile. In fact, that's not the way you must manage. A ready conquest is slightly valued, and you had better keep him

off with promises just when he least expects to be re-
buffed. Let him pound upon your door and call you
names; don't let it disturb you. He may swear he's
through with you, but don't worry. He'll be around
again tomorrow. Nothing is better for a jaded appetite
than some food, acidy or bitter, that re-awakens the taste
of your palate. A breeze astern may be quite welcome
to a ship becalmed, but many a vessel has gone on the
rocks because a storm was hitting too much sail. What
makes of matrimony such a tepid affair is that each party
to the bargain is free to gain access to the other at will.
Remember this; and have the slave occasionally bang the
door in your lover's face. And now I am coming to the
really intimate and mischievous part of the business in
which I am foolishly advising you to my own undoing.

When your innocent young man has fallen in your
snares, you are to lead him into thinking that he is the
only cockerel on the dung-pile. But later on, by slow
degrees, you are to imply that there are others who have
or are or may enjoy your favors. It is important for you
to practise this simple device to act as a spur on his
glutted desire. Competition makes a horse-race, and it
is good for the jaded appetite to feel the loss of food. I
am speaking from personal experience and I must can-
didly admit that these little setbacks add quite a fillip to
one's romantic ardor. Don't let him notice anything
definite; but pester him with imaginary rivals for they
are infinitely more effective than real ones. Pretend that
some man's servant is forever at your door and troubling
you with offers from his master. Pretend to be in con-
stant fear of your jealous husband and his prying hire-
lings. And even if you are free from every supervision,

pretend to be in constant dread of unexpected discovery. Although nothing should prevent him from entering at your door, insist that he climb romantically through the windows at the hazard of his limbs, and don't forget to greet him at his entrance with a mysterious and frightened expression. At the proper moment, your maid can rap ominously on the door, and, ashen-faced, you are to clasp him to your bosom and say: "We are undone." At this point, if it amuses you, stuff him hastily into a cupboard and let him sweat a while. Occasionally let him have his fun without these dramatic interludes, for if he gets nothing for his pains, he is likely to appraise his conquest against the effort that it costs him, and consider himself sorely cheated. So far, I have not considered the stratagems required for eluding the watchful gaze of a cunning husband. A wife should respect and obey her husband; that is only fitting and all law and decency require it. But that you are to spend your life in dull servitude seems hardly reasonable or fair to me, and so I will say a few things at random about eluding your guards. If your husband had as many eyes as Argus, you should still be able to give him the slip. Nothing prevents you from writing a letter while you are bathing. He can't prevent your maid from carrying these letters to and fro: she can hide them in her slipper or beneath her tunic. Suppose your husband suspects and seeks these missives about her person. Nothing prevents you from inscribing your sentiments on the body of your servant, and she will thus become the living letter, bearing your secrets on her shoulder-blades. You can write with fresh milk and your script will be invisible until your lover pours a bit of charcoal dust across the writing.   Remember how Acrisius moved heaven and earth to keep Danae intact, and still he failed and became a grandfather against his will.   He cannot keep you absolutely under lock and key; sometimes you will go to the theater, to the circus, or to a festival, or even to a religious celebration.   He may stand outside the women's bath, guarding your drapes, but if your lover has failed to gain entrance into the bath itself beforehand, he is not deserving of your favors.   You can always feign illness and have a female friend sleep in your room at night.   To have an accomplice of that sort is worth a good deal.   There are more ways of entering a room than through a door, but even so, you can get the guardian of your chamber drunk or drugged, according to your need and fancy. Your female friend can even grant him some trifling favors, leading him to believe that others are to follow, and thus you may buy his good will.   But why discuss so many devious methods when quite likely a trifling tip can buy any servant in your house? Both gods and men are bought with gifts; a large enough present might even shut the husband's mouth.   But don't tip more than once a year, for with these fellows it becomes a malady to crook the hand in cunning supplication.   What I say to men about guarding against their friends applies equally to you.   It may annoy you to discover that the chum of your bosom, who so obligingly lends you a room as a meeting-place for you and your lover, has but lately quit that same bed, where she has groaned with pleasure in the arms of that self-same paramour.   Don't employ maids that are too pretty, for they are likely to understudy your part.

Consider my folly and observe how I've bared myself to all the fatal blows of women. See how my glib tongue has run away with my caution and how I, the bird, have taught the fowler the methods for laying snares; the hind has taught the hounds how to trace out her lair. And yet I feel content. I have advice to give and so I give it, regardless of the consequences.

Pretend to be enamored when you're not, for no man is such a dolt as not to like affection, nor can anyone be so ill-mannered and misshapen but he will readily believe that you adore him, if only your manner is persuasive enough. Practise all the tricks, the sighs, the tears, and the seductive affectations—which ought to come to you naturally—and you can make any man believe anything you wish.

And if you hear that he's gallivanting about with someone else, don't rush at him with fury and make a fuss. Just think it over quietly and don't believe everything you hear. Remember Procris and her sad fate, caused by an over-abundance of credulity.

On the gentle, undulating slopes of Hymettus there bubbles a clear spring whose brim is framed with fragrant herbs and grasses. A soft carpet of many colored flowers is spread there, and although, properly speaking, it is no forest, the low shrubs and a few pines make the scene one of idyllic enchantment. The tender tips of the plants are set softly a-tremble by the passing zephyrs. Cephalus, wearied from the chase, would frequently desert his companions and throw himself exhausted into the grass to rest. One day, some passing gossips heard him whispering, "Come, tender Zephyr; abide with me and cool me from the heat that does oppress me." The busy-bodies had no sooner heard his innocent exclamation than they hastened forthwith to notify Procris, his spouse, that her husband was disporting himself in amorous dalliance with another, and that they had but a few moments before heard him affectionately discoursing with her in the woodland brake. Poor Procris was distraught with grief and nearly swooned when she heard of her husband's duplicity. Her anguish drained the blood from her cheeks until she was as pale as those belated clusters of grapes which the first hoar frost has painted. The ripe white cherry is not paler than was Procris when she heard the name of her unknown rival. She threw herself into the dust and cursed the fortunate Zephyr who had robbed her of her husband's affection; she clawed herself till the blood flowed from her lacerated bosom. Then, suddenly, bethinking herself of vengeance, she raced across the countryside until she neared the glade that the gossips had indicated as the trysting place of the lovers. Softly, not to arouse their suspicion, she treaded her way twixt gorse and bracken, carefully avoiding all dried and crackling branches that might forewarn the lovers of her approach. A thousand troubling thoughts beset her distracted heart, as Procris, seething with jealous rage, came nigh to the spot where Cephalus rested. Rapidly her mind rehearsed the possible developments were she to spring upon the lovers unawares. It is the unhappy gift of a great love that it believes readily some dread fatality is soon to end the happy dream of its existence. Poor Procris anticipated and dreaded the next few moments, and as she came upon recent footprints in the grass, she paused momentarily to control a gasp. The hot noonday sun stood high overhead when Cephalus, passing close to his unseen spouse, threw himself into the grass and said, "Sweet Zephyr, come to me, thou cooling breeze."

And like a flash of lightning that on a dark and stormy night illuminates the landscape for miles around, the truth appeared to Procris. She grasped her palpitating heart with an exclamation of uncontrollable joy. Her color returned to her cheeks as she stretched out her arms in longing for her husband's embrace.

Cephalus, alarmed at the sound that she had made, suspected the presence of some wild animal and quickly jumped for his bow. And no god stayed his hand, no miracle intervened. With one swift unerring dart, he struck his mistress, and with a cry of anguish, she fell at his feet. Cephalus threw himself on the turf beside her; distraught with sorrow, he vainly pleaded with her passing spirit to stay. And the Zephyr that had caused the error of rash Procris carried away her spirit on a soft and gentle breeze. She died within the arms of Cephalus; and holding his mouth pressed close to hers, he inhaled her dying breath.

But let us not waste further time by pointing morals and drawing apt illustrations to bear out some point in our argument. Let us discuss how you are to conduct yourselves at public banquets, dinners and festivals. Don't come too early and stay your frolicsome spirits till after nightfall, for it is reasonable that eyes bedewed with wine will think the plainest girl quite charming. Consider what the charitable light of the moon may do for your imperfections and you will act wisely to delay your appearance. Eat the food delicately, with the tips of your fingers, and don't leave markings of grease all over your face. Wipe your hands frequently. Don't glut yourself, for it is unlikely, if Helen had stuffed herself like a pig, that the son of Priam would have loved her as he did. If she had produced objectionable table manners, she would have caused him to regret the abduction. You may drink with a little more freedom, for Love and wine are natural playmates. But hold your liquor like a lady; don't stagger about when you're tipsy and wave your arms. The drunken woman is invariably disgusting and makes one think that she is anyone's for the asking. Don't fall asleep at the table, for if you do, you deserve to be raped by any scoundrel that happens along.

I am slightly embarrassed by what is about to follow, but encouraged by Venus, I will now proceed to tell the most important thing of all. Make up your mind as to what posture best becomes you when you enter the battlefield of Love. If you have a pretty face, lie on your back; if your hips are comely, find occasion to display them. Remember that Melanion bore Atalanta's thighs upon his shoulders; if yours can bear comparison with hers, put them in the same place. If you are short, let your lover play the jockey. Andromache, who was as tall as Hector, never did anything like that, but don't let it worry you. If you are unusually tall try to find a kneeling position; if your legs are good and your breasts without a flaw, stretch yourself sideways upon a couch, and let your hair fly loosely about your shoulders. If the gate of your transgressions has been widened beyond the point of comfort, then by all means turn around and lift your back to the fray. The least fatiguing method is to lie on your side.

No oracle in Egypt or in Greece has given better advice than I am giving you and you should listen in rapt silence and attention. Respond to your lover from your innermost being and share with him equally the pleasures that abound. If meanwhile you can think of some witty or naughty things to whisper in his ear, let nothing detain you. And if you are a stepchild of nature and the whole thing is more or less boring to you, it is your duty to pretend the ecstasies you do not feel. In any case, you have my sympathy if Love means nothing to you. Be careful and don't pretend too much excitement: time your gasps and cluckings of exuberance so that they may appear reasonable. The shrine of bliss should have its secrets, and the woman who has enjoyed the pleasures of Love and suddenly demands payment is a fool. Don't keep too bright a light in your bedroom, for there are some things that profit by dim illumination.

And now ungird, for I have done. The swans are ready to bear me aloft, and you, my young and promising pupils, emulate my precepts and grave upon the trophies of your conquests:

"OVID WAS MY MASTER."

LOVE'S REMEDY

WHEN Love had read the title to this book, he said, "Clearly Ovid is determined to wage war upon me." Nothing could be further from the truth, for no standard-bearer in your cause has served you more faithfully than I. While others burn with a tepid, wavering flame, I am always consumed with love. And even at this wretched moment, I am more in love than I have ever been. I have organized and tabulated the whole business of loving which was hitherto but a meaningless instinctive welter of passion. Reason supplants accident in these matters, all thanks to myself. Do you believe that I am about to betray you and retrace my own footsteps? I have no intention to undo my labors.

If you are in love with a woman who requites your affection, raise high aloft your sail of bliss, and let the prospering breezes bear you onward. But if you are smitten with some worthless baggage and every passing hour gathers a toll of tears, then harken to my remedies and abide by my advice. Pause before you suspend your hapless carcass from a beam or plunge a dagger into your already wounded heart. Cupid, a lover of tranquillity, will surely welcome my efforts in behalf of an unfortunate lover who is otherwise destined to die, a vic-

tim to his passion. If by the skill of my art I preserve
your life, this child must surely approve my pacific en-
deavors. He is king in the realm of dalliance and of
play, and his keen arrows are never tinged with blood;
it is the business of his stepfather Mars to go about drip-
ping with gore. It is more fitting for Cupid to harken
to the tender whispers of his mother Venus, for her ad-
vice will cause no battles to be fought, nor bereave a
mother of her children. Content yourself, O Cupid,
with conspiracies that shall equip an anxious husband
with the horns of cuckoldry, and the plots of lovers parted
by adverse circumstances. Act as the sponsor at sport-
ive brawls for Love's sake and be content with the wrath
of the suitor who batters at the unyielding door of his be-
loved. Be satisfied with tears; for if it be your will to
claim a life, your flaming torch, meant to illumine Love's
delights, will serve to light a funeral pyre.

And Love, hearing my plaintive chant, lifted his
wings and granted that I fulfill my self-imposed mission.
Now those of you to whom I have imparted the secret
arts of Love and who, in spite of all my cunning, have
failed and been deceived, learn now the ways of healing
your wound. The plant whose poison will infect you
grows from the self-same soil as the herb whose balm
will cure you. Roses and nettles often spring from the
same clod of earth. The son of Hercules, injured by the
javelin of Achilles, was healed by the weapon that dam-
aged him. My advice is equally good for men and
women and do ye both harken to me. If the examples
that I give are not pertinent to your particular di-
lemma, they may by comparison be beneficial to you.
My mission is a simple one: I wish to free you from

bonds that cause you grief and to extinguish the fire that consumes you. Had Phyllis been one of my pupils she would have lived a longer span. She sought the lonely shores nine times; had I been her preceptor, she would have come more frequently. Could Dido have harkened to the rich fruit of my experience, she would have refrained from destroying herself. Nor would Medea have slaughtered her innocent offspring in rage against her faithless husband. Tereus, beside himself with longing for Philomel, would never have been changed into a bird, and as for Pasiphae, she would have been cured of her passion for the white bull. Phædra would have forgotten her incestuous madness; and could I have dealt with Paris, then Menelaus would have lived tranquilly with Helen, and Troy would never have been conquered by the Greeks. If Scylla could have read my poems, Nisus had never lost his precious purple lock. Harken unto me, my pupils, and free yourselves from sordid, morbid passions. Let me steer your craft, bearing your troubled souls, securely to the promised harbor of peace. You read your Ovid to be instructed in Love; read now the same Ovid to be cured. I shall be your defender and I shall remove the malady that gnaws at your heart. Co-operate with me, and our efforts will be crowned by success.

Let us invoke Apollo, inventor of poetry and medicine, (for I am both poet and doctor) and beseech him to protect his spokesman.

If at the beginning of a love affair you have some misgivings, then turn and flee ere you are too deeply in love; for once the malady has gotten hold upon you, it may prove too powerful for reason. Halt, therefore, in the very beginning, while there is still time. Time brings all things to fruition: rounds out the grape upon the vine; strengthens the frail blade into a sturdy stalk. The tree whose gracious shade shields you from the sunlight was once a tender shoot; originally you could tug it from the earth with one slight pull, but now its sturdy roots dig deep into the earth. Consider carefully the chances pro and con in a new love affair, and cautiously withdraw your neck from a yoke that will hold you relentlessly. Your chance to fight it off is strongest at the outset, for it is futile to administer medicine when the disease has had a chance to ravage your body. Do not postpone a remedy, no matter how painful, if you can apply it today and your chances of a cure are thereby enhanced. If it seems unpleasant today, the prospect shall not improve by tomorrow. A lover has always excuses for postponements at his finger-tips. Your cure cannot begin too soon. With the first symptoms of your malady, you must administer a powerful anti-toxin. At their source all rivers start as rivulets, and only as they proceed and are strengthened by various tributaries, do they gain force.

If Myrrha at the very outset had realized the scope of her sin, she would never have become a tree. Many a slight wound neglected becomes an incurable and deadly ulcer.

It is difficult to part from a pleasant folly and so we keep postponing until the virus has spread into our blood. Once the tree has firmly set its roots into the earth, or your heart has been entwined powerfully in the coils of some fatal amour, it is difficult to uproot and untie. Still, though I am arriving tardily upon the scene,

—called in at the very last moment—I shall, nevertheless, endeavor to free you and set your spirit at ease. The son of Poeas, when wounded, took a sharp dagger and with one bold stroke slashed off the affected part. He lived long afterwards and is even reputed to have ended the Trojan War.

It is better to act with dispatch in the beginning of your malady, for afterwards all remedies are going to be slow and painful. Having missed the opportune and early moment, however, you had better wait until the crisis of your malady has passed. It is impossible suddenly to halt a fiercely racing charger. A swimmer who can reach the far-side of a river by gliding at least partly with the current, but insists on cutting straight across, is foolhardy indeed. I don't expect that you, who are perhaps willful and proud, will casually abandon your mad course and listen to the voice of caution. Sooner or later, when you will be sore from reiterating your grievances and perhaps a little weary from fruitless endeavor, it is more likely that you will benefit from my advice. It is useless to tell a mother not to weep at her child's funeral, and only a madman would choose such time to speak of resignation. At first, let the full tide of grief submerge her heart, and only after she has been numbed by the realization of her sorrow, can you casually begin to utter soft words of consolation. In medicine, it is perhaps the most important thing to intervene at the proper moment. The draught of wine that comforts you on one occasion may do you infinite mischief upon another. Let the cure begin when the moment is ripe or you will but aggravate the malady.

When you have reached that point of your disillusionment when the outside voice of a sympathetic bystander can be of assistance to you, it will be time for you to harken to me. Love is the child of idleness, as slothfulness begets sensuality. It behooves you, therefore, to be active, and you may succeed in breaking the painful shafts of Cupid and putting out his torch. As the poplar longs for the pure stream of water, and as reeds crave the swampy sodden soil, so does Venus delight in idleness. Love is the natural enemy of toil; busy your idle hands and you will have taken the first step towards your cure. Laziness, gaming, an overabundance of sleep and an indulgence in spirits may do you no serious damage, but they rob you of energy and resolution. You leave your fortress unarmed and Love can capture you with ease. Cupid is ever found in the company of idleness and he shuns the haunts of the active and industrious. If your mind sets itself no definite aim, it will fall prey readily to his whisperings.

We have a court of justice in which the codes of law are being interpreted. Perhaps your friends are in need of an attorney? Get yourself a job as attorney. Or join the army and take an active part in our various campaigns. All soft and sensuous delights will flee from your mind as you pursue the Parthian foe and win distinction on the battlefields. Thus you may win a twofold triumph, over Love and the Parthian, and bring back the trophies of your conquest to the altar of your god. Venus, wounded by a spear, desired her lover to continue the war. And why did Aegisthus commit adultery? He had nothing to do. All the other princes were engaged in everlasting battles before Troy, and

Greece had shipped off all her forces into Asia. With the best of intentions, Aegisthus had no wars to fight nor were there any cases to plead, as all the law-suits in Argos were abandoned. Unwilling to do nothing, he did what he could: he became involved in a love affair.

In this fashion Love finds an ingress into our hearts and remains there. A very good cure for your malady would be to go to the country, which is full of simple yet absorbing tasks. Tame the willful oxen to bend their necks beneath the yoke and cut the stubborn earth with the shining ploughshare. When the soil is furrowed, sow the grain; and soon your labors will be rewarded by a bounteous harvest. Work, and the branches in your orchard shall be laden with abundance and each tree bend beneath the weight of its fruits. In the country, soft-murmuring brooks pass glitteringly between shadow and sunlight, and gentle sheep browse on the fragrant hillside. On high, sure-footed goats prance from crag to crag, and in the evening, they return, their udders filled with milk. A curly shepherd lad upon his reeds plays some simple rustic melody; beside him on the ground, slumbering uneasily, lie his dogs, the guardians of his flock. From beyond a woodland copse, a lowing cow can be heard crying for its calf. A swarm of bees has been dislodged from its hive and its ample store of honey is being removed. Spring is rich with flowers; summer with the ripening of its corn, and autumn with the harvest of its fruits. Every year, the vineyard bears its rich burden of grapes, and every year its fruition is renewed. The fields are relieved of their corn and the farmer binds it into sheaves that glow like molten gold in the sunlight. How multifold are the occupations of the country! How pleasant to wield a pruning knife, insert an alien twig and see the tree bedeck itself with foreign foliage! And once the pleasures of these growing, ripening things have laid their soothing balm upon your heart, then Love, defeated, shall totter forth and leave you cured.

Consider also the diversions of hunting. Often has Venus been put to flight by the sister of Apollo. Tramping the forests, accompanied by a hound, you may hunt the hare, and set your traps on the slopes of the hillside; capture the cautious stag; and conquer the boar with your deadly spear. At night, you will be weary unto death from these exertions and readily forego the attentions of women for the solacing embrace of slumber. If these exertions prove too strenuous, you can go bird-hunting, which is less arduous and still diverting. You can go fishing and carefully bait the hook. By such means as these, you will eventually be cured of your fatal affliction.

Remember that you must go as far as possible from the spot where your malady was first conceived. You must do this no matter how many sound reasons you can discover for remaining. The mere idea of such a proposition may fill your eyes with tears, but the more unfeasible it seems to you, the more urgent ought to be the haste of your departure. Go even though it rains, or is a holiday or some special occasion of celebration in your family; let nothing keep you from your journey. Don't figure how far you have come but how far you still have to go, and don't linger for the purchase of a wardrobe or for any other silly excuse that will hopelessly detain your cure. Don't turn your head longingly on Rome but run like the Parthian and save your skin as he does.

I believe in drastic treatments only, for there can be no cure without pain. When you are ill, they deny you all the good things you crave and feed you nothing but bitter physic, and yet you suffer it willingly enough to save the health of your body. You must submit to the same treatment to save your mind, for it certainly is as precious. I admit it will be difficult in the beginning; at first the ox has difficulty with the yoke and the colt refuses harness. It may be hard for you to quit your home and family but don't fool yourself: the chief reason will be Love, and your homesickness is a mere pretext. By all means, leave! The diversions of the journey, your traveling companions, and the changes of persons and places will at once tend to console your wounded spirit. After you have gone, remember that you must stay away, for it is possible that embers of the fire that consumes you are still smoldering treacherously beneath the ashes of your surface indifference. To return prematurely will undo all the efforts you have wasted on your cure. It will be fatal to come back and find that your absence has merely given you a keener appetite for what is bad for you. You are free to believe that you can be cured by drugs and incantations; but believe me, it is all a lot of antiquated nonsense. I have no miracles with which to soothe your languishing soul. No dead will rise out of their graves, no witch shall cast her spells and make the earth a gate for your delivery, nor will the sun grow pale by the casting of a charm. The Tiber in his usual manner will flow into the sea and the moon proceed in her due course, for it is not by spells of magic that the illness can be banished from your heart and Cupid cannot be frightened by the childish trickery of quacks equipped with burning sulphur. Consider how little it availed Circe to possess the herbs of Persa, when the winds were bearing away the vessels of Ulysses. She did all within her power, and it was great, to delay his departure. She who could change men into diverse shapes was unable to cope with the cruel flame of Love that was consuming her and that continued to burn within her long after Ulysses had departed.

When he was making ready to set sail, she pleaded with him to remain, and by divers arguments, endeavored to hold him to her side. Humbly she avowed that at first it had been her hope to become his spouse, and though she was a goddess and a daughter of the sun, she begged his pardon for having held herself worthy of such a high position. She begged him to await the turning of the tides and the coming of more favorable winds; she pointed out that there were no Troys to be conquered and that upon her island they could dwell in happiness and peace; she warned him of the treacherous storms at sea and the unpromising condition of the weather. Gravely did Ulysses harken unto her, and quietly proceeded to set sail. And as his vessels disappeared from her sight, she at once set about with magic incantations; and with cunning art she sought to still the fires of her passion, but she failed. So if you seek aid of this sort, you are foolish indeed.

It may be necessary for you to remain in the capital, not for any subterfuge that Love inspires you with, but for some really important reason. If you are courageous, you shall win nevertheless and free yourself even under these adverse conditions with one sure blow from your dangerous affliction. Keep always before your eyes the multitudinous transgressions of your mistress and hold within your breast a constant mirror for her infidelities. Remember the cruelty of her treatment and how frequently you spent the night upon her doorstep. Make an accounting of all she has cost you in peace of mind, in gifts and in health. Recall the common louts who now enjoy her favors and you will be sowing the seeds of hatred in your heart against her.

But lately, I was much enamored of a certain wench whose temperament was ill-suited to my own. I immediately bethought myself of my own remedies and proceeded to doctor myself. I have to admit I was a wretched patient. In recounting to myself what awkward legs she had, I had difficulty in keeping from my mind the truth that they were more than ordinarily shapely. In harping on the ungainliness of her arms, I recalled in anguish that they were very beautiful and well modelled. I pointed out to my harassed heart that the strumpet was squat and shapeless, but the difficulty of the matter lay in the fact that she was nothing of the kind. I accused her of being greedy, and this indeed was the only fault I could justly accuse her of. You will notice how closely related the good and bad invariably are and it merely is necessary to exaggerate a virtue so it become a fault.

Proceed then in the following fashion: If she is charmingly plump, insist that she is dumpy; if she's a brunette, say she looks Ethiopian; if she's slender, say she's a skeleton; if she is pleasantly coquettish, say she is brazen; if she is modest, call her witless. Do your utmost to have her expose her failings. If she has a hoarse voice, insist that she sing; and if her movements are awkward, make her dance; if she stutters, insist that she talk to you freely; if her breasts are unsightly, make her expose them on every occasion; if her teeth are poor, keep on telling her jokes; if her eyes are sensitive, make her cry. Call on her in the morning before her toilette is completed, for you may believe me that what we see of women is the least part of them, and their precious garments cover a multitude of imperfections. Dropping in on her unexpectedly you may see her looking her worst, with boxes and bottles full of beauty aids, the unguents running in greasy streams down her cheeks, her hair standing all awry about her head, and the whole room reeking with a stench that will turn your stomach.

I am about to tell you something more intimate but I must admit there are some matters one cannot readily discuss. You will have to read between the lines and make out my implications as best you can. I have been severely criticised of late for the freedom of my language. I am consoled by the knowledge that my work gives pleasure to a multitude and is celebrated the world over; and I am solaced by the knowledge that slander did not halt on the threshold of the great Homer himself. Those situated upon the high places are ever subjected to calumny, as the winds forever hurl themselves upon the highest peaks of the mountains. Let those who are outraged by the frankness of my Muse endeavor to regain their sense of proportion. Remember that each subject has to be treated with the proper method; that wars are appropriately sung as Homer sang of Troy; that tragedy needs to be treated in a lofty and austere manner;

that noble rage requires the ponderous method. My Muse must wear a variable garment: a mild elegiac form must serve to chant of Cupid and his quivers.

I am consoled by the fame that I already enjoy and I hope to continue, in spite of the tongue of malice, just as I have begun. This is the only answer that I deign to give my detractors, and so let me proceed with my advice. When the night approaches upon which your fair one is to grant you the first delights of her person, lest you have too much exuberance in the enjoyment of her, going as you do charged with a full quiver, pay first a fruitful visit to some other charmer and take the first keen edge off your appetite. The second affair is bound to be less fierce.

Persuade your mistress, when you are about to copulate with her, to assume the posture that will least become her, and nothing can be easier than that. You cannot conceive how vain they are, and how they deem themselves beautiful under all conditions. See that the room is brilliantly lighted and take note of the infinite blemishes of her body. And when you are exhausted, nauseated to fatigue, filled and glutted to the over-brimming of your spirit, and wish that you had never touched a woman, then gaze and linger long on all her failings and deposit them securely within your mind for future reference. You may object that these are trifling resources; and I will agree that singly each of my remedies could avail but little, but joined together, they can help you considerably. Besides, a bull dies from the bite of a viper, and a hound of average size can hold a boar at bay. Hold on to each shred that I offer and you will conquer.

I have forgotten to consider that mental reactions differ as do the faces that we sport. Many things that I consider unpardonable might throw you into fits of rapture. There are men who are fatally shocked at the sight of those parts that have given them pleasure; others who, noticing trophies of the battle upon the bed that they have but recently quit, will be utterly revolted with their mistress. I do not counsel you with needlessly gruesome and vigorous remedies, such as concealing yourself to behold your mistress performing those natural functions that decency has prescribed us to perform in solitude.

I advise you, if it is feasible, to have two mistresses at the same time, for thus one passion shall moderate the other. Rivers lose their force when they split and branch off, and the fury of a fire can be diminished by making several small ones out of a big one. It is always advisable to fish with more than one hook in the water, and the man who has the forethought to equip his bow with two strings, has made certain of victory. If you have been so foolish as to retain the affections of but a single mistress, lose no time to find another immediately. Minos forgot Pasiphae by conceiving a passion for Procris and his second love banished the first from his heart. Oenone would have had unchallenged sway in the heart of Paris had he not conceived a passion for the adulterous Queen of Sparta. Philomela outrivaled her sister in beauty and thus she won from her Odrysian, her spouse. I could weary you to death with examples but it must be obvious that the new love always triumphs over the old and the mother of many children bears the death of one more easily than she who, falling over his prostrate form, calls out: "My son! My only son!"

I preach no innovations; there is a hallowed tradition on this subject. Remember how Agamemnon loved the captive Chryseis. The maiden's father raised such a fuss that the whole neighborhood rang with his groanings. The couple was getting on famously but the old fool insisted that he'd have his daughter back no matter what befell, and with the help of Achilles, the old man finally prevailed. After she had returned to her father's roof, Agamemnon, missing her sorely, was reminded of another maiden, the fair Briseis, who shared the couch of Achilles. Being a king and wielding a powerful scepter, Agamemnon voiced his wish in such unmistakably serious terms, that shortly afterwards he had forgotten his former love in the arms of the fair Briseis.

Follow his example. Find yourself another woman, and let your affection hover uneasily between the two. If you are troubled to find them, read my *Art of Love*. Voyage out upon the sea of Love courageously and soon your ship will be laden with beautiful wenches. And if my advice is any good and you will listen to it even if your heart were burning with the fires of Aetna, your mistress will think you colder than ice. Pretend that you are through with her even if you are not; and assume the calm you do not feel, while laughter hides your unshed tears. I don't insist that you break with her at the height of your passion; but learn to pretend adequately when there is no need for it. A calm, however false, if it is assumed with sufficient regularity, can eventually become a sincere detachment. Frequently, in order to avoid more drinking, I pretend to be asleep, and have just as frequently fallen asleep indeed. I have sometimes been much amused by a man pretending to be passionately in love in all sincerity, and was like a hunter caught in his own snare. Love comes into your heart by habit, and by habit you must learn to get rid of it. Your mistress, let us say, has promised on a certain night to lie with you. When you get to her house, you find that the gate is shut in your face. Be tranquil; make no fuss; just simply walk away. The next morning make no mention of the affront and pretend that the whole thing doesn't really concern you very much. I shall be much surprised if this treatment will not upset her a good deal. Don't be too critical and don't analyze too closely the reasons for your doing one thing or another. It is advisable even to hide your own tactics from yourself. In any case, be brusque with her; and I think her arrogance will melt before your own. If you pass her house and she invites you pretend to be engaged on pressing business; and if she offers to sleep with you on a certain night, pucker your brow and tell her you will be unable to come. It will be worth it in the end to discipline yourself thus; besides, you can find consolation readily enough in the arms of some other woman.

Surely these treatments are not too severe. I always try to reconcile pleasure with good sense. Naturally, as the people themselves vary, the treatment has to vary along with them. Some maladies require an operation; while some are cured by medicine. If you are too weak to leave the town as I advise you, then don't attempt to shake off your fetters. Your malady has got you by the throat? Well, then, it is useless to fight. You must find something for the thirst that's driving you mad and drink to your fill from the middle of the river. Drink more than enough, so much in fact that you vomit up everything you have imbibed. Throw yourself at her night and day; have your fill of her in every way and manner; and she shall prove the means of curing your ills. Remain with her even after you could leave her with a quiet heart; never quit her house and keep her up until her very presence nauseates you.

But he who banishes Love must first of all rid himself of jealousy; for if he is forever in distress lest he lose her, his mistress will have a continual and vicious hold upon him.

By the Collinian gate there stands a temple in whose lofty halls a great god holds sway; his name is Oblivion. Hither come the sick, the lame, the blind, the halt, and all those lovers whose passion is unrequited. And in this temple the god whispered to me: "Ovid, you who alternately kindle and extinguish the flames of affection, add this, my maxim, to your lessons: Let every lover balance the favors and the ills of an amour, and he will be cured of his passion. Every one has sufficient ills to bear even if matters prosper fairly well. If you have borrowed a sum of money, it will trouble you, and if you lend it, it certainly should; if you have a stern father, all your other happiness will be over-shadowed by his severity; if you have married a poor wife, you will blame her for your failure; if you have a prospering vineyard, you will fear the blight of vermin that may rob you of your harvest; if you have a ship at sea, laden with treasure, the treachery of the ocean may well give you cause for uneasiness. One man fears for the life of his son in the wars and another for the virtue of his daughter who is marriageable." Thus spoke the god ere his dream-like figure vanished, and I wondered if he himself were nothing but a dream.

Avoid all solitude; it is disastrous for you to be alone. Your only salvation can be in a throng. When you are lonely, all sorts of mad and melancholy fancies will come to torment you. The vision of your favorite mistress shall be ever before you, and this is the reason why the night is so much harder to bear than the day. For then you seek the solitude of your chamber, your friends have left you, and there is no company to cheer you. Don't lock yourself into a secret chamber to hide your tear-stained visage behind curtained windows. Let us hope you have at least one trusty friend who will not desert you in this crisis. Quite likely it was the silence and the solitude of the forest that brought such grief to Phyllis. The poor distressed maiden, like a mad Bacchante at the feast of Bacchus, would fly about the forest with disordered tresses, and fling herself upon the ground in an ecstasy of wild despair. She would cry the name of her faithless lover to the unheeding waves, and when she came down to the seashore for the ninth time, along that narrow pathway that ran through the dense foliage, if only the poor hapless creature could have had someone beside her to admonish or to cheer her, her fate surely would have been less disastrous.

Remember, my female listeners, (for my advice is pertinent to both men and women equally) to shun solitude, for you too may share the fate of the unhappy Phyllis. A certain pupil of mine, who had religiously followed all my advice on how to cure Love, was well-nigh safely in the harbor and had left the treacherous tides behind him, when suddenly he came upon two lovers unawares. The exhibition of their passion sent the miserable youth out again upon the eternal sea of unrest. Steer clear of such as are infected with the malady on their own account, for Love is a fearfully contagious disease, in which one readily feels the symptoms of another person. Like a barren field that suddenly is watered by an errant stream and blossoms forth in full luxuriance, so Love, lying barren in our hearts, may suddenly burst forth at sight of two impassioned lovers.

I am afraid that I can hardly mention all the necessary precautions. A friend of mine was well-nigh cured of his affliction when a neighbor of his suddenly mentioned, in terms of high eulogium, the mistress that my friend was anxious to forget. At once all his old wounds re-opened. It is difficult to protect your house against fire when your neighbor's roof is all aflame. Keep away from her usual promenades and don't let any actual duties make you cross those streets that she is likely to walk on. You're simply starting the trouble all over again and you'd do a darn sight better to move to another hemisphere. An empty stomach can ill abide a well laid dinner table without being tempted to partake; the sound of running water will make your thirst ten times as keen. It is hard to catch the bull when he gains sight of a likely heifer; and the fiery stallion neighs loudly at sight of a mare.

Since you are getting cured and you have gone through a good deal of trouble in affecting this, you had better remember to steer clear of her mother, her best friend, her maid, and everyone connected with her. Suddenly some wretch of a servant will be turning up, delivering a letter, wiping his eyes very likely, and full of hypocritical snifflings. Don't be foolish and inquire how she is getting on; just shut your mouth and you will never regret it.

Finally don't keep recounting reasons why you must break with her, for these arguments lead nowhere. Just be quiet until you are really through with her. If you rush around and tell the whole world that you don't love her any more, you are giving undoubted proof of the exact opposite. Just drop her by slow degrees, imperceptibly, steadily and surely, and you cannot fail to be rid of her in the end. A turbulent mountain stream, for all its impetuous gurgling, doesn't go very far, while the river, slow-moving but imperiously bent upon his way, keeps going ceaselessly through many lands. Your affection should be like a cloud that melts imperceptibly into the heavens. Only a gross barbarian can be filled with hate right after a great affection. Stop very slowly paying those minute little courtesies and attentions which I have told you about.

If you find that you hate the woman, the chances are you are still not through with her; very possibly, still love her; but in any case, that your state of mind is one most difficult of cure. Let you not be at daggers' points with the woman you have but lately cherished. It frequently happens that a man will bring official charges against a woman, heap disgrace upon her and yet be still in love with her.

An acquaintance of mine made a public scandal the other day when his mistress approached in a litter. He was going to hand her a writ and requested in a loud voice that she descend from her conveyance. She followed his request, but no sooner had her foot touched the ground and he beheld her in the familiarity of her gracious loveliness than he flung himself at her feet and cried out, "You have won the case." He threw away the tablets and fell into her arms.

Don't rush into law courts. You can do a lot better by setting up, piece by piece, a wall of indifference. Let her keep your gifts; don't remonstrate; and don't make a riot. Leave her slowly, using the weapons I have armed you with, and remember that sometimes one must make a slight sacrifice. Recall the face and figure of your rival; remember the anguish she has caused you, the doors locked in your face, the broken vows, the mischief and the trouble; then you will readily get into a suitable frame of mind to abandon her. Don't fuss with your appearance and spend a lot of money getting yourself all togged out to make an impression on the woman you are trying to get rid of. Let your actions be casual and indifferent, as with any other acquaintance.

I think the greatest obstacle to your success will be your own conceit. Most likely you flatter yourself into thinking that she is still in some mysterious and secret way quite fond of you. Don't be an ass. They have learnt the art of weeping opportunely and telling lies that sound like the sheerest veracity, come straight from the heart.

Your emotions will be tossed about like a pebble on the beach. Don't explain the reasons for your breaking it off and don't estimate the extent of your sorrow out loud. Let the true scope of your grief be your own secret. Don't endlessly reiterate her misdeeds and don't trouble to listen to her justifications. Let it seem as if you were wronging her. She will be only too ready to believe that this is so and it will add to your strength. I am not playing myself up to be another king of Ithaca, casting Love's weapons into the river and clipping his wings; nor do I propose to slacken his bow. I am satisfied to give advice. Listen to me, and Phoebus will continue, so I trust, to smile upon and prosper my endeavors. I swear that I can hear him present even now, for I have heard his sacred lyre, and it is thus his presence is made manifest.

Tyrian purple, when compared with other dyes, makes them look absolutely trashy. You will do well, in the same manner, to compare your mistress to the really great beauties of the world or to that nameless beauty that exists in the heart of every man, and you will blush for the woman of your affection. Paris favored Juno and Minerva but where were they when Venus put in an appearance? And don't dwell only upon the face but consider bearing and accomplishments.

I am now going to suggest what may seem a little matter, but as it has stood me in good stead, I advise you to follow my example. Don't treasure the letters of your mistress and don't re-read them, for it is a difficult matter to withstand the charm of an old romance brought so vividly into your presence again. It is likely to weaken the strongest character. Throw the letters into the fire and let you hope that the flames are destroying at the same moment the missives and your affection for the writer. Don't cherish any replicas of her likeness; it is useless to keep about one these lifeless images that merely recall the source of one's disaster. Avoid all places where your romance has flourished; they will cause you needless depression and serve you no purpose. Every bench will recall the happy moments you spent sitting there in her society, every path your pleasant walks with her and every bed the rapturous delight you shared in her arms. A wound but recently healed will re-open under such trying conditions, and a convalescent should not expose himself to needless dangers. A slight ember can be made into a fierce conflagration by bringing sulphur to bear upon it. You are to avoid all such places as might prove rich in reminiscences. The heart of the mariner rejoices when he has safely passed the treacherous straits of Scylla. Avoid the rocks of Acroceraunia, where Charybdis ceaselessly regurgitates the waters she has swallowed.

There are other accidental remedies that may help you. Had Pasiphae been poor, her lecherous longings would have been less luxurious. Voluptuousness follows in the train of wealth. No man chose Hecale and no woman took Irus: they were both terribly poor. Poverty provides a lean diet for affection. Of course, this is no reason why you should wish to be down at the heel, but in any case, avoid going out to theaters and to festivals until you are quite cured of your illness. The sound of the music is not likely to be of help to you, and in the theaters they are forever enacting some imaginary love affairs, whose culminations one way or the other are not likely to cheer you.

It pains me to admit this—but in heaven's name avoid all poets who chant of Love. Steer clear of Callimachus, of Sappho and of the poet Teos, for they will upset you no end. Tibullus, continually raving about his Cynthia, will burden your heart, as will Gallus and Ovid, whose verses have a strange influence on lovers.

The chief trouble, of course, will be a rival. Convince yourself, at no matter what cost of logic, that your mistress sleeps in boring celibacy. Remember for how long Menelaus left his wife and remained quietly in Crete undisturbed by his separation from her, but no sooner did Paris carry her off than he decided that life was burdensome without her. The sorrow of Achilles, when Briseis was lost to him, was tenfold because she went to the couch of another. And believe me, he had good cause for his tears. He did what I should have done in his place, and I am no more sensible than he.

May the gods grant that you may pass the door of your late mistress and that your strength be great enough quietly to dig the spurs into the sides of your horse when in front of her house. Pretend that her dwelling is the cave of the Sirens. Better still, learn to look with casual detachment on the coutenance of your late rival, and even if there be some slight twinge of annoyance at sight of him, learn to greet him with passable friendliness. Once you are able to embrace him with sincerity, then, my friend, you have been cured.

Acting somewhat in the fashion of a physician, I shall now prescribe for you a diet. Avoid all eating of things that have a bulbous appearance and such foods as might act upon you as aphrodisiacs. Eat rather such things that have a sedative quality about them, and avoid wine, which has a tendency to increase sexual desire, excepting if drunk in excess. Do therefore drink nothing at all or so much that you will drown your sorrows; but avoid all moderation.

My great task is now completed and you may crown my tired head with laurel. I have steered you towards the harbor of our promise, and youths and maidens healed by my chant will raise their voices in high thanks to their poet.

THE ART OF BEAUTY

AND now, my dears, I shall teach you the art of making up your faces; impart to you the methods required to perpetuate your charms. Effort makes fruitful the barren ground and wipes out noxious weeds, cultivation removes the sourness from the apple, and the tree properly pruned will bear new rich fruit. Art transforms all surfaces with beauty; it gilds the high ceilings and hides the dark earth with marble edifices. Wool is dyed many times in Tyrian purple and ivory is carved with curious devices to suit our luxurious tastes.

In the olden days when Tatius was king, the Sabine women spent more time and thought on the appearance of their fields than on their own toilette. In those days, the robust, high-complexioned matron, squatting on her stool, would spin from morning until night. When her daughter brought the flocks back from the meadows, she would drive them into the shed, and, with a rough hand, make a huge fire from faggots and logs of her own collecting.

But your sisters are less robust and they are accoutered in costumes heavily embroidered with gold; they spray delicate perfumes upon their hair and wear precious rings upon their fingers. Around their necks and in their ears they wear pearls from dusky India. And yet

it ill behooves us to begrudge them all this finery and the
time they require to adorn their persons, since men now-
adays favor exquisiteness of attire. In fact, the male on
his own account has become so luxurious that women
can hardly keep abreast of him.

It is your duty to look your best and it is unimpor-
tant what method Love pursues to spread his nets. Sim-
plicity is at no time amiss. Some women, buried in a
rural community, know how to dress their hair most
admirably. If Athos were to hide them from the world,
they would still dress carefully—for Athos. They are
pleased to dress for the sake of dressing, even if no one be
there to see them—and all young women love to show
themselves to their best advantage. Dress is indeed a
good deal more potent in kindling love than are magic
and miracles. Disdain the pillules and philtres made of
herbs and juices and avoid the flux of mares in heat. In-
cantations avail little against serpents, and rivers will not
flow up hill to their sources. You may bang to your
heart's content on the brass of Temesa, and still the moon
will not come down to earth.

First of all, be careful about your manners. Manners
are extremely important, for time will ravage your beauty
and the smooth prettiness of your face will be charted
with wrinkles. Some day your reflection in a mirror
will fill you with distress and regret. But a pleasant de-
portment is a lasting possession nor can the burden of
the years deprive you of it.

Sleep long and well and I will teach you how to make
your skin exquisite and white. Take about two pounds
of barley and two pounds of vetches and pour over the
lot a mixture of ten eggs. Let it dry in the air and after-

wards have it pounded beneath a mill stone. Pulverize the first horns dropped from a lusty stag and add it to twelve narcissus bulbs that have been peeled; have the whole mixed together in a mortar, but first add about two ounces of gum and Tuscan spelt, and about eighteen ounces of honey. Any woman using this cosmetic will have a face of dazzling whiteness.

Bake white lupines and beans, six pounds of each, and grind them to powder. To this add white lead, the foam of red nitre and Illyrian iris. This must be well kneaded for such a length of time until only one ounce remains. To this add the sticky matter from the nest of a halcyon, and there you have a perfect cure for pimples and blackheads. I advise as a dose half an ounce at a time. To make it adhere properly you should add honey from Attica.

Incense is pleasant to the gods, but it can serve in other places besides their altars. Incense mixed with nitre is very good for blackheads. It requires four ounces of each and one ounce of bark gum; add to this a little bit of oily myrrh; mix the whole together, force it through a sieve, and bind the result with honey. Certain people advise that fennel should be added to the myrrh; nine scruples of myrrh and five of fennel. To this add a handful of dried rose leaves, a little sal ammoniac and male frankincense. On this you are to pour some barley water; let the sal ammoniac and the frankincense be equal in weight to the rose leaves. Apply this, and after a few times you will be the proud possessor of a delightful complexion.

I have seen a woman rub her cheeks with powdered poppies which had first been soaked in cold water.

THE LOVES

BOOK ONE

EPIGRAM

WE WHO *in the beginning were five books have now been reduced to three; the poet Naso has preferred to have his work thus. It may give you little pleasure to read us; nevertheless, your burden has been lessened by two books.*

I. The poet explains how he came to chant the matters erotic instead of singing in strains heroic.

Arms I was about to sing, and the violent deeds of war I was about to trumpet forth in ponderous numbers, with matter and measure suitably combined. All verses were of equal length until Cupid came unexpectedly upon the scene and laughingly absconded with a foot of one verse.

Who gave you, cruel youngster, this right over poetry? We bards belong to the train of the Muses and are not of your company. What if Venus were suddenly to abscond with the arms of the golden-haired Minerva; or the golden-haired Minerva proceeded to fan the flame of love? What sort of sense would there be if Ceres reigned over forest and dell while the quiver-bearing maid would supervise the tilling of the fields? What would you think if the curly-headed Phoebus were to wield the warlike spear while Mars were equipped with the Ionian lyre? You have a great, aye and a potent, realm for your dominion and you are not in need of further powers. Or is everything, everywhere, your property: the vales of Helicon, the lyre of Phoebus?

My new song began well with lofty strain and stately measure, when the next verse, through your interference, became whimsical and slight. I have no subject suited to these light strains, neither a boy nor a girl with long and well-kept locks.

This was the tenor of my complaint, when he, without further ado, chose from his quiver a likely shaft, fashioned especially for my undoing. He stoutly bent his moon-shaped and resilient bow and said, "Poet, here I give you ready matter for your song!"

Unhappy me! who became the target of his marksmanship and am now all aflame and in whose erstwhile vacant heart Love sits enthroned.

Farewell, heroic wars, with stately measures, for I am about to deck my Muse with fragrant myrtle and play upon my lyre a more subtle, sensuous theme.

II. Describing the triumph of Love.

What can be the reason that my couch seems so unyielding and my counterpane refuses to stay in place. Sleeplessly I pass the long and weary night, with every bone in my body aching. If it were Love, surely I ought to know. Perhaps it has stolen into my heart so secretly that I was unaware of its having taken lodging in my breast.

Mayhap it would be fitting for me to resist, but I dread that this will merely add fuel to the inward-stealing flame. I had better yield, for the burden well carried grows lighter and the flame waxes more furious when the torch is moved about. Recalcitrant oxen suffer more than those who yield their necks willingly to the yoke. The restive stallion is tortured by the bit while the gentle mare has less pain in willingly assuming the harness. The stubborn and unyielding suffer much more than those who graciously submit to the servitude of Love.

Lo, I confess! I am your latest victim, O Cupid, and I stretch out my submissive hands to be bound by your laws. There is no need of warfare; peace and tranquillity are my hope and prayer; and it will add little to your credit to have vanquished me unarmed. Bind your brow with myrtle and yoke your mother's doves before your chariot, and as you pass, the people all around shall cry aloud your triumph. And in your train will follow captive youths and maidens, and as you lead them on in stately pomp, I, your most recent spoil, shall be there, nursing my new wound, bearing my bonds unresistingly. Conscience and Modesty, with hands tied behind their backs, and all the others that are foes to the camp of Love, shall tremble before you.

The assembled throng will cheer aloud your triumph and by your side shall be Caresses, Error and Madness, your handmaidens that invariably follow in your train. It is with an army of this sort that you vanquish gods and men, for without their aid you would be weaponless.

And as you pass in joyous triumph, your blessed mother will applaud your conquests from Olympus and scatter down upon you the roses that are offered at her altars. Your hair and wings shall be studded with gems, and the wheels of your chariot shall be golden. And as you pass, your flame shall burn a goodly number in the throng and your weapons will not cease to wreak havoc, even if you should wish to desist. It was thus with Bacchus, whose harnessed tigers could cause no more dread than your span of birds.

And since I am a member of your troop, it is needless for you to waste your efforts in conquering me. Note how your kinsman Caesar shields the vanquished.

III. Recommending the ways and manners of poets who make the most faithful lovers.

Let the maiden who has lately made me her prey give me her love or give me reason to love her forever. I have asked for too much? Well, then, let her permit me to love; and may Cytherea harken to my invocation.

I am willing to be your slave for many long years to come; and I know how to love with a pure and enduring faith. If my lineage is not unduly aristocratic and my ancestor was but a mere knight and my fields are not ploughed by numberless ploughshares, and if my parents guard frugally their limited income, yet is Phoebus my ally, and his nine companions. The finder of the vine is also on my side, and Love protects me and makes me a gift for you. I am filled with good faith, of a deportment without reproach and I am simple and of a becoming modesty. I am not fickle, flitting about among a thousand amours, and you alone shall be my everlasting care. May it be my happy lot to live with you the years spun out upon the threads of the Sisters and to be mourned by you when I have passed on. Give yourself to me as a happy theme for my songs and I promise that they shall be worthy of their cause.

The fame of Io frightened by her horns, and of Leda who was beguiled by a bird, and Europa carried away on a pretended bull whose horns she grasped with virgin hands—the fame of all these, I say, has been made great through songs. And you and I shall equally be known through all the earth and evermore shall my name be coupled with yours.

IV. He conspires with his mistress before they are about to meet at a public banquet which her husband will also attend.

Your husband will attend the same banquet with us, and may that dinner, I pray, be his last! What suffering to be a mere fellow guest and gaze upon the woman that I love with pretended indifference! Is it destined that it shall be merely another's privilege to touch your hand, to put his arms about your neck and feel the warmth of your breast? Be not astonished that after the wine had been served, the Centaurs and Papiths went out to combat for Hippodamia. I am not a dweller of the forest nor are my members ambiguously equine, and yet I am hardly able to keep my hands from you.

Learn your duties as I teach them to you, and don't throw my words to the east or south wind. Arrive before your husband—and yet I don't see much advantage if you do. When he presses you upon the couch, recline beside him readily, but in secret touch my foot. Keep your eyes upon me and watch carefully the language of my mimicry. My brow shall tell you much without a word; my fingers will trace sentences with wine upon the table; and when you are reminded of the wanton treasures of our love, then put a tender finger to your rosy cheeks. If some secret grievance against me is troubling you, let your hand hold the lowest part of your ear. If you are pleased with my discourse, twist your ring slowly about your finger. And when you call down upon the head of your spouse the curses he so well deserves, lay down your hand upon the table in the manner of those pronouncing a prayer.

When he concocts a mixture of wine for you, bid him to drink it himself, and secretly advise a slave to serve you with the kind that you prefer. The cup intended for your drinking, I shall manage somehow to press first to my lips. Don't permit him to put his arms about you, nor let your secret charms be touched by him. But more than all of these, don't let him kiss you, for my uncontrollable wrath shall get the better of me, and I shall arise before all the world to declare myself your lover, to insist that every kiss of yours is mine and claim my property.

Most of these trespasses I shall see, but there are others, hidden by the drapes one wears, that shall cause me greater anguish. The pressing of limb to limb and thigh to thigh, I fear all this because many of these trespasses I have myself wantonly wrought, and so I can well understand the many secret little sins one can commit in public. My lady-love and I have frequently exchanged some hasty endearment beneath the cover of her robe. I know you will not do this, but lest perchance someone may think your actions doubtful, remove the mantle from your shoulders. Encourage your husband to drink, but add no endearments to these supplications; and secretly keep filling his cup. When once he is quite drowsy with liquor, some opportune plan may occur to make us happy. When we rise to leave, attempt to get lost in the crowd; I shall be there. And seek to touch me if even for a few moments.

Consider my unhappy and degraded state that prizes itself fortunate with a few stolen moments of bliss. I shall be separated from you when the night comes on, for then your husband shall shut you up within his dwelling, while I follow from afar and pour my tears upon your cruel door. And then he shall take kisses from you, aye, kisses—and all the rest that I must steal in secret, you must give him as his right and due. But do it all against your will, like one that is made to yield by force; let your favors be reluctant, and let him find Venus unpropitious. If my prayers have any weight, she will grant him no delight; and if she does, may you at least have no delight from him. But whatsoever be the fortunes of the night, tell me at least upon the morrow in a truthful voice that you were most unkind.

V. His joy at having obtained the favors of his mistress.

It was a humid, sultry day, somewhat past noon, when I laid myself upon the middle of my couch to rest. One shutter of my window was open, and the light in my room had the faint glow of twilight in a woodland, just when Phoebus is taking leave, or when the night having departed, the day has not yet fully dawned. It was the sort of light that is auspicious to the timid modesty of shrinking maids. The door is opened and Corinna comes, draped in a tunic, with her fair hair parted, falling in subtle ringlets on her neck. She is fair as the famed Semiramis when passing to her bridal chamber and Lais, loved of many men.

I ripped her splendid tunic though it scarcely hid her charms while she struggled for the frail shelter of her garment. And even thus, struggling as one who would not be overcome, was she overcome, without much difficulty. Standing before me, bereft of her drapes, in all her glorious body was not the slightest sign of blemish. Her shoulders and her arms that I was permitted to gaze upon and to touch defied all rivalry, and her tender breasts seemed formed for caresses. Her body felt smooth beneath her faultless bosom, and I gazed in ecstasy at her long and beautiful side and her youthfully fair thigh.

But why recount each separate charm? I beheld naught unworthy of praise and I clasped her nude and exquisite form to mine.

Who does not know the rest? Pleasantly weary we both lay in quiet repose.

May my fate hold many a noonday such as this!

VI. He excoriates the door-keeper of his mistress who denies him admittance to her dwelling.

Janitor, what a fate is mine! Move the surly door bound on its surly hinge and open up the portals for me. What I ask is small enough: just stand it half-ajar, wide enough to give me room that I may slip through side-wise. My frame is very lean from loving long and my flesh is wasted with desire. Love has taught my soft footsteps to pass the watchful guard and keep my feet from stumbling.

Once I was in dread of night and its phantoms and I marvelled at those who ventured abroad in the dark; but Cupid laughed as did his mother and whispered in my ear: "You too shall become valiant," and then came love; and now I fear no shades that flitter fitfully at night, nor any arms raised up to deal me doom. I fear only you, and prostrate myself at your feet, for you can hurl the only thunderbolt of my undoing.

See how your door has been bedewed with my tears. Unworthy varlet of a gate-keeper, when you were stripped and ready for the scourge, did I not intercede with your mistress in your behalf? And now, when you are free to repay this act of grace, you are unwilling to return the favor that I merit. The night is swiftly pass-ing, so lift the latch and open up the door for me. And so you may be loosened from the chain you bear, nor have to drink eternally the slimy waters of slavery.

But you listen with a heart of iron while I am vainly entreating you, and the door stands unyielding in its oaken brace. Only beleaguered cities bar their doors as a measure of protection. We are in the midst of peace. What foolish caution makes you now in dread of arms? What fate awaits your enemies if you deal thus with a hapless lover? The night is going, minute by minute, so lift the bar from off the door.

I lead no armed guard. Indeed I would be com-pletely alone if cruel Lover were not at my side, and him, even if I desired, I could not dismiss, unless at the same time I chose to be divided from my very self. I am accompanied by Love, a slight quantity of wine, that now courses through my throbbing temples, and a little wreath that is falling from my perfume-laden hair. Surely you are not afraid of arms and escorts such as these? Come, open up the door before the night is gone.

You will not listen to me? Perhaps sleep, and may it be your undoing, has closed your ears to my entreaties. I recall how wide awake you were when I tried to escape your gaze, scoundrel. In all probability you have a love who is now sleeping by your side. Your lot is infinitely superior to mine; I wish I were so comfortably situated. Unbend, hard chains, and take the bar from off the door.

It seems to me there is a sound as of hinges turning and that the door is slightly shaken. I was deceived. It was the beating of the wind upon the panels of the portal, and the deceitful breeze has borne away my hope. Remember thy stolen Oritheyia and come hither, Boreas, and break down this heedless door. The whole city is wrapped in a mantle of silence, and moist with the dew. But the night is passing; so away with the door!

In frenzy I shall return better armed; with crowbars and with torches I will assault the unresponsive dwelling. Take heed! Night and Love and wine are not the best counsellors for self-restraint. They know naught of shame and fear; and I have tried all forms of entreaty and now you are moved not at all by my threats. You are harder and more unyielding than your doors and you are unfit to guard the threshold of my love; you ought to be the keeper of a dungeon. Lucifer is already beginning to move his axles, and the morning bird is rousing all wretched mankind to its tasks. Let this chaplet fallen from my unhappy head rest here upon the senseless doorstep, and when she sees it there in the morning, it will be a witness of the night I passed in wretchedness.

And you, door-keeper, unworthy as you are, take my last farewell, unyielding, undisgraced by the admission of a lover. And you, cruel gateposts, with your rigid thresholds, and you, doors with unfeeling beams, fellow slaves of the lout who guards you, fare you well!

VII. *He regrets having maltreated his mistress.*

If there is any friend within the reach of my words, let him put shackles upon my hands, for well have they deserved them. Madness made me raise my reckless hands against my lady, and she has been crushed by my furious blows. It proves me capable of laying hands on my revered parents and of offering to strike the gods themselves.

Yet did not Ajax lay low the flocks upon the fields and Orestes ask for weapons against the mystic goddesses? Does this not partially at least atone for having lifted my hands against my mistress? Truth to tell, her disordered appearance became her well. She looked beautiful in her distress; something like the Cretan maiden, as she wept while the winds bore before them the sails and false promises of perjured Theseus; Cassandra was thus when she sank down at the shrine of sacred Minerva.

Madman or barbarian though I was, yet she uttered no reproach. Her face was far from silent and accused me far more audibly than words might have done. Each tear was my accuser, though her lips were sealed. I wish my arms had dropped from their sockets or that I had lost some part of myself. I had practised my strength to my own undoing. If I had struck the least of the Quirites in a mob, I would be fittingly punished. Am I to go free when I have raised my hand against my mistress? I should be shackled as I deserve. The son of Tydeus was the first to strike a goddess. I am the second, and certainly his crime was the lesser. He had been cruel with a foe, but I injured one that I professed to love.

What victory is mine to celebrate with laurels and with incense, and were the retinue following my car, shouting triumphantly my conquest over a girl? And where is she, to walk before me, downcast, with loosened hair, dressed all in white, endeavoring to hide her wounded cheeks? How much more fitting had it been for them to be marked by the pressure of my lips and for her neck to bear the imprint of my caressing teeth! And if I was unable to control myself, and I was swept along by my fury like a raging torrent, would it not have been sufficient with the threats I uttered and the shouts I leveled at her, or to have torn her gown down to her middle where her girdle would have come appropriately to her rescue?

Instead I tore her hair and left the marks of my nails upon her cheeks, while she faced me, bereft of her senses, as white as a block of marble hewn from Parian cliffs. Her helpless limbs trembled like the branches of a poplar shaken by the breeze, like reeds set a-quiver by a passing zephyr, or the surface of the water ruffled by the south wind. And the tears kept flowing from her eyes like water from melted snow. Then I began to comprehend the full extent of the mischief I had done. And for every

144

tear she shed, I felt my blood was being spilt. Three times I attempted to cast myself beneath her feet and she repulsed me fittingly enough.

But let you not desist: strike me and claw me up, sparing neither my hair nor my eyes. No matter how weak the hand, wrath will give it strength. Or at least do hastily remove the sad signs of my vicious temper and straighten out your precious locks.

VIII. He curses an old bawd who tempts his mistress to become a prostitute.

There is a certain bawd by the name of Dipsas who has never looked with sober eyes upon Memnon's mother, her of the rosy steeds. She is well versed in magic and incantations and by her cunning knows how to turn the rivers back upon their source. And she knows well the power of potions and mixtures; she knows how to distil the poison of the mare in heat, the threads to set in motion the magic wheel, and can, at will, make clouds appear or disappear up in the sky. I have seen her draw blood from stars, and I suspect she flits about at night covered with the plumage of birds. Rumor bears me out in claiming that she has double pupils and that she summons from the grave the long buried dead and with mystic incantations opens the earth.

This old crone has chosen as her task to undo with devious mischief a certain union. By accident I overheard some counsel that she gave while I lay concealed behind a double door.

"My fair one, you have yesterday gained the favor of a certain youth of wealth. He was so securely hooked, he could not keep his eyes from your face. And it is fit-

ting, for surely there is no one more beautiful and de-
serving of affection. You lack only appropriate ap-
parel that would well become your person. You ought
to be as fortunate as you are fair, for if you are wealthy I
shall not suffer from want. Mars, with a contrary star,
has impeded your aspirations, but now with Venus fav-
oring, there is nothing to delay your fortune. At a suit-
able moment a wealthy admirer has turned up, with a
face deserving of yours, and were he unwilling to buy,
he would deserve to be bought."

My lady blushed.

"Blushes are becoming to a pale face but the pre-
tended blush is the most profitable one and the real one
is likely to be a dead loss. With eyes chastely lowered
into your lap, you will appraise each suitor according to
the gifts he brings.

"When Tatius was king, the simple Sabine woman
would not be wife to more than one; but the men now
off to the wars have their souls tested by Mars, and Venus
reigns supreme in the city of her Aeneas. It is a holiday
for beauty, and chastity is practised by the neglected ones
that are too simple to go out and ask first. Penelope at
the test of the bow made trial of the strength of her
suitors, and the bow was made of horn. The stream of
life passes smoothly and is gone before we know, and the
years speed on at full pace, drawn by swift horses. Bronze
becomes polished with use; a beautiful garment begs to
be worn; an abandoned house crumbles with age; and
beauty unused becomes old. No mere one or two will
serve your purpose: your spoils can be rich only from
many. The wolf has a successful forage by attacking a
whole flock.

"What does your fine poet have to offer besides his verses? You can have the letters of a thousand lovers to read. The very god of the poets is dressed in gold and plays upon a lyre studded with jewels. The man who gives you ample gifts should be superior to Homer as far as you're concerned. And don't disdain him because he once had to purchase his freedom; 'the chalk-marked foot' is a foolish reproach. Take along your grandfathers if you're poor; lineage counts for nothing here; and if he ask your favors for nothing, simply because he has a pretty face, let him go out and earn you gifts from a lover of his own.

"Be modest in your requests while you are catching them, but once you are holding them securely, you can dictate your own terms. It will be suitable upon occasions to pretend Love, but be careful that it pays you to dissimulate. Deny your favors to them with various excuses such as headaches, and blame it at certain times on Isis. After a while, relent a little, lest your lover grow weary from too many repulses. Let your doors be unfeeling to prayers and wide open to one who comes laden with gifts. Let the lover you receive hear your words of dismissal as you send the other packing about his business. Sometimes when you have done him some needless injury, get furiously angry and accuse him first of having injured you, and while defending himself, his own accusations will take flight. But don't remain angry too long, as it may have serious consequences. Learn how to weep at will; and you must learn to swear falsely if the matter warrants it, for Venus is deaf to the deceits of Love. Have your servants properly trained so that they will suggest appropriate gifts to be purchased

147

for you, and have them tactfully require little trifles for themselves. Remember to have your sister and your maid and your mother each pluck your lover on their own account. Where there seems little pretext for requesting further gifts, produce a cake and say it is your birthday.

"Don't let him feel that he loves you without a rival; it would be a dangerous security for him. You must give his passion an opponent. Let your couch be crumpled as if a previous visitor had been to see you, and let him note about your neck the marks of passion. Show him the presents that another sent you, and when you have taken from him what he gives, then proceed to borrow what you will never return. Let your tongue be cunning in covering up the traces of your thoughts, for poisons are best hidden in honey.

"If you will harken to my advice, the value of which I have tested by long experience, you will continue to consult me frequently while I am alive, and pray for me when I am dead."

She was still talking when my shadow betrayed my presence, and I could scarce control my hands from tearing out her hair and clawing up her withered cheeks. Her eyes were swimming from wine and she was most repulsive to behold. May the gods deny her a resting place in her helpless old age and may she suffer hard winters and eternal thirst!

IX. *The poet compares Love and War.*

Every lover is a soldier in the camp of Cupid and the age most suited for the wars is the one best equipped for Venus. An old soldier and an old lover are equally ludicrous. The spirit that a captain requires from the valiant soldier is the same that the maid requires from the man who would be her lover. Both must stay awake through the night. When occasion requires, they must rest upon the ground, one guarding the door of his captain, the other the door of his mistress. The soldier travels great distances. Send but his mistress before him, and the lover will go from one end of the earth to the other. He will climb the snow-capped mountains; he will cross the rivers swollen with rain; he will plod through drifts of snow and embark upon the seas without consulting favorable winds or waiting for pleasant weather. Soldier and lover alike will bear the cold of night with indifference and think nothing of snow and rain. One will keep his eye upon the foe of his country; the other observes the movements of his rival, the foe of his amour. The soldier besieges a fortress; the lover the threshold of his mistress; one storms the gates; the other at the doors.

It is frequently politic to catch the enemy unawares, when he is sunk in sleep. Thus fell the lines of Rhesus of Thrace. So do lovers frequently take advantage of a slumbering husband and bestir their weapons while the unsuspecting foe is sleeping. It is the task of soldier and lover to pass by guards and sentinels that are ever on the watch for both of them. Mars and Venus are of variable temper, and frequently the vanquished rise again.

Love is not for the spiritless, and it puts the soul to infinite tests of bravery. Achilles was aflame with passion for Briseis; Hector left Andromache for the wars, and it was she who placed upon his head the helmet. The greatest of warriors, the son of Atreus, stood rapt at sight of Priam's daughter. Mars himself was caught and felt the bonds of the smith—no story was better known in all the heavens. I always sought the easy and effortless ways of dalliance, taking my proper repose in the shade of some favorable tree, but love for a woman has torn me from my pleasant ease, and sent me off to camp, where I am ever prepared for action to do service at night. If you would not lose all your spirit, then enlist in the army of Love.

X. He remonstrates with his mistress for her greediness.

Like her who was carried from the Eurotas in a Phrygian ship to be the cause of war to both her lords; like Leda who was deceived by the swan and his brilliant plumage; like Amymone going through the thirsty fields carrying full urns upon her head—like these you were; and in loving you I feared the swan and bull and whatsoever form Jove has taken in the cause of Love.

But now I am afraid no longer and my heart is still. Your charms no longer haunt my senses and I am changed. And if you would know the reason—very simply then, it is because you have set a price upon yourself. You can no longer please me now. As long as you were suffused by a sweet simplicity, I loved you body and soul; but now your beauty has been spoiled by a fault in your heart.

Love is a naked child; his youth and lack of raiment are a sign of his freedom, and the child of Venus does not offer himself for profit.

He has no pockets in which to keep money. Venus and Cupid are not warlike gods that they should draw soldier's pay.

It is the harlot's privilege to barter her body for gain to anyone who offers the proper price that she demands. Even the harlot hates her trade which compels her to do what you do of your own free will.

Look at the beasts of the field, for example, and you will note that the mare claims no gift from the stallion, nor the cow from the bull; the ram offers nothing to his favored ewe. Only woman sells her favors and is hired. You can buy from her what delights you both, and she measures her price by the amount of joy you both share. You would wish that our pleasure be your gain and my loss, although we both contribute to bring it about.

A witness may not perjure himself for gain, nor a juror deviate in his estimate of a situation because of a bribe. It is ignoble to defend a guilty wretch with hired eloquence, and a court which is profitable is false. It is equally base to swell one's fortune by a revenue from one's amours and to peddle beauty at a price. No gratitude can go for a love that is purchased, for the payment is acquittance in full and your lover is not in your debt.

Do not ask a price for your favors, my fair ones, for this gain will bring you no good fortune. It proved not profitable for the holy maiden to bargain for the Sabine armlets. A son once pierced the mother who bore him and a necklace was the cause of her pain.

And yet it is not disgraceful to require gifts from the wealthy, for they have the wherewithal to grant them. Pluck from the full vines the heavy clusters and let the rich fields give you their fruit. A poor lover gives you his service, his zeal and faithfulness. Let each bring to his mistress what he has.

My gift is to sing the glories of my fair one and thereby make her famous with my art. Garments, however rich, eventually fall to rags, and gems and gold will be broken and lost; but the glory that my songs bestow is everlasting. It is not the giving that I object to; it is the asking and the stipulation of a price that I find despicable and hateful. What I refuse to give at your command, cease only to insist upon it and I will give you lavishly.

XI. *He sends Nape with a letter to her mistress.*

Nape, dexterous at setting in order the ruffled locks of my fair one, thou art the chosen one among handmaidens; thou art adroit at the giving of signals and often hast thou persuaded the wavering Corinna to seek me out. Take now these tablets hastily to your mistress. Your heart is kind and yet you are not simpler than befits your station. I do believe you too have felt the darts of Cupid, so aptly do you comprehend the measure of my campaigns. Should she ask you how I feel, tell her that I live but in the hopes of her favor; the rest she will learn from the tablets I entrust to your care.

Even now, while I am speaking, the moments fly; so hasten to give her the missive while she is still free and observe carefully her visage while she peruses my letter. Regard her eyes, her brow, and when she answers me, see that there is not a big space with a little writing upon it. See that the lines are tightly packed, with some post scriptum scribbled on the outer margin.

But better still, (for what need is there of wearying her with writing) just let her send a single tablet bearing the treasured word: *Come*. And if this could be accomplished, I would take my conquering tablets, and binding them with laurel, hang them in the midst of the shrine of Venus. Upon the outside I would write:

"Naso dedicates his faithful aids to Venus that but a moment past were only common maple."

XII. He denounces the tablets for returning with bad news.

Weep for me! My tablets have returned with sad, depressing news. "Sorry, not today," was the unhappy legend they bore. As Nape had gone out upon my errand, she had tripped upon the doorstep. Be more careful in the future and walk more soberly. Away from me, foul funereal tablets, common pieces of wood, and you, filthy smear of wax, that say me nay. I suspect that this wax was gathered from the hemlock by Corsican bees and sold to us as wrapping for its vile honey. Your rosy hue is probably derived from blood. I shall cast you upon the crossroads and may the passing wheel of a cart break you asunder. And the man who converted you from a tree into objects for utility had impure hands. And on the tree itself, some wretch was hung no doubt. It probably furnished the wherewithal for a cross. In its branches the vulture sought his repose and the screech-owl made its nest. And to such tablets, doomed to misfortune, I entrusted my message of love. They would more fittingly have borne some miserable plea to be read by some sour-visaged judge. They would have been

THE ART OF LOVE

more deserving to bear the accounts of some miser who could weep over them for the pittance he had spent. You are double-dealing, in accordance with your name, and your very number stands for an ill-omen. I pray that old age may wither you and make you foul, and that the wax upon you grow colorless from disuse.

XIII. *He begs Aurora to slacken her pace.*

Aurora is already rising over the ocean, coming from her too-ancient husband, and her golden hair is bringing us the day. Why is she in such haste? Now is the time when I delight to repose myself in the tender arms of my love; and this is the moment I particularly cherish to feel her close at my side. Now comes the slumber that is deep, while the birds are chanting their liquid notes. You are unwelcome to youths and maidens; so check with rosy fingers the reins of your steeds.

Before your coming, the seaman can observe the stars and guide himself more surely on the pathless waters. At your coming, the traveler, however weary, must rise to continue on his journey, and the soldier assume the arms of battle. You are the first to see man slaving on the fields and the first to summon the steer beneath his yoke. You cheat boys of their slumbers and you give them over to their masters. And many do you send early in the morning before the court, where they suffer tremendous losses at a single word. Neither lawyer nor plaintiff is fond of you, and you make ready the new labor for the tired hands of women. What man, unless he were bereft of a mistress, would wish that maidens should rise early? Often I have longed that you should be supplanted by the stars and that the winds should break the axle of your chariot or that your steeds should trip upon some dense cloud and fall. The son you bore was black and he was the color of his mother's heart.

I wish Tithonus would tell all he knows, and I am certain no woman would be disgraced more universally than you for her vile career. How quickly you fly to leave his ancient embraces, and yet when you are close to Cephalus, you slacken the pace of your steeds.

Why must I be troubled in my love affairs because you are burdened with an eternally aging spouse? Was I the go-between who arranged the match? See how charitably Luna bestows long hours upon the lovers of the world, and her beauty is not less than yours. The father of the gods, in order to see you less often, once made two nights into one to favor his desires.

Thus I scolded; she heard me, blushed, and appeared in the heavens at the usual time.

XIV.   To his mistress who has lost her hair.

I used to plead with you to stop doping that hair of yours with dyes and ointments; now you are happily relieved of my chiding, for you have no hair left to trouble about. Remember when it touched your thighs and its texture was so fine that you feared to dress it? It was delicate like the subtle thread the busy spider weaves upon deserted beams. Its color was not dark nor golden, but a mingling of both. In the shady vales of Ida, the lofty cedar exposes such a tint when it is stripped of its bark.

You were able to comb it in a hundred ways without causing yourself pain, and neither the needle nor the comb was able to tear it. Your hair dresser was fortunate, and I have never seen you angry with your servants. In the morning, I often saw you when your hair was not dressed, lying languidly upon a purple couch. Even so, in seeming neglect, it looked beautiful, like the abandoned locks of a Thracian Bacchante resting wearily upon the turf.

And though they were delicate, they were tortured continuously and had to yield themselves to iron and to fire, and bend themselves into close, curling ringlets. I used to cry out and protest against these barbarous proceedings, pointing out aptly how their curls quite naturally put to shame the artificial ringlets she prized so highly—to no avail! Her iron heart proceeded on the chosen course unheeding of the voice of reason.

And now those tresses that Apollo and Bacchus could desire for their own heads are no more. They could brook comparison with the tresses that the nude Dione holds aloft with dripping fingers. And now you can lay aside your mirror, foolish girl, and wonder at the sight that meets your eye. No vicious rival has enchanted you and no witch from Haemonian land has laved it with magic waters; nor has a treacherous illness robbed you of your hair; nor evil tongue diminished your locks. Your loss was wrought by your own hands, and you yourself distilled the poison that did the mischief.

Now you will have to import the tresses of some captive woman from Germany and you will wear the bounty of a race that we have conquered. When afterwards some flattering gaze will rest upon your hair, you will blush and think that it is the borrowed plumage from another head that brings you favor. And yet, you will remember sadly the day when you could boast as good a crop of your own.

What have I said? Crushed, scarcely able to control her tears, she covers her face and hides her blushing cheeks. In her lap she holds all the hair she had of yore and looks reproachfully upon me.

Calm your heart and cease your weeping! Obviously your loss can be repaired and shortly you will be admired for tresses that are truly your very own.

XV. *Against the enemies of poetry.*

Biting Envy charges me with lazy years and calls my work the product of a futile wit. I am accused that, abandoning the fashions of our fathers, I fail to seek glory in the life of a soldier, that I am unskilled in the methods of the law courts, and do not raise my voice for the common cause in the ungrateful forum. The work I am thus charged with neglecting is commonplace but I am in the search of glory through all the ages for I seek to be known through my songs all through the earth. Homer shall live as long as Tenedos shall stand, and Ida as long as Simois shall roll his gushing waters to the sea. The poet of Ascra shall live as long as swelling grapes will grow upon the vine and Ceres fall beneath the stroke of the curving sickle. The son of Battus shall ever be sung throughout the earth for he may not sway through genius but he sways nevertheless through art. Naught can impair the glory of Sophocles; Aratus shall live as long as sun and moon endure; as long as lying slave, hard parent, treacherous bawd and cunning harlot shall be found, so long Menander's name shall be known. Ennius, the rugged, and Accuis, the spirited, have names that shall outlast eternity. What generation shall fail to know of Varro or forget the golden fleece? The verses of Lucretius shall perish on the day of doom. Tityrus and the harvests, and the arms of Aeneas, will be read as long as Rome shall be capital of the world; and as long as Cupid is equipped with bow and torch, Tibullus and Gallus shall be known to Hesperia's sons. Aye, and though great rocks and the iron ploughshare perish with the time, their songs shall be beyond the reach of death.

Before the power of songs let famous monarchs bow their heads; and let what is common and tawdry excite the marvel of the mob. For me the golden Apollo ministers cups from the Castalian fount, and on my locks I bear the myrtle that dreads the cold, and let this ever be known by all lovers. It is the living that envy gnaws upon, for after death, each man's fame is what he justly deserves. And so I rest assured, for I am tranquil that when the final fire has burned me out, the greatest part of me shall still live on.

BOOK TWO

I. *Why he continues to sing of Love.*

This, too, is my work, Naso's, born at Sulmo, among the humid Paeligni, and I am a singer of my worthless ways. And this, too, am I writing in the service of Love, and be ye gone from me, ye austere ones. Ye are not fit to be my audience nor listen to my tender, muted strains. I choose as my readers the maiden who is not calm at sight of her lover, and the untaught youth, simple and straightforward, whose heart has hitherto been untouched by passion, and such as, wounded by the same weapons as I, may wonderingly see their own trouble described so aptly that it will lead them to exclaim, "He is recounting my own mishaps."

I began to sing, nor was my utterance feeble, of the wars of heaven, when earth made her attempt at vengeance, and steep Ossa was piled upon Olympus. I hurled the thunder clouds of Jove that he had used to save his heaven.

But then my mistress closed her door in my face, and hastily I dropped Jove with all his lightning. May he pardon me, for his bolts availed me little in the face of a blow that was greater than any he could deal. And so I have assumed my proper weapons, the airy, bantering line of elegy, for its gentle strains have softened the hardhearted door. Songs bring down the horns of the moon and recall the white steed of the departing sun; they burst the serpent's jaw, and make the waters run back into their source. Song has made unyielding doors to open and lifted bolts that were made of oak.

What use is it to sing of brave Achilles? What will the sons of Atreus avail when one of them wandered about aimlessly and the other was dragged to death by the Haemonian steeds? But some tender maiden, at the behest of my chance, has come graciously to give herself to the poet in lieu of payment for the praise that he bestowed upon her. This is sweet recompense, so fare ye well, ye famous names, for I do not seek your favors. But you, O fair ones, turn your faces towards me, while I sing to you the songs that Love dictates to me.

II. He reproaches Bagoas for denying him access to his mistress.

Do you, Bagoas, whose occupation it is to guard your mistress, attend, while I say a few apt words to you. Yesterday I saw a very fair maiden walking in the portico of Apollo, and immediately I was sorely smitten with her. I sent her a note and she replied, "It cannot be;" and when I asked her, "Why not?" she replied that you guard her too attentively.

If you are wise, my good fellow, don't make such efforts to merit hatred. If you are sufficiently feared you will eventually be destroyed. Her husband, too, is very silly, for he takes pains to guard something that no

thievery could diminish.   But let him go on in his fool-
ishness and think she will be chaste; but let you be less
foolish, and exchange freedom for freedom.   You will
be wise if you conspire with her.   Consider: you, a slave,
conniving with your mistress.   If you are afraid to do it
openly, you are free to pretend.   If you see her reading a
letter, you may believe it is from her mother.   A stranger
approaches?   After you have seen him twice, he's a
stranger no longer.   She insists on visiting a sick friend?
Obviously the friend is quite well, but it is not for you
to judge her secret malady.   If she is late in coming home,
don't weary yourself with waiting; go to sleep.   Don't
concern yourself too much about what happens at the
temple of Isis or at the amphitheater.   As an accomplice
you will reap rich rewards for contributing so trifling a
thing as silence.   You will become a favorite, rule the
house, suffer no blows, and the rest of the slaves will
cower at your feet.   The husband will be supplied with
dexterous pretexts and he will approve what she devises.
Remember that while he wrinkles his brow and ponders
deeply, he really does what his wheedling wife wants
him to do.

Sometimes you will do well to quarrel with her and
let her pretend to weep and call you her executioner.
You can charge her with various trifling trespasses that
she can easily explain away, and will make you out to
be the very Cerberus of watchdogs.   It is thus by false
accusations that the true ones will be hidden, while your
honor will grow and your savings accumulate.   Follow
this counsel and shortly you will be a free man.

Story-tellers wear chains tied around their necks.
Tantalus seeks for a drink the midst of water and

catches forever the escaping fruit; it is his punishment for having a garrulous tongue. I have seen a man in shackles because he told a husband that he was a cuckold and proved it. It was a mild punishment, of course. You may believe me that no man welcomes accusations, particularly if they are proven true; for if he is calm, your tattling tongue whispers to indifferent ears; while if he loves his wife your foolish braying is merely making him wretched.

Consider that a trespass, however obvious, is hard to prove. The wife is likely to come off without harm, for even though her spouse has seen, he will disbelieve his eyes and give himself a lie. At the sight of her tears, he will offer to punish the cause of her sorrow, and in this contest the odds are heavily against you. You will get a flogging, while she sits on the lap of your judge. I am not conspiring to commit crimes: there are no poisons to be mingled and no swords are flashing. It is simply required of you that you grant us the means to seek our love in safety, and what can be more modest than such a request?

III. To the inflexible eunuch.

Unhappy me! that you, who are the guardian of my mistress, are neither man nor woman, and so you are denied the blissful knowledge of a mutual love. Those who rob young boys of their gender ought to suffer the same. How readily you would be compliant to the entreaties of a lover if you yourself had ever burned for a woman. You are unfit to be a soldier; the spear does not become your hand. You must forego many enterprises, and your only chance is to gain the favor of your mistress, so ply her with deserving deeds and let this service bring you ample rewards. What other thing can you accomplish? Remember that the time is ripe and that her years are apt for Love's delights while she is still in the possession of her charms. How pitiful to have her beauty perish in neglect!

Besides, we can easily elude you, for what two have willed can ever be accomplished. But we think better of requiring your assistance; and you can profit by our confidence.

IV. The conditions suitable and necessary for an affair of the heart.

I don't offer to defend my faulty ways nor spread an armor to shield my questionable morals. I admit my shortcomings, and having owned them, I furiously attack my sins. I hate what I am, yet I cannot help being what I hate. How difficult to bear the burden that one longs to lay aside.

I lack the strength to control myself; I am tossed about like a ship on a restless flood. There is no definite sort of beauty that calls out my passion, for indeed the causes of it are multitudinous. Sometimes I am aflame for some fair one who with modest eyes looks down upon her lap, and I am completely fetched by her innocent demeanor. Sometimes I like a saucy jade because she is no country bumpkin and there are promises of an easy conquest upon a soft couch. If she seems austere, like a Sabine matron, I am certain she would yield but is too deep in her conceit. If they are learned

and well-read, they win me by their intellectual accom-
plishments; if they are crude, their simple ways endear
them to me.

Some fair one says that Callimachus is rustic by
comparison to me. What can I do but love the one who
loves me in return? Another severely criticizes my poetry,
and I would fain clasp her in my arms to convert her to
my Muse. I am enchanted by the soft step of one and
tempted to soften the step of one who walks less grace-
fully. One has a charming voice, so that I long to in-
terrupt her with kisses; another plays upon the strings
with cunning hands; a third knows how to dance with
supple art; and I take fire from every cause. Hippoly-
tus himself, were he in my place, would become a very
Priapus.

I love one because she's so tall, like the ancient daugh-
ters of heroes, and lying down will cover a full couch
length. Another I find apt because she is short. If she
is badly dressed, I imagine her appropriately gowned;
and if she is carefully attired, all her physical advantages
are glaringly set forth.

I love the white-skinned and the golden-haired but I
do not take a dusky skin amiss. I am fetched by dark
locks hanging on a snowy neck. Remember, fair Leda
had black locks. Has she got golden curls? Aurora's
hair is saffron. To all these varying colors, shapes and
sizes, my love will readily attune itself. Youth steals my
heart, but I am readily smitten with the charm of ma-
turity.

In other words, whatever fair ones worthy of the sim-
plest praise are found in this, our city, I offer my love as
candidate for all their favors.

*V. He reproaches his mistress for her unfaithful-
ness.*

Surely no love is worth all this.   Get you hence,
Cupid, with your quiver! How frequently I long for
death,—whenever I think you false, my pretty one, who
seem to be born for my eternal undoing.

I am not judging you by any trifling intercepted note,
nor any secret gifts that I am puzzled by.   I wish that
my misgivings were founded upon such slender evi-
dence. Ah, miserable me! why have I so excellent a
case? How I envy the man who can boldly defend his
mistress! Happy is he to whom she says, "It isn't so!"
what iron heart does he possess to ply her with further
troublesome questions.

I saw your guilt with mine own eyes, after the wine
had been served and you thought I was asleep. I saw
you both speak trembling words with the wrinkling of
your brows and the nodding of your heads.   And the
table was scribbled o'er by your wine-stained fingers;
your eyes spoke volumes and your speech had secret
meanings that are not ambiguous to me. And when the
guests were gone and none was left but just a drowsy
youth or two worn out with drinking, I saw you sharing
shameful kisses in which the tongue played an import-
ant part.   Obviously they were not endearments that a
brother and a sister may casually exchange.   They were
not the sort that Diana gives to Phoebus but rather of that
variety that Venus oft bestowed on Mars.

When I could contain myself no longer, I arose and
cried, "What is the meaning of this? How does it come
about that these joys, meant to be shared equally between

you and me, are thus offered casually to an intruder?"

This I said and such other things as the wrath of the moment prompted me. She stood before me, her face covered with blushes, like the sky grown ruddy with the bride of Tithonus, like roses mingled with lilies, or the moon in labor with enchanted steeds, or the Assyrian ivories that are tinctured to prevent them from turning yellow. Very much like one of these was the color she displayed and never in her life had she been fairer to look upon. Her eyes were lowered to the ground and her face was suffused with grief. Undoubtedly her sorrow made her comely. In my fury, I wished to fly at her and tear her neatly plaited locks and to dig my nails into her cheeks.

But looking at her face, I felt my arms drop to my side, for she was protected by a great armor. A moment previous I had been filled with cruel rage and now I felt weak and humble, and suddenly entreated her to give me kisses. She smiled, complying with my request, and she gave me such as would make the irate Jove drop from his hand the three-forked bolt. My torment is great, for I am much afraid that my rival has tasted such heavenly food as this. They tasted better than usual and contained a certain something newly learned. I consider this new voluptuousness a bad sign; it isn't merely that she kisses rather close, and yet her doing so troubles me. Some great master has had a great reward for his teachings.

VI.   He deplores the death of a talented parrot.

Our parrot, feathered mimic from India, is no more, so come flocking, ye birds, to his obsequies. Come all ye feathered minions, weeping and clawing your cheeks; tear your feathered plumage in place of hair; and instead of the long trumpet, let your songs sound out. If you, Philomela, are lamenting the deed of the tyrant of Ismarus, that lament has been fulfilled by its term of years; turn hither to the hapless funeral of an uncommon bird. —There was great cause in sorrowing for Itys—but he has been dead a long time.

All you who cross the liquid air in flight, grieve, you, friendly turtle-dove, above all others. The life that you shared with the deceased was full of harmony. Your faithfulness cheered him to the very end.

And yet what profits all her loyalty, what benefit from her beautiful color, what indeed availed that clever voice adept at mimicry? Naught, naught could serve to keep that hapless bird alive. There was no plumed creature on this earth could better imitate the speech of man; and you may well mourn him whose wings were like fragile jasper and whose beak was punic red.

Fate was envious of you and took you away. You were of a mild and pacific nature and a prattling lover of peace. The ill-natured quail, forever battling with her kind, survives and lives to a good old age. You were no glutton, for you were fond of speech and your busy beak had little time for eating. Nuts made a meal for you, poppy seeds brought you happy slumber, and drops of pure water slaked your thirst. The ominous vulture prospers, as does the kite drawing threatening circles in the air. The daw, harbinger of rain, and ravens, despised by Minerva, thrive and live on.

The parrot, loquacious mirror for the human voice, a treasure brought from the ends of the earth, is gone.

The choicest things are blighted soonest by the greedy hands of Fate. Thersites saw the funeral of Protesilaus, and Hector perished before any of his brothers.

I call to mind the pious prayers of my fair one in her fear for you, prayers swept by the unheeding winds over the sea to the south. The seventh day approached, your last on earth, and Fate with a barren distaff all unwound, stood over you. With a dying effort, you lifted your almost immobile tongue and cried out, "Fare you well, Corinna!"

At the foot of a hill in Elysium is a shady grove of dark ilex where the humid earth is green with ever-blooming grass. If we may trust in tales of old, this is the spot in which the pious winged creatures of the air gather and near which no impure fowl approaches. Here one can find gracious swans and the long-lived phoenix, unique of its kind; here the bird of Juno spreads her plumage for her own delectation, and the gentle dove kisses her ardent mate. Seated among this chosen company, our parrot, by his choice vocabulary, gathers about him his feathered followers.

His corpse is covered by a small mound on which a trifling stone bears this legend:

"You may judge from my very monument the
esteem of my mistress.
I was skilled in speech beyond the
abilities of a bird."

VII. He defends himself against the suspicions of Corinna.

Am I to be forever the target of fresh complaints? Even if I disprove your accusations, I am wearied by these constant quarrels and recriminations. If I but glance casually at the highest row in the theater, you immediately pick on any of the women present there as a fitting excuse for an argument. If any passing fair one give me but a casual glance, you insist upon diciphering the strange meaning of her silence. If I unthinkingly give praise to some female, you are ready to fly at me; but you are equally grieved if I disparage her, for you suspect that I am merely covering a treacherous enterprise. When I look calm and rested, you accuse me for my lack of ardor, and when I am pale, you insist that I am perishing with love for another.

I wish that I at least merited your disapproval. How easy it is to bear calmly such accusations as are caused by actual trespasses. But you are in a constant fury about nothing; as an example of what needless abuse accomplishes, look upon the long-eared, pitiable donkey, staggering about drowsily, his spirit broken by ceaseless punishment.

And what is your latest charge against me? Cypassis, whose deft fingers govern your hair, is supposed to have co-operated to dishonor your couch. I hope I am more favored of the gods, that wishing to sin, I should have to seek the sordid embraces of a slave. What man of spirit would desire to spend endearments upon a body that has felt the lash? Besides, this one lives only to ministrate to your fair tresses, and I would never dream to become involved with a faithful servant of yours. I would make a fool of myself: she would repel my advances and tell you of my dishonest proposals. I swear by Venus and the bow of her winged child, I am not guilty.

VIII. *He asks Cypassis for another rendezvous.*

Cypassis, most perfect of hair-dressers, whose hands are fit to coil the tresses of goddesses; who, in the treasured moment of my stolen delight, has proven more than charming; how fitting are your endeavors in the service of your mistress but how much more fitting in my own. Who could have tattled of our liaison; how did Corinna get wind of this affair? Is it possible that I blushed or that some tell-tale word unguardedly passed from my lips?

As for my having insisted that only a madman would lose his heart to a slave—let us consider how the Thessalian was taken with the charms of the slave Briseis. The Mycenean chief languished for Phoebas, another slave. I am not greater than the son of Tantalus, nor more proud than Achilles, and I am content to accept what has been sufficient for kings.

When her wrathful gaze was fixed upon you, I noticed how your cheeks were suffused with blushes. Remember what I looked like, swearing to my faithfulness by the name of Venus.

Great goddess, bid the warm south wind carry far away o'er the Carpathians a harmless perjury sprung from a simple, guileless heart.

As a fair return for my endeavors in your behalf, my dusky Cypassis, it is becoming that you pay me this very day with the treasured price of your caresses. Don't shake your head and say me nay, pretending new fears. It is sufficient for you to earn the favor of only one of your masters; and if you gainsay me, I shall be compelled to turn informer and confess your duplicity.

I am ready to admit my own guilt and advise your mistress where we met, how many times, Cypassis, and how many ways, and what they were!

IX. *He reproaches Cupid for treating him unfairly.*

(a)

Wherefore, O Cupid, lodged as you are in my heart, though helping me little, (for surely never did man have a more indifferent ally) wherefore do you harm me? I am a soldier wounded in his own camp, and your torch burns friends when it were greater glory for you to conquer your opponents.

The hero of Haemonia assisted at the cure of him whom he had struck down with a spear. A hunter ever keeps pursuing the quarry that flies and what he overtakes he leaves behind him. Having surrendered to thee, we continue to feel the weight of your persecutions. What satisfaction can there be to blunt your barbed shafts on barren bones? There are so many people, men and women, utterly bereft of love; it seems they would tempt your powers more readily. If Rome had failed to seek for further conquests, we would now be but a hamlet filled with thatched cottages. The weary soldier is permitted to retire on the acres that comprise his grant, and the race horse, once retired from the course, is permitted to browse in peace upon the pastures. Covered docks receive the worn-out ship, and when the gladiator lays aside his sword, a harmless foil is granted him.

I, too, weary from having served in many wars of woman's love, desire that, my labors finished, I should live in peace.

(b)

If some god were to say to me, "Have finished with your loves," I would plead with him not to insist, so sweet a poison are the fair. When I am weary with love and the passion of my heart has cooled, my spirit is seized by a tempest of wretchedness. As a stubborn, hard-mouthed horse carries his helpless master at a fearful pace while the rider vainly tugs the foaming bit; as a mariner about to put his foot on the approaching land is suddenly swept out upon the sea; so am I oft turned from my course by the capricious gales of Cupid.

Wound me, child; I have dropped my defenses and stand unarmed before you. This is a place to exercise your strength; let your hand strike here and let your arrows fly. They scarcely know their quiver because of me. Fools, who will sleep the whole night through and consider it a blessing, is not sleep a counterfeit of death? And is there not ample time to find repose for all eternity? I am satisfied to harken to the deceitful words of an unfaithful maiden, for no one can rob me of hope. Let her speak lovingly or chide me, grant me her favors or repulse me, I shall still continue to cherish my madness.

That Mars is fickle is your fault, Cupid. Your stepfather wields doubtful arms after your own example.

You are light and can feel the changing winds more swiftly than your wings, and you grant or deny your joys most uncertainly. And yet, if you and your beautiful mother will listen to my prayers, you will set up your thrones in my heart to rule there forever. And let fair women, too, be your subjects in that realm, a great and constant throng, and you will be adored by peoples twain.

X. He reproaches Graecinus for putting foolish notions into the poet's head.

I believe it was you, Graecinus, who told me that it was impossible for a man to love two women at the same time. It is to you I owe my downfall; to you I owe being trapped without defense, for I am even now in love with two damsels. Each is beautiful and both have taste in dressing. It is impossible to decide which one is more accomplished: one pleases me more until I meet the other; and the other seems fairer until I see the first. Like a ship that is driven by erratic winds, I am now going for one and now the other; and I keep veering about purposelessly. Why does the lady of Eryx add to my troubles? Were not my difficulties, to keep one love going, enough? Why plaster a shady tree with leaves, or add stars to a twinkling sky, or carry waters to the sea?

Still, I am better served than if I had no love at all and were alone. May the austere life suit my enemies, and may it behoove them to sleep in celibate peace in the midst of an empty bed. What care I if cruel Love breaks in upon my slumbers, so long as I am not the single burden of my bed. Let my strength be wasted by one, and if that is insufficient, by two. I shall meet the test. I am lean, but strong; I lack bulk but no sinew, and joy shall re-strengthen the vigor of my loins. No mistress has ever been deceived in me; although I have often made merry through all the night, I was never quite washed out in the morning. Blessed is he who is worn out in Love's combats; and may the gods grant that my end come thus.

Let the soldier offer his breast to hostile darts and purchase glory with his blood. Let the greedy merchant hunt for wealth, and let his lying mouth be glutted by the waves that have grown weary of bearing his bark. I prefer to perish in the embrace of Venus, exhausted by her delights, and let those weeping at my funeral accord me reverence and say truthfully that my death was consonant with my life.

XI. He begs Corinna to desist from her prospective voyage.

The pine that grows a-top of Pelion first taught men the evil ways of the sea, while the astonished waves looked on and wondered at the frail craft that rashly sailed between the thunderous rocks and bore away the fleece. If Argo had been overwhelmed, and his life extinguished by the roaring waters, mayhap no wandering oar would now trouble the treacherous seas.

Corinna is about to desert the couch well-grooved from contact with her and she means to seek adventure on treacherous uncharted paths. Now I must lift my prayers and tremble at the west wind and the east, at frosty Boreas and at the balmy breezes from the south.

Your gaze, Corinna, will vainly seek to rest upon the fair security of towns graciously shaded with leafy arbors; you will behold only the deep blue waters of the unfaithful sea. The water here is unrelieved by delicate shells and softly-tinted pebbles, for those embellish the shallow surf. Only thus far ought maidens fair to venture, for all the rest is dangerous and gloomy. There lie the waters of Scylla and Charybdis and there are the rocks where the ominous Ceraunians rise from the sea. Yonder lie the darkened folds from where the Syrtes sally forth. Beware of all these things and believe all the warnings you may hear.

Once the cable is loosened and the curving keel bent outward from the shore, it is too late to look lingeringly back upon the land. It is then the troubled sailor trembles at unfavoring winds and feels the close approach of death, who is no further from you than the surface of the water. But when the Triton smites the towering waves, your face will blanch and you will call to aid the high-born stars, the fair sons of fruitful Leda, and realize that she is happy that remains on land.

It is much safer to lie upon your couch, to read a book and let your gentle fingers strum upon the Thracian lyre. But if my reasonable admonitions are destined to be borne away upon the flying gales, may Galatea prosper your voyage. It would be a tragedy if such a beauty were to perish. As you are borne away, remember me, and may you return with a favorable wind. May the breeze be a strong one that brings you back, and let the mighty Nereus slope the sea towards our shore and let the waters of the tide rush hither. And when Zephyr inflates the sails, I shall be the first to sight the oncoming

177

vessel and cry out, "Yonder are my gods approaching."
And I shall hold you fondly in my arms and greedily
snatch your kisses.   And any man who wishes that your
return be delayed shall be a victim of my ire and buried
in the yielding sands where we shall have a couch and
table.

And there, when the repast is served and the wine has
been poured, you will tell me many thrilling tales of
threatening danger safely passed, and how, while hasten-
ing back to me, your spirit feared neither headlong winds
nor the dark unfriendly hours of the night.   How
eagerly I shall believe you, even if it is all lies, for why
should I not flatter the desires of my heart?   May Luci-
fer in the lofty sky with flying steed full speedily bring
about that propitious hour.

XII.   *His joy in obtaining the favors of Corinna.*

Strew about my temples the laurels of triumph, for
victory is mine: Corinna is within my arms, in spite of
husband, keeper and unyielding door.   This troop of
enemies overcome, is a victory deserving special celebra-
tion, for it was accomplished without the spilling of a
drop of blood.   It was not a question of climbing walls
or conquering towns surrounded by cunning moats that
were to be taken by subtle stratagems ... but a woman.

When Pergamum fell, conquered in a war two lus-
trums long, from among that crowd of men what part of
praise fell to the son of Atreus?   But I need share my
glory with no other soldier and I may claim that I
achieved my victory unaided.   I was myself the captain
and the army, cavalry, infantry and standard-bearer.   No

fortunate accident favored my achievement, and I can claim my triumph has been won by art.

My cause was not a novel one. Had the daughter of Tyndareus not been stolen, Europe and Asia would have been at peace. Woman caused a war among the Lapiths and the Centaurs, and the Trojans set afoot new battles in the realms of just Latinus. And woman it was, when our city was still young, that sent the Sabine fathers out to battle against their sons-in-law.

I have seen bulls contend for a snowy mate that watched their rage and spurred them on. And Cupid, who commands many, urged me to bear a standard in his campaign without bloodshed.

XIII. He prays to Isis for the welfare of his foolish mistress.

Corinna, rashly seeking to be rid of the burden in her womb, lies languishing in peril of her life. This action on her part in a performance so dangerous causes my wrath, but my anger grows pale before my fear. And yet it was I that caused her difficulty, or so I choose to believe, for my certainties are frequently just peradventures.

Great Isis, who art fond of Paraetonium and Canopus, of Memphis and Pharos covered with swaying palms, where the great Nile flows swiftly through seven mouths into the sea, I beseech you by the revered face of Anubis (and may Osiris ever love your rites, the sluggish serpent glide about your altar gifts, and horned Apis be your comrade!) turn towards us your countenance and spare us both: giving life to my lady, she will grant life to me. She was ever zealous in her ministrations to you on the days allotted for your service, where the Gallic squadron rides by your laurel trees.

And you, who ease the labor of women in their pangs, when their bodies are tormented by the hidden burden, do you attend in charity, and harken to my prayers, Ilithyria! She is deserving of your aid, and I beseech you, bid her live! And I, accoutered in festive robes, shall offer incense on your smoking altars, and bring you gifts to lay at your feet. My offerings shall bear the legend: "Naso, for Corinna who was saved." Do most graciously give me occasion for both gift and legend.

And you, Corinna, if it be right amid these fears to utter warnings, let this be the last battle in such dangerous strife!

XIV. He explains to Corinna the grievousness of her fault.

What profit is it to women that they are free from the gruesome battles of war and do not have to go to battle arrayed in armor, nor suffer wounds inflicted by the spears of their enemies, when they so readily do damage to themselves.

She who practised the first abortion and plucked forth the tender life ought rightfully to have perished of her own invention. To avoid a few wrinkles around your belly, you insist upon leaving on the sands a bloody carnage.

If these fashions had always been in favor, the race of mortal men would long have perished from the earth. Fortunately, some one was found ready to cast abroad

the seeds a second time after the flood. What if Thetis
had refused to bear her rightful burden, or Ilia had slain
her twins. It would have been the doom of a city des-
tined to rule the world. Had Venus laid rash hands on
her heavy womb, the world would have been orphaned
of its Caesars. And what would have become of you,
my fair one, had your mother cherished such notions?
And though I am destined to perish of love, it is a fate
preferable to having my life extinguished by an unnat-
ural mother.

Why pluck green grapes before their time? Let what
is destined to grow ripe fulfill itself; a short delay bears
in its train the gift of life. Why will you butcher your-
selves with instruments and poison your unborn chil-
dren? The maid of Colchis undid the life of her chil-
dren, and Itys was murdered by the hands of his mother.
But each of these cruel parents had a tragic reason for
being avenged on an unfaithful husband. What Tereus,
what Jason goads you on to rend your bodies with sense-
less hands? The tigress of Armenia would not do such
to her unborn young, nor would the lioness in the wilds
of the forest. Yet tender women do indulge therein,
but not without consequences, for oft one slays herself
in the process and is borne to the fire while the populace
cries out: "She has well merited her fate."

XV. *The poet addresses his gift destined for his
mistress.*

O little ring without value besides the love of the
giver, you are destined to grace my lady's finger, and may
she receive you a welcome gift.

Your fate is fortunate, for you will be borne upon her hand—and I envy my own gift. If by the art of Circe, or Proteus, it could come about that I should be transformed into your shape, I would congratulate myself upon the transformation. Then would I wish that my lady would often fondle her bosom and put the ring-bearing hand within the soft confines of her tunic. And no matter how close my hold would be upon her finger, I would, with wondrous skill, manage to free myself and fall into the secret places of her fair body. She would use me to seal her missives and hold me to her lips the while. If she would wish to place me within her jewel casket, I would refuse to part from her, and keep a firm hold upon her finger.

I would grace you well, my life, nor be a burden to your tender hand, and you could wear me in the spraying rain of your warm bath. I only fear my passion would prove stronger than the charm of magic and that that ring would play a human part.

But why hope for the impossible? Go on your way, little gift, and let my lady feel that with you goes my love.

XVI. To Corinna, from his country home at Sulmo.

I am now at Sulmo, a small land but wholesome, with channeled streams. Though the sun be fierce, and the earth cracked with heat, and the star of the Icarian dog blaze forth, the fields of Paeligni are ever watered by waves, and from the tender soil the fruitful plants are rising. It is a land rich in corn and grapes, and in some fields there rises the tree of Pallas. The lush herbage, crossed by softly gliding streams, covers a fertile soil.

But my heart's flame is not here, or—better phrased —she who puts my heart afire is afar, but the flame is with me. If I were placed twixt Castor and Pollux without you, I should grumble at my seat in high heaven. May those who made the endless roads upon the earth ignobly perish; or else they should have ordered it so that maids might everywhere accompany their mates, else what reason is there for the roads? Then, if it were my lot shiveringly to cross the windy Alps, I should do so with a cheerful heart, if only my lover were at my side. Were she with me, I'd calmly steer my ship through the Libyan Syrtes and fearlessly spread my sail to the unpropitious south. I should calmly approach the monsters crying from the maiden's groin, nor shrink from the winding gulfs of Malea. I would quietly cross the waters which Charybdis, glutted with sunken ships, regurgitates.

If I had to face these dangers out where Neptune holds sway and the waves sweep afar the assisting gods, then let at least your arms be about my neck. Your burden should be sweet and ease my stroke. Often the young lover swam across the waters to see his Hero.

But here, without you, surrounded by the fields and vines, all teeming with a busy life, the prospering countryside, drenched with running streams, and the cool caressing breezes that sway the rich branches of the trees, I seem to be dwelling not in the healthful Paelignian land nor in my father's house, but in Scythia, or among the fierce Cilicians, or the rude Britons, or on the rocks reddened with Promethean gore.

The elm loves the vine and the vine abandons not the elm; why am I always separated from my mistress? Remember how you swore ever to be my comrade, swore by your eyes which are my happy stars. The words of women, like falling leaves, go willy-nilly before the whim of wind and wave.

If in your heart you still retain some slight feeling towards me, then hasten to transpose your emotions into deeds, and you yourself with sure hands command the flying manes of your steeds in my direction; and wherever she passes, bow down, ye mountains, and let the winding ways be straightened!

XVII. To Corinna, who thinks too highly of her beauty.

Before those who believe it shameful that a man be the slave of a woman, I shall most certainly bow down to bear their ire. Well let me lose my name and be proven base if she who is the queen of Paphos and Cythera were only to ply me with milder fires. Had I but fallen prey to a more merciful mistress, instead of a merely beautiful one—for beauty breeds arrogance—my fate must needs have been less pitiful. Corinna's fair face makes her a scourge to me. Well does she know herself, and the image in her glass has taught her haughtiness.

And even if your charms make you proud and bear promise of great conquests, why should you scorn me in comparison with yourself? Great things may well be coupled with lesser ones. Calypso was smitten with a mortal and kept him by her side against his will. Was not the daughter of Nereus wed to the king of Phthian, while Egeria wed Numa, who was skilled in law? Venus married Vulcan, who limped wretchedly about his forge, and my very verses are unequal though the rhyme is perfect. Do you, my light of love, take me on any terms, and let you mete out law to me as if in the midst of the forum.

No cause shall I give you for complaint, and you will be grieved to see me leaving; our love shall be lasting and we shall be proud to avow it. Felicitous songs, instead of great possessions, are mine, and many a maiden languishes to be glorified by me. I hear that there is one who goes about prating that she is Corinna. What would she not give to have it truly so? But sooner can the cold Eurotas and the poplar shaded Po glide between the same banks, than anyone but you should serve as the spur to my Muse.

XVIII. He justifies his Muse to a fellow poet.

While Macer has brought his poem to the time of Achilles and the conspiracy of the chiefs, I dally in the shade of Venus, and Love is crossing all my heroic ventures. How frequently have I pleaded that my love leave me to myself, and in response she came to sit upon my lap. How frequently have I said, "I am ashamed," and she has tearfully wound her slender arms about my neck and plied me with kisses. Thus am I vanquished and summon back my Muse from singing of arms, in heroic strain, and turn again to the follies of my own campaigns.

I did begin to sing of scepters, and through my effort tragedy became popular: surely that was a fitting task for me. But Love laughed at my scepter, and grasping my unkinglike hand, drew me away. My lady joined in my undoing, and now Love triumphantly carries in his train the buskined poet.

I do what I can: I teach the art of Love—and I am made sufferer by my own teaching. I write the words that Penelope sends to Ulysses, the sad plaint of abandoned Phyllis; what is to be read by Paris and Macareus; and what Jason, Hippolytus and his sire receive as news. Also, I write what poor Dido indites, while in her hand she holds a drawn blade.

Sabinus has returned swiftly from the ends of the earth and brought back letters written in far distant places. Penelope has recognized the seal of Ulysses; Aeneas has written to Elissa, and there is a missive for Phyllis, if she be living. A letter has come for Hypsipyle from Jason; and Sappho, learning that her love is returned, has now only to surrender the lyre she has vowed to Phoebus.

You, Macer, who sing of arms, cannot entirely neglect to chant of Love wherever it befits. Paris and Helen and their famous crimes are in your songs, as is Laodamia accompanying her master in death. If I judge you right, these things you sing a little more gladly than the strains of war, and you are slowly passing out of your camp into mine.

XIX. *To a careless husband.*

If you feel no anxiety about losing your wife and you neglect to watch over her, you fool, then guard her at least for me. When anyone can freely have access to her, an affair with her loses its charm. What is forbidden is doubly desirable. The man who claims what another readily concedes is bereft of feelings. Let us hope while we fear, and fear while we hope; let us suffer trials and misfortunes. I do not care for the sure and undeviating path nor do I long for what will never wound me. The clever Corinna, properly appraising my weakness, has shrewdly utilized the means for capturing me: often has she feigned various maladies while she was wholly well and most frequently has she upbraided me when I was guiltless. And when I had been stirred and the indifferent flame of my infection had been fanned anew, she would turn about and be conciliatory towards me. With winsome ways she would be compliant to my prayers, and soothe me with sweet words. What kisses she would shower upon me—and how many of them!

You, too, who most recently have captured my eyes, be frequently disturbed and pretend to be afraid of scandalous disclosures; occasionally rebuff my advances and be deaf to my entreaties. Permit me to lie in vain upon your doorstep and to freeze before your dwelling in the shivery night. Thus love grows sturdy and remains well through many years, for ruses such as these are the nourishment of a long-lasting passion. A love grown fat and careless from compliance cloys, and is as harmful as too many sweets in our diet. Danae, sequestered in a brazen tower, was made a mother by Jove. Juno guarded Io, changed to a horned beast, but this only enhanced her charms in the eyes of Jove. He who desires the casual and easy, let him pluck leaves from trees and drink the waters of the passing streams. If you would be a mistress long, you must deceive your lover. Well will I suffer from my own advice, in spite of which I do insist it galls me to be indulged. What seeks me I fly; and what eludes me, I seek.

But you who are careless of your mistress close your door before nightfall and inquire constantly who beats upon your doors. Discover why the dogs keep barking in the night, what is contained on the tablets that the conspiring slave girl brings and takes, and why your lady spends the night so frequently out of your bed. Let these troubles disturb you; and make it difficult for me —and worth my while to overcome your care. One who will abscond with the wife of a fool is likely to steal the sand from the seashore.

You are hereby warned that unless you guard her better, I shall trouble no more about her! I have borne this long enough, in the hope that you would come to guard her better so that I might have some delight in tricking you; but you are slow and seemingly will stand for anything. Your foolish complaisance is going to end a perfectly good love affair.

Unfortunate me, who have no difficulty in seeing her at any time I please. Is the night never going to lurk dangerously about me? Am I to be fearful of nothing? Shall I have no fitful gasps to disturb my slumbers? Will you do nothing to make me wish you evil? What do I want with a simple fool—with a husband who plays the pimp? He ruins my joy with his good nature. There may be some who are pleased with silly ways, but if you want me as a rival, you will have to make it a little more difficult.

BOOK THREE

I. Tragedy disputes with Elegy the possession of the poet.

Ancient, and spared by the ax for numberless years, here stands a grove. In the midst thereof is a sacred spring, and a cave covered by overhanging rocks. One could believe some god dwelt in this place, and from all sides comes the sweet chattering of birds.

While strolling in this ancient forest, questioning what future work my Muse should venture on, came Elegy with plaited locks and one foot slightly longer than its mate. Her comely form was robed in gauze, her face o'er-spread with love, while the fault in her carriage added further charm. There came, too, Tragedy, with grave strides, her locks shading a darkened brow, her robe trailing behind. In her left hand she held a kingly scepter, and on her foot was the Lydian buskin.

And she spoke thus: "Is there no end to your love-making, O poet of only one theme? Your worthless doings are the gossip of dinner tables and are discussed upon the cross-roads. Frequently, while you pass, some-one will point you out and say: 'There goes he who is consumed with love.' You may be unaware of all this sordid notoriety, but your actions are the common property of the town, for most shamelessly have you blazoned abroad your amorous exploits. It is high time that you were stirred of a greater thyrsus. There has been enough of this foolish dalliance. Begin now upon serious work. Your theme embarrasses your genius. It will become you far better to chant the deeds of heroes. Your Muse has been trifling with such light matter as is fitting for a maiden's song and your first youth has been devoted to the light affairs of youth. It is time that I, Roman Tragedy, win fame through you; you have the gift and may fulfill my needs." Thus she spoke to me, and her manner was impressive, while the other cast a sidelong glance at me and smiled.

"Why be so ominously ponderous, O haughty Tragedy?" she asked. "Can you be naught but heavy? Of course I do not pretend to compare your lofty, high-flown strain with mine, for your queenly bearing overshadows me. I am light, and Cupid, the care of my heart, is also frail; nor am I stronger than the theme I sing. The mother of Love would be but a rustic jade without me; to be the comrade and the go-between of this goddess, I was conceived. The door forever sealed against your austere buskin opens of itself to my blandishments. And I have earned this power by bearing much that your haughty would never endure.

"I have taught Corinna to elude her guards and to tamper with the tightly barred door; to glide softly from her couch with her robes ungirdled, and to move in the darkness with unstumbling feet. Often I have been scribbled on unyielding doors, unashamed that I was scanned by the passing stranger, and once I slept in the bosom of a slave until the danger had passed. And once when you sent me a birthday gift, the dear hands tore me in twain and drowned me in a cup of water. It was I who first swelled the fruitful seeds of your mind, and it is because of me that she now stands there and claims you for her own."

Then I said, "I beg you both to listen most attentively. One tempts me with a mighty scepter and lofty accouterments, and my tongue already curls a glorious speech, while the other bids fair to give everlasting glory to my lovers. Join and let my verses be short and long. Indulge your singer for a short time, O Tragedy, for you are eternal—and what she asks is but brief."

She was moved by my prayer—so let the tender loves come hasting while I am still free, for close upon me there presses a greater task.

II. *At the circus.*

"Do you think I sit here because I am fond of pure-bred steeds? And yet, I do sincerely wish that your own favorite may win. I came especially to talk to you and to tell you of the great love you have stirred in my heart. You look at the races, and I look at you: let us both gaze at what delights our eyes.

"Happy the driver who wins your praises for he is fortunate to have enlisted your favor! I hope that my fortune will not be less, and when I dash out with a fearless heart, I will urge on my steeds, now giving free rein, now cutting their backs with the whip, now grazing my axle on the turning post. When I catch a glimpse of you as I race, I will stop dead and let the reins drop from my hands. Remember how near Pelops came to falling

by a Pisaean spear while looking on the face of Hippo-
damia. Of course, he won through the favor of his mis-
tress, and may we all be indebted for our victories to our
loves.

"Don't try to draw away from me: it will avail you
naught; the line compels us to sit close. This is the great
advantage of sitting in the circus, where the space is care-
fully ruled out. Yet you, there, on the right, be careful;
you are pressing my lady too close. And you, too, in the
back, draw in your knees; you are inconveniencing her.

"Your cloak hangs down too far; it is trailing on the
ground. I will help you gather it up. The envious
wrap covers such pretty limbs. And the more one sees—
ah! the wrap is envious indeed! Atlanta had such limbs,
and such had Diana at the chase, pursuing bold beasts,
less bold than she. I was aflame before I saw so much;
what will my unhappy fate be now? You add fire to fire
and water to the sea. And what do I now suspect about
those charms that are well-hidden beneath your tunic?

"Would you like me to fan you? Or isn't it warm
at all, and is it merely the heat of my heart that makes
the air oppressive? There is a speck of dust defiling you.
Away from this snowy body!

"Now starts the procession; let all attend. This is
the time to applaud. First comes Victory with wings
outspread; O goddess, come hither and assist my love.
Then comes Neptune in whom I have no interest, for I
distrust the sea. Follows Mars; let the soldiers applaud,
but my delight is peace, where Love is found. But there
is Phoebus; let him be gracious to soothsayers; and
Phoebe gracious to huntsmen; Minerva applauded by
craftsmen; while the country dwellers cheer Ceres and

Bacchus. The boxer courts Pollux, the horseman Castor, but we applaud Venus and your child potent with the bow. Smile, O goddess, on all my adventures and make favorable the mind of my new mistress. Let her suffer me to love her.

"The goddess has nodded and given her assent. Promise what she has conceded, and I say, with her permission, you shall be the greater goddess. I swear to you by all those present, and by the train of all the gods, that I am asking you to be my queen forever.

"Your feet are dangling uncomfortably and you will do well to rest them on the grating. The circus is now clear but for the praetor, who has just given the starting signal to the four-horsed cars. I know the one you want to win; he's bound to be successful, for he has your favor. But look what the miserable man is doing; he has circled the posts leaving a wide margin, while the next one stays close and gains on him. Scoundrel, what are you about? You will lose my love the wish of her heart. Pull the left rein with all your might! Ah, we are favoring a good-for-nothing. But let us call a fresh start; come on, friends, let us toss our togas in. Good! Now they are calling them back. But for fear some waving toga may spoil your hair, I would advise you to hide your head in the fold of my cloak.

"And now they are off again. With reins let loose, the many-colored rout comes flying by. Come on! Get past him! Use your chance in the open space—and see that you fulfill our vows!

"Ah, well! The prayers of my mistress are fulfilled —but mine remain. The charioteer has now received his palm, while mine is still to be won."

195

She smiled, and her speaking eyes held a promise for me.

"That will do for this place. You can render the rest somewhere else."

III. He pleads with his mistress to abandon her false oaths.

It is difficult to believe in gods. She has sworn a false oath and still she is as beautiful as ever; her hair is just as long as it was before she blasphemed; her cheeks were rose-colored then, nor is their beauty diminished now. She had a small and comely foot; its daintiness has since in no way been impaired. She was tall and exquisite and she is still well-grown and beautiful. Her eyes were sparkling and they sparkle still, although they have often lied to me. Certainly the gods are also indulgent to the fair and their eternal perjuries, and beauty has divine privileges. A short while gone, she swore by my eyes and hers, and only mine are pained.

O god, if the deceitful thing has hoodwinked you, why must I bear the punishment for her transgressions? The daughter of Cepheus you doomed to death for her mother's ill-starred beauty. Is it not enough that your backing is without weight, and that she pokes fun at you as well as me? Am I to suffer for her perjury and be deceived and a victim to boot? Either god is just a name for the ignorant rabble, or he is too susceptible to a pretty face. It is only against men that Mars girds on his sword, and we are the targets for the spears of Pallas. It is against us that Apollo bends his bow and upon us fall the bolts from the hands of Jove.

The gods fear to offend fair women and dread those who have no awe for the gods. Do any women ever place incense on their altars? It is high time we men showed more courage.

Jove hurls lightning on sacred groves and temples but spares the fair. How many of them deserve his bolts, yet the hapless Semele was the only one who suffered.

But why do I complain and scold at heaven? Surely the gods have eyes and hearts! Were I myself divine, would it not be easy for women to cheat my divinity? I would myself insist that all they swore was true. Nor would I be a stodgy austere sort of god.

But you, my lady, be more careful with your oaths and have pity for my eyes.

IV. He reproaches a husband for the strict surveillance he places upon his wife.

Cruel and foolish husband, who sets a guard over his wife, how vain is your precaution, for certainly the only safe guide she can possess must be her own nature. She only is really pure who would remain pure if she were wholly unguarded; and certainly she who remains virtuous because she is too closely watched has in reality no virtue whatever. The body can be kept under control while the mind commits the most unimaginable folly. And even the body cannot be wholly guarded; for with every door locked, you may still unknowingly harbor a traitor within. The woman who is free to err, errs less, for supervision and restraint add power to the seed of sin. Listen to me, and you will cease to spur on to wrong-doing by forbidding. You will achieve a good deal more by indulgence.

Not long ago I saw a horse take the bit in his mouth and career like a flash of lightning; but the moment he felt the slackened reins upon his flank, he stopped of his own volition. We hunger forever for what is denied us; the sick man languishes for what will be his certain undoing.

Argus, equipped with a hundred eyes in front and a hundred eyes behind, was still deceived by the cunning ways of Love. Danae, in her chamber of rock and iron, became a mother, although she had entered it a maid; but Penelope, unguarded, remained faithful among her throng of youthful suitors.

Caution invites the thief, for few desire what another concedes. Your fair one is not desirable because of her overpowering charms, but because of the great love you show for her. It leads one to suspect that there is more to her than is obvious to the naked eye. It is not fitting that a free-born woman be kept like a slave or that she tremble at your sight. What profit if she be chaste merely to prove a boast to your watchfulness?

It is not at all urbane on your part to be upset when she plays you false, and you certainly show little acquaintance with city manners. In Rome, the sons of Mars were born not without reproach: Romulus, the child of Ilia, and Ilia's child, Remus. If you would have a chaste wife, why trouble to marry a beautiful one? It is a difficult combination and never found intact.

If you are wise, you will be indulgent. Drop your stern look. Be gracious. Don't insist eternally upon your rights, and cherish the friends your wife will bring

—there will be plenty of them. You will be popular without much effort, always surrounded by smiling youthful faces, and you will see lots of presents around the place which you haven't paid for.

V. *An evil dream.*

It was night and I was slumbering, when a certain vision terrified my spirit.

At the foot of a hill there was an ilex grove, in whose branches the birds were singing. Nearby was a grassy lawn, humid with the trickling of gentle waters. I had sought refuge from the heat in the shadow of the trees, when turning, I saw an exquisite white heifer come to crop the rich herbage near the grove. Her coat was whiter than the freshly fallen snow, more shining than the foam on newly gathered milk. Beside her walked a bull, undoubtedly her happy consort, who occasionally pressed her side with possessive grace.

The bull reclined upon the ground and majestically chewed his cud. I saw his tired eyelids slowly droop and eventually he fell into a peaceful slumber. Suddenly, there came out of the air a swiftly flying crow that settled on the ground and with a wanton beak struck three times upon the breast of the snowy heifer. Afterwards the crow arose and flew away, carrying in its mouth some white tufts of hair. Another while passed, and the heifer, bearing a livid mark upon her breast, looked up and saw not far away some other bulls a-pasturing. Cautiously she looked about, then quickly ran toward them and was lost in the herd where the grass was most abundant.

I went to consult him who augurs the meaning of dreams and asked him to tell me the substance of my vision. Carefully, he harkened to my words, and after pondering them well, he said:

"The heat you meant to avoid was the flame of your love; the heifer was your mistress; and you were the bull, her mate. The crow was a pandering old dame who is meddling with her heart. The heifer's lingering before she left the bull gives token that you will be deserted in your bed; the dark stains on her breast are the signs of unfaithfulness in her heart."

He had spoken while I shivered with cold; the blood had left my face, and I stared into a night of darkness.

VI. To a stream that impedes his progress.

O stream, whose muddy banks are covered with reeds, stop for a moment, as I am in haste to see my mistress. There is no bridge nor boat to carry me across, for you were small, and at your deepest you did not rise above my ankles. But now the snows have melted and come down from the mountains, and their waters, muddy and turbulent, have made you into a whirling river. What does it avail that I have hastened hither, resting little upon the way, if now I am to be balked upon this shore? Now do I wish for the pinions that the son of Danae wore, when he carried away the severed head of Medusa; now do I wish I had at my command the car from which the first seeds of Ceres fell upon the untilled grounds. But these things are the tales of bards of olden times; no one has ever seen them and no one ever will.

Still, do you, river, listen to me—trespassed as you
have on the land either side of your banks—and return
within the limits of your usual bounds. You will merit
eternal hate if it be because of you and your transgression
that a lover has been kept from his mission. Rivers ought
to assist all lovers, for their waters have often trembled
with this sacred emotion. The Inachus languished for
Bithynian Melie, and his cold waves grew warm with
love. The siege of Troy had not yet been two lustrums
long, when the Neaera ravished the eyes of Xanthus.
Alpheus flowed into many lands urged by his great love
for an Arcadian maid, and Peneus hid Creusa, the prom-
ised bride of Xuthus, in the land of the Phthiotes. Re-
member Asopus, in love with Thebes, the child of Mars,
destined to have five daughters on her own account. And
what became of the horns of Achelous? It was Hercu-
les that broke them off. Aye, and what he would not
have done for all Etolia, Deianira alone was able to ob-
tain. The rich Nile that flows through seven mouths
and hides so well the home-land of its source, could not
drown out the fires that Asopus' child, Iuanthe, had
kindled in his breast. Enipeus, desiring to embrace the
daughter of Salmoneus without wetting her, commanded
his waters to recede; and thus commanded, they retired.

Nor shall I overlook the flowing waters that moisten
the fruitful fields of Argive Tibur—you, whom Ilia,
with hair disheveled and cheeks that showed the marks
of nails, charmed in spite of her distraught appearance.
Weeping over the crime of her uncle and the wrongs of
Mars, she wandered bare-footed through the lonely
places. Anio, beholding her thus, looked out from his
sweeping floods, and from the waves his hoarse voice

shouted: "Why do you thus tread my banks, O Ilia, and what has become of your gorgeous raiment? What are you seeking? Why is your hair falling loosely about your shoulders? What is the cause of your weeping and why do you beat your breast with an impassioned hand? Surely he has a heart of iron who, unmoved, can see the tears fall from your eyes. Fear naught, Ilia, for my royal hall shall be prepared for you and my waves shall pay you honor. You shall become my mistress, served by a hundred nymphs, for a hundred or more make their home in my stream. Do not reject my offer, you, sprung from the Trojan blood, and you shall have gifts surpassing far my promises."

Thus he spoke while she listened with downcast lids, letting the tears fall in a soft rain upon her bosom. Three times she tried to fly, but lacking strength to run, she at last called out with trembling lips the wrongs that she had suffered.

"Now do I wish that my body had been buried in the tomb of my ancestors when it was still the body of a maid. A vestal but yesterday, today disgraced and denied my rightful place at the altar-fires of Ilion, am I now to be invited to a casual marriage? Why do I remain alive, a target for the jeers of the crowd? Allow me to die, who am but destined to suffer shame and disrespect."

Thus had she spoken; and abandoning herself completely to her grief, she stretched out her arms and threw herself upon the waves. The smooth-gliding stream took her softly to his breast, and bearing her securely aloft, took her as his rightful bride to his bed.

You, too, I am most certain, have been warmed by love for some fair maiden, but your trespasses are covered by soft, shaded arbors. While I have been speaking to you, your turbulent path has grown deeper and wider. Why do you delay my joys? What wrong have I done to you? Why do you lay yourself across the path of my desire? What sort of stream or river, even if you were the most famous on all the earth—but you have no fame or name. You are just a gathering of fitful, accidental rivulets; you have neither source nor destination. Your origin is dependent upon the erratic course of the weather; the accidental rain or snow-storm has begotten you. And so you run a muddy course in the winter, but crawl along a dusty bed in summer's heat. What thirsty wanderer has ever found refreshment from your muddy waters, and who has ever lifted up his voice and said: "May you flow on forever!" You are injurious to flocks and fields—but these troubles matter nothing to me who am concerned but with my own affairs.

Fie upon such a stream! Shame upon him! And what a fool am I to have talked of the loves of great rivers in his unworthy presence and to have sounded their great names before this obscure piece of moisture. To think that before him I spoke of the Nile, of Achelous and Inachus, when all he deserves is that the summer suns be ever fierce and the winters without snow.

VII. He reproaches himself for having failed his mistress.

How fair and how accomplished she is! And have I not hungered madly to possess her? And yet I have held her in my embrace to no purpose whatever. I must confess it, to my everlasting shame, that I lay torpid like an inanimate hulk upon her couch, without strength or achievement. In vain were her longings and my writhings; naught would stir my hapless member into life. Despite the twining of her ivory arms about my neck, those arms as white as the snows of Thrace; aye, despite her tongue which cunningly entwined my own, and her luscious thigh pressed amorously where it is wont to do the greatest good, I remained lifeless. She showered upon me endearing names and said all the sweet nothings that a woman can and does say upon such an occasion; but my members lay as if they had been drugged with hemlock and had no notion of the path to duty. Lifeless I was, like the trunk of a tree, a statue, or a mass of clay, and she had good cause to wonder whether I were indeed a man or just a stuffed dummy.

What fate awaits me in after years if now, in my youth, I produce such a lamentable fiasco. Well do I blush for my young years—for I am but a youth and a man, although my mistress has reason to disbelieve both. She left her bed pure as a vestal virgin, or like a sister who had come to bid her brother farewell. I am distracted, for only recently I dutifully paid my respects twice to the fair-haired Chloe, thrice to the white-skinned Pitho, thrice also to Libas; and encouraged by my Corinna, nine times in one night I acquitted myself most honorably.

Has some witchcraft benumbed my carcass, some poisonous herb or magic incantation caused my distress? Has some aged crone written my name in crimson wax and plunged a needle into my vitals? The rich corn can dwindle into sterile grass through a witch's spell; springs can be made to run dry, great oaks to wither, grapes to dry upon the vine, and fruit to fall rotting from hapless boughs, by a cunning incantation. Perhaps, by the same magic my nerves have been undone, and my body turned into unfeeling ice. But think of the shame of it; it was the shame itself that robbed me of my strength, and was, at least in part, the cause of my disaster.

How beautiful she was as I looked upon her and touched her, for I was as close to her as the shift she wore. Her contact would have made the King of Pylos grow young again, and Tithonus would have been stirred by curious promptings for his years. Ah! what a woman I found in her! And what a man she discovered in me! What prayer, what vow may I now have recourse to, when surely the gods already regret that they placed into my unworthy hand so rare a prize?

I was mad with longing to gain entrance to her house; I did; to kiss her; I kissed her; to sleep with her; I slept with her.

But what avails my good fortune, when I turn out to be a king who wields no scepter? Like a miser, surrounded by his riches, I gloated over my wealth and was incapable of using it. I was a Tantalus, consumed with thirst although surrounded by water, and beheld the fruit that I was destined not to touch although close to my out-stretched hand. I was a husband who honorably leaves his wife untouched when he goes to seek the altar of the gods.

Perchance you will console me by suggesting that she failed to shower me with endearments most passionate and enticing. Ah me! indeed she did her utmost; the hardest adamant and the sturdiest oaks would have trembled and been moved; she would have shaken any living thing that you could call a man. But I was neither living nor a man. What are the songs of Phemius to the deaf? What is a pleasant picture to the blind Thamyris?

What joys had I anticipated and what ecstasies had I imagined! My body belied my expectations and was limp like a faded rose. But now, and it is high time, behold how it is rejuvenated, clamoring to be up and about, seeking for work to be done. Shame, shame upon you, most worthless part of me! I know these promises, which you have failed to fulfill when the occasion arose but you did not. You have deceived me and my mistress, and I have fallen into disgrace because of you.

She did all in her power to incite me by the cunning manipulation of her hand; until, convinced that all her efforts were in vain and that my body could in no way be brought back to life, she gave up in disgust. "Why do you come into my bed against your will?" she asked. "What sort of folly is this? Have you fallen the victim of some enchantress, or have you been sowing your strength upon other women?"

And then, attired in but the flimsiest of garments she jumped out of the bed and sped away to fetch her maid, who came forthwith fetching some water; for my mistress would not have her servants know that the combat had come to nothing.

VIII. *To his mistress, who has chosen his rich rival.*

And who, at this time attaches any importance to the liberal arts; who deems that tender verse is worth a dollar? Time was when genius was cherished above gold, but now to be poor is considered the height of vulgarity. My mistress was pleased with my little books, but I must say they were more fortunate than I, for after praising them she closed the door against my face, and I am free to wander about unmolested.

A newly-rich knight, who won his gold by the dealing of wounds and who grew fat on the blood of others, has replaced me in her esteem. How can you, with your exquisite arms, embrace so repulsive a creature? How can you let him clasp you to his bosom? Know that on his head he was wont to wear a helmet and that in one hand he held a sword, while with the other, upon which he now sports an ill-becoming ring, he bore a shield. That same right hand that freely touches you has frequently been stained with blood; cherished by you now, it once dealt death.

Where is your erstwhile tenderness of heart? Look at his battle-scarred body, with which he earned his fortune. Ask him to tell you, for no doubt he can recall, how many throats he has slashed. Do you touch his gruesome hands without a qualm, you greedy one, while I, the stainless priest of Phoebus and the Muses, sing in vain before your unyielding doors?

Ah! ye who are wise or seek wisdom, follow not in our footsteps, but learn rather to seek glory upon the fields of battle. Place the death-dealing spear above the adroitly chiseled verse; for great Homer himself would meet with no better fate in these wretched days.

Jove, who knew well the potency of gold, turned himself into the price of a maiden's betrayal; until the price was forthcoming, the father was obdurate, the maiden chaste, the tower of iron, and brazen the door. But when the astute wooer had hit upon a glittering disguise, all opposition yielded, and the maiden willingly opened her arms.

When ancient Saturn ruled in the heavens, all the metals were held in the dark embrace of the earth: copper, silver, gold and iron were hidden in the depths. There were better, greater gifts than harvests that had to be labored over. Freely and untilled the fields brought forth their riches of fruit and honey, and all good things were in abundance. No laboring oar then stirred the waters, and the shore was the boundary for the paths of men.

Your own cunning, O humanity, has been your greatest foe, and your craft is your own undoing. What use is there to build enormous towering walls around your cities; what use to wage endless wars; and what purpose has been served by crossing the sea, when you already possessed sufficient lands for your needs? Why not rise up in the air and attempt to conquer heaven as well? Aye, and haven't you even done that already? Have not Quirinus, Liber, Alcides and Caesar each their temple?

We turn up the earth to seek gold instead of to plant wheat; the soldier seeks gold in return for his blood. The senate is closed to the poor, for gold is the merit that qualifies for office; gold it is that gives the juror weight, and degree to the knight.

Let them keep it all. Let the Campus and the Forum be in their hire and let them decide war and peace; but in their fierce greed, let them not purchase our loves also. Let them leave something that a poor man may aspire to. But now, though a woman be prudish as a Sabine dame, a rich wooer can eventually treat her like his captive. I am denied admittance by her guards because she trembles at her husband, but were I to arrive with lavish gifts, guard and husband would abandon the house to me. O, if only there were some god to avenge a neglected lover and rob the parvenu of his ill-gotten gains.

IX. *Upon the death of Tibullus.*

If the mother of Memnon and the mother of Achilles bewailed their sons, and they as goddesses were not insensible to the awful blows of fate, then you, too, Elegy, unbind your tresses, for a great singer in thy strain, Tibullus, has been raised upon the pyre. Behold the child of Venus, quiver reversed and bow broken, approach with unlighted torch. His wings are drooped, and with aggrieved hand he beats his breast. His tear-stained curls fall forward about his neck, and he is shaken by sobs. Thus came he forth from the dwelling of the fair Iulus, mourning the death of Aeneas, his brother. Nor was the heart of Venus less grieved when Tibullus perished than when the fierce boar pierced the groin of her young lover. We are called sacred, we bards, and favored of the gods: there are some who even avow that there is a divine fire within us. But death is inexorable and pays no heed to tears or distinctions. What availed the Ismarian Orpheus his parentage, or that he had stopped the beasts and overpowered them by his songs? The same father mourned Linus, whom Apollo bewailed in the deep forest upon his unresponsive lyre. Then we have the Maeonian singer, the bard who is the unfailing spring for poets who draw nigh to drink at the Pierian fount. His voice was also stilled and he was lowered to the depths of dark Avernus. Only the poetry escapes the burning pyre; the work of the poet alone is immortal. The great tale of Troy's siege and conquest and the story of the unfinished web will be eternally remembered. Thus Nemesis and Delia are famed forever more, one as the last and the other as his first love.

What purpose are our sacrifices? What avail the sistrums of Egypt? What profits your repose apart in a faithful bed? When thus the virtuous are swept away by fate, I may be forgiven for being tempted to doubt the existence of the gods. Live the good life and you will perish; be faithful in your acts of worship, and in the very act death will drag you to the grave. Put your power and your passion into lofty poetry, and lo! Tibullus lies dead! His remnants scarcely fill an urn. Is it really you that the flames have consumed and have unshrinkingly reduced to ashes? Such flames would not hesitate to reduce the blessed dwelling of the gods to ruins. Venus turned away her face, and there are some who say her tears flowed unrestrained.

And yet his lot has been fairer than had he died among the Phaeacians, unhonored and unknown. At least his mother closed his dying eyes and bestowed the proper honor to his ashes; his sister came with hair disordered to help bear the poor mother's grief. So did

Nemesis and Delia approach and print on your faded lips a final kiss, and stood beside your pyre.

"I am the happier," said Delia, "for you lived as long as I inspired you."

"Do not bewail my loss," said Nemesis. "It was I who held his hand as he lay dying."

Yet if aught survives beyond mere name and shade, in the vale of Elysium, then Tibullus will abide. May you come forth to meet him, learned Catullus and Calvus, your temples encircled with ivy. And you, too, Gallus, if the charge that you had wronged your friend be false, come and lavish of your blood and of your life. Your shade is comrade to these, if there be a shade that survives the body. You have increased the number of the blessed, Tibullus. Rest quietly his bones in the protecting urn, and may the earth lie lightly upon your ashes.

X.   He reproaches Ceres for her cruelty.

The time for the festival of Ceres has come and my mistress is in retreat and rests in a lonely bed. O golden Ceres, who comes with delicate tresses crowned with wheat, why must your festival put a ban upon our pleasures?

All the nations of the world call you the giver of gifts, and there is no one who envies man his blessings less than you do. Before you came, the peasant did not bake his bread, nor did he know the meaning of a threshing floor. Only the oak, our earliest soothsayer, gave him acorns, and these and rude herbs were the only food he knew. It was Ceres who made the seed to swell and cut with a curved sickle the colored locks of the corn. She first put yoke upon the stubborn neck of the steer and turned the glebe with the ploughshare.

Hardly a goddess, one would suspect, who would enjoy the tears of lovers and whose worship would entail that they sleep apart. Although the goddess of the fields, she is no simple rustic with heart devoid of finer sentiments.

The Cretans will serve as my witnesses, and they are not absolutely false, for in Crete Jove was nurtured, and it was here that he who sways the starry heavens drank the tender milk of childhood.

We have faith in their witness, approved by their foster-son; and Ceres herself, I believe, will endorse my statement. At the foot of Ida, in Crete, it chanced that the goddess espied Iasius piercing with powerful hand the side of a wild beast. Looking upon him, her heart was flushed with love. But love was hastily replaced by shame and just as quickly was shame dislodged by love again. Then you beheld the furrows of the field grow dry and the seed return but a minute harvest. The mattock had wrought upon the earth and the curved share had dug into the dour glebe and the husbandman had strewn the grain equally over his ploughed fields, but his hopes and prayers came to nothing.

The goddess, whose care guarded his fields, was away dallying in the deep forest, and from her long tresses, the wreath of corn had fallen. Only Crete had a fruitful harvest, for wherever the goddess passed, her footsteps were laden with rich crops. Ida, once covered with woodlands, was now loaded with corn, and the wild boar fed richly upon it. Minos, the law-giver, wished for seasons ever like this, and hoped that the love of Ceres would endure.

The pain you would have suffered, O fairhaired goddess, if you had been compelled to sleep away from your lover, I am now forced to undergo on your hallowed day of mysteries. Why must I be sad upon the day when you have recovered your daughter, a queen of only lesser state than Juno herself? A festal day such as this calls for love and song and wine: such are the gifts most fitly tendered to the gods that rule the world.

XI. He recalls the numerous trespasses of his mistress.

(a)

I have endured a great deal and for a long time. I am through with you. My heart is tired, and you had better leave me. Now that I have claimed my freedom and shaken my shackles, I am ashamed that I was not ashamed ever to bear them. Victory is mine, for I have vanquished Love, and though it has taken me a long time, I at last trample it beneath my feet. I shall persist, and whatever pain I have, I will some day be glad that I endured it. Often enough a bitter potion brings succor to the languishing.

How can it be that I have stood so much, cast my body down, free-born though I be, to play the guardian for you and your lover, comfortably snug inside, while I kept a night-long vigil before your door? I saw your lover issue forth exhausted and with a weakened frame, tired from Love's battle, but this is nothing to the fact that he saw me, too. May my enemies suffer the like!

Haven't I always hung on to you, been guard and lover and companion to you? Rest assured that this is partly why people desired you; it was my love that won you the love of others. It is useless to recall your lies and perjuries, or the coquetries you practised at the banquet table, and the secret signals you exchanged with your lovers. When I was told that she was ill, in what a panic did I run to see her, and found her well enough to have entertained my rival.

Many such tricks have I endured, and others it is not worth recalling. But I have changed, so find someone else who will more graciously submit to your treachery. My craft is decked with votive wreaths and harkens expectantly to the sea's swelling waters. Don't waste your embraces nor the words that once could sway me; I am no longer the fool I once was.

(b)

My fickle heart is drawn now this way now that, by love and hate in various directions, with love getting slightly the better of it. I insist on hating if my strength holds out; if not, I shall love unwillingly. The ox loves not the yoke he bears, but hating it, he bears it none-the-less. Flying from your baseness, I am drawn back by your beauty; I despise the wickedness of your ways, but I desire your body. Thus I can live neither with nor without you, and I do not seem to know my own heart's desire. I wish you were either less beautiful or less evil, for your charms are mated to a base soul. Your actions merit contempt while your face pleads for affection. Ah! poor me! It has more power over my heart than your misdeeds.

Forgive me by the laws of our comradeship and by all the gods who lend themselves so willingly to your false oaths; by your face that bears to me the image of some high divinity; and by your eyes that have taken mine as captive. Whatever you may be, you will ever be mine. You have the choice whether you would have me love you because I want to, or because I am constrained. Let me rather spread my sail, and prospering by a favorable breeze, fly, than that I love you against my will.

XII. He regrets having spread abroad the fame of his mistress.

What day was that, ye birds of mournful plumage, on which you chanted omens ill-boding to my love affairs? What ominous star is rising counter to my fate, or what god shall I complain is making war upon me? She who but now was my own dear, whose only love I was, I must now share with many.

And well do I deserve it, for it is my own fault, as my verses have made her the talk of the town. Most cunningly I have sounded abroad her charms. Why did I appoint myself the crier of her beauty? Through me she has been put up for auction; I am the pander that has helped her to please and assisted her prospective lovers to find a way to her door. What be the good of poetry I am very much in doubt about: it has always been my bane and stood in the way of my good fortune. Here was Thebes and Troy and the bravery of Caesar, but I would sing of Corinna's beauty instead. I wish the Muses had turned their back upon me when I first touched verse; and Phoebus had refused his aid when I was young about the business. Still, the custom being to accredit the testimony of poets in such matters, I must confess that I would not have liked it if my verses had counted for naught.

We poets made Scylla steal the treasured locks from her sire and made her hide the fierce, devouring dogs in her groin. We have put wings on feet, mingled snakes with hair and made the child of Abas victor with a winged horse. We also stretched Tityos through space and gave to the vicious dog three mouths. We made Enceladus hurl a spear with a thousand arms and had the hero snared by the voice of the Siren. We enclosed in the skins of the Ithacan the east winds of Aeolus, and made the crying Tantalus thirst in the midst of a stream. Niobe we turned into a rock and we changed a maiden to a bear, and it is we who made the bird of Cecrops sing Odrysian Itys. That Jove transforms himself now into a bird, now into fleece, or crosses the water as a bull with a maiden on his back, has all been done by poets. We thought of Proteus and those Theban seeds, the dragon's teeth; that there were cattle that spewed flames out of their mouths; of Auriga's sisters weeping tears of amber; of ships that now are goddesses of the sea; of the ill-starred day when Atreus gave his dreadful feast; and the rocks that followed the stroke of the lyre.

Unlimited is the imaginative power of the poets, tramping ceaselessly upon the truths of history. My praise of my mistress should have been taken with a grain of salt: I have been undone by your foolish credulity.

XIII. The festival of Juno.

Since the woman I wed was born at fruitful Falisci, it chanced that we came to visit the walls once brought low by Camillus. The priestesses were preparing the festival of Juno with solemn games and a heifer of native stock. I was tempted to tarry and to observe the rites although the road that leads to the scene of its performance is rather steep. There is an ancient grove of dense foliage that obviously forms the home of some divinity. There is an altar to receive the prayers and offerings of the faithful, an artless altar, built by the devout of olden times. From here, when the pipe has sounded in solemn strain, the cavalcade advances in its annual pomp. Snowy heifers are led amid the cheering of the populace, heifers reared here in their native meadows, and promising calves, as well as pigs, and bulls, with horns curved over the threatening brow. Only the she-goat is hateful to the goddess; her tattling tongue is supposed to have caused Juno to abandon her flight through the woods. Even now, children assail the gossip with their darts, and she is prize of the one who lays her low.

Wherever the goddess passes, youths and shy maidens go before, sweeping the paths with trailing robes. In the Grecian manner, the maidens' locks are pressed by gold and jewels, and they carry the sacred vessels in their keeping. Their feet are decked with gold, and deep silence holds the people as the procession comes on, and the goddess comes in the wake of her priestesses.

From Argos is the form of the pomp. After Agamemnon fell, Halaesus fled the scene of his crime and the riches of his father-land, and wandered in exile over many lands and seas until he founded with auspicious hands these lofty walls. It was he who taught the Faliscans the sacred rites of Juno. May they be ever propitious to her people and to me.

XIV. To his mistress.

Considering your beauty, I do not forbid you a few frailties. What I am annoyed by is that they are no secret to me. I am no censor who dogmatically insists upon your chastity; I merely ask that you pretend a little more successfully. She who denies her sin with some appearance of truthfulness, has really not sinned. It is only the proven fault that is dishonorable. What sort of madness is this to harangue the town in the light of day about the secret things that pass in the night? The common trollop, who receives the unknown son of Quirinus, carefully bolts the door and makes some fair attempt at privacy. Not you! You will casually expose your trespasses to the mercy of vicious tongues and play the informer on your own transgressions. Change your method and imitate, at least, the virtuous and modest of your sex, and make some pretense of honesty, though none exist. Continue in your evil ways but deny them, at least, and have the decency to use becoming speech in public.

There is one spot that calls for lechery. Fill that to your heart's content and let your blushes be absent in so doing. But once removed from there, cast aside all wantonness of conduct and abandon lewdness simultaneously with your couch. In assuming your robe, assume an innocent face, and let your modest aspect belie the harlot.

Cheat the world, cheat me, permit me to misunderstand through ignorance, to enjoy a fool's faith in an unexisting character.

Why must I so frequently observe the despatching and receiving of love letters? Why am I compelled to notice the sordidly crumpled state of your couch? Why must I come upon you and find your hair disordered by something more than sleep, and see the marks of teeth upon your neck? You insist on dragging your trespasses before my eyes. If you care nothing about your reputation, at least spare mine. My mind totters, and I suffer the agonies of death each time that you confess your sins, and through my anguished frame the blood runs cold. I love you, then, and try in vain to hate, although I would be gladly dead, but dead with you.

I shall not spy upon you, be certain of it; nor follow you to discover what you are hiding. It shall be part of the bargain that I be deceived. If, in spite of this, I shall discover you in the midst of some fault, and my eyes be witnesses of your shame, see that you deny what I have my own self observed; and my eyes will yield to your words. It will be an easy conquest for you, achieving your victory over one who is eager to be vanquished; all that you need is a tongue that will stubbornly insist: "I didn't do it." When you can be successful by a few words, then if your cause fails you, conquer through your judge.

XV.   He bids farewell to his Muse.

Seek a new bard, mother of tender Loves; I have come to the last turning post my elegies shall graze, the elegies whose singer I am. Nor have I been dishonored by these songs I chanted, child as I am of the Paelignian acres and heir of a line of sires who bore a knightly name—nor was their dignity gratuitously achieved yesterday in some trifling exchange of arms.

Mantua boasts of Virgil, Verona has Catullus, and I shall be the glory of the Paelignians, who bore honorable arms when Rome was menaced by confederate hosts. And some passing stranger, looking upon Sulmo of the many streams, may say: "O you, who did beget so distinguished a poet, you are, in spite of your minute dimensions, a mighty city!"

Beloved child, and you, Venus, his equally beloved mother, pluck up from my fields your golden standards. The horned god Lyaeus has dealt me a thwacking blow with a weightier thyrsus, and I must smite the earth with steeds bent upon a greater course. Farewell, unwarlike elegies, and my congenial Muse, farewell. When I shall once have passed on, my work shall still live after me!

OVID'S ELEGIES

————

Translated by

CHRISTOPHER MARLOWE

BOOK ONE

P. OVIDII NASONIS AMORUM

LIBER PRIMUS

ELEGIA I.

Quemadmodum a Cupidine, pro bellis amores scribere coactus sit.

We which were Ovid's five books, now are three,
For these before the rest preferreth he:
If reading five thou plain'st of tediousness,
Two ta'en away, thy labour will be less;

With Muse prepared, I meant to sing of arms,
Choosing a subject fit for fierce alarms:
Both verses were alike till Love (men say)
Began to smile and took one foot away.
Rash boy, who gave thee power to change a line?
We are the Muses' prophets, none of thine.
What, if thy mother take Diana's bow ,
Shall Dian fan when love begins to glow?
In woody groves is't meet that Ceres reign,
And quiver-bearing Dian till the plain?
Who'll set the fair-tressed Sun in battle-ray
While Mars doth take the Aonian harp to play?
Great are thy kingdoms, over-strong and large,
Ambitious imp, why seek'st thou further charge?
Are all things thine? the Muses' Tempe thine?

Then scarce can Phoebus say, "This harp is mine."
When in this work's first verse I trod aloft,
Love slaked my muse, and made my numbers soft:
I have no mistress nor no favourite,
Being fittest matter for a wanton wit.
Thus I complained, but Love unlocked his quiver,
Took out the shaft, ordained my heart to shiver,
And bent his sinewy bow upon his knee,
Saying, "Poet, here's a work beseeming thee."
O, woe is me! he never shoots but hits,
I burn, love in my idle bosom sits:
Let my first verse be six, my last five feet:
Farewell stern war, for blunder poets meet!
Elegian muse, that warblest amorous lays,
Girt my shine[1], brow with seabank myrtle sprays[2].

ELEGIA II.

Quod primo amore correptus, in triumphum duci se a
Cupidine patiatur.

What makes my bed seem hard seeing it is soft?
Or why slips down the coverlet so oft?
Although the nights be long I sleep not tho;[3]
My sides are sore with tumbling to and fro.
Were Love the cause it's like I should descry him,
Or lies he close and shoots where none can spy him?
'Twas so; he strook me with a slender dart;
'Tis cruel Love turmoils my captive heart.

---

[1] Sheen.
[2] Dyce's correction for "praise" of the old eds.
[3] Then.

Yielding or striving do we give him might,
Let's yield, a burden easily borne is light.
I saw a brandished fire increase in strength,
Which being not shak'd, I saw it die at length.
Young oxen newly yoked are beaten more,
Than oxen which have drawn the plough before:
And rough jades' mouths with stubborn bits are torn,
But managed horses' heads are lightly borne.[1]
Unwilling lovers, love doth more torment,
Than such as in their bondage feel content.
Lo! I confess, I am thy captive I,
And hold my conquered hands for thee to tie.
What needest thou war? I sue to thee for grace:
With arms to conquer armless men is base.
Yoke Venus' Doves, put myrtle on thy hair,
Vulcan will give the chariots rich and fair:
The people thee applauding, thou shalt stand,
Guiding the harmless pigeons with thy hand.
Young men and women shalt thou lead as thrall,
So will thy triumph seem magnifical;
I, lately caught, will have a new-made wound,
And captive-like be manacled and bound:
Good meaning, Shame, and such as seek Love's wrack
Shall follow thee, their hands tied at their back.
Thee all shall fear, and worship as a king;
Io triumphing shall thy people sing.
Smooth speeches, Fear and Rage shall by thee ride,
Which troops have always been on Cupid's side;

---

[1] "*Frena minus sentit* quisquis ad arma facit."—Marlowe's
line strongly supports the view that "bear hard" in *Julius
Cæsar* means "curb, keep a tight rein over" (hence "eye with
suspicion").

Thou with these soldiers conquer'st gods and men,
Take these away, where is thine honour then?
Thy mother shall from heaven applaud this show,
And on their faces heaps of roses strow:
With beauty of thy wings, thy fair hair gilded,
Ride golden Love in chariots richly builded!
Unless I err, full many shalt thou burn,
And give wounds infinite at every turn.
In spite of thee, forth will thine arrows fly,
A scorching flame burns all the standers by.
So, having conquered Inde, was Bacchus' hue;
Thee pompous birds, and him two tigers, drew;
Then seeing I grace thy show in following thee.
Forbear to hurt thyself in spoiling me.
Behold thy kinsman[1] Caesar's prosperous bands,
Who guards the[2] conquered with his conquering hands.

ELEGIA III.

Ad amicam.

I ask but right, let her that caught me late,
Either love, or cause that I may never hate;
I crave too much—would she but let me love her;
Jove knows with such-like prayers I daily move her.
Accept him that will serve thee all his youth,
Accept him that will love with spotless truth.
If lofty titles cannot make me thine.
That am descended but of knightly line,

---

[1] Old eds. "kinsmans."
[2] Old eds. "thee."

(Soon may you plough the little land I have;
I gladly grant my parents given to save;[1])
Apollo, Bacchus, and the Muses may;
And Cupid who hath marked me for thy prey;
My spotless life, which but to gods gives place,
Naked simplicity, and modest grace.
I love but one, and her I love change never;
If men have faith, I'll live with thee forever.
The years that fatal Destiny shall give
I'll live with thee, and die ere thou shalt grieve.
Be thou the happy subject of my books
That I may write things worthy thy fair looks.
By verses, horned Io got her name;
And she to whom in shape of swan Jove came;
And she that on a feigned Bull swam to land,
Griping his false horns with her virgin hand.
So likewise we will through the world be rung
And with my name shall thine be always sung.

Elegia IV.

Amicam, quoarte quibusque nutibus in cæna, presente viro, uti
debeat, admonet.

Thy husband to a banquet goes with me;
Pray God it may his latest supper be!
Shall I sit gazing as a bashful guest,
While others touch the damsel I love best?
Wilt lying under him, his bosom clip?

---

[1] "Temperat et sumptus parcus uterque parens."

About thy neck shall he at pleasure skip?
Marvel not, though the fair bride did incite
The drunken Centaurs to a sudden fight.
I am no half horse, nor in woods I dwell,
Yet scarce my hands from thee contain I well.
But how thou should'st behave thyself now know'
Nor let the winds away my warnings blow.
Before thy husband come, though I not see
What may be done, yet there before him be.
Lie with him gently, when his limbs he spread
Upon the bed; but on my foot first tread.
View me, my becks, and speaking countenance;
Take, and return each secret amorous glance.
Words without voice shall on my eyebrows sit,
Lines thou shalt read in wine by my hand writ.
When our lascivious toys come in thy mind,
Thy rosy cheeks be to thy thumb inclined.
If aught of me thou speak'st in inward thought,
Let thy soft finger to thy ear be brought.
When I, my light, do or say aught that please thee,
Turn round thy gold ring, as it were to ease thee.
Strike on the board like them that pray for evil.
What wine he fills thee, wisely will him drink.
Ask thou the boy, what thou enough dost think.
When thou hast tasted, I will take the cup,
And where thou drink'st, on that part I will sup.
If he gives thee what first himself did taste'
Even in his face his offered gobbets [1] cast.

---

[1] So Dyce for "goblets" of the old eds. ("Rejice libatos illius ore *cibos*.")

Let not thy neck by his vile arms be prest,
Nor lean thy soft head on his boisterous breast.
Thy bosom's roseate buds let him not finger,
Chiefly on thy lips let not his lips linger;
If thou givest kisses, I shall all disclose,
Say they are mine, and hands on thee impose.
Yet this I'll see, but if thy gown aught cover,
Suspicious fear in all my veins will hover.
Mingle not thighs, nor to his leg join thine,
Nor thy soft foot with his hard foot combine.
I have been wanton, therefore am perplexed,
And with mistrust of the like measure vexed.
I and my wench oft under clothes did lurk,
When pleasure moved us to our sweetest work.
Do not thou so; but throw thy mantle hence,
Lest I should think thee guilty of offense.
Entreat thy husband drink, but do not kiss,
And while he drinks, to add more do not miss;
If he lies down with wine and sleep opprest,
The thing and place shall counsel us the rest.
When to go homewards we rise all along
Have care to walk in middle of the throng.
There will I find thee or be found by thee,
There touch whatever thou canst touch of me.
Ay me! I warn what profits some few hours!
But we must part, when heaven with black night lours,
At night thy husband clips thee: I will weep
And to the doors sight of thyself [will] keep:
Then will he kiss thee, and not only kiss,
But force thee give him my stolen honey-bliss.
Constrained against thy will give it the peasant,
Forbear sweet words, and be your sport unpleasant.

To him I pray it no delight may bring,
Or if it do, to thee no joy thence spring.
But, though this night thy fortune be to try it,
To me to-morrow constantly deny [1] it.

ELEGIA V.

Corinnæ concubitus.

In summer's heat, and mid-time of the day,
To rest my limbs upon a bed I lay;
One window shut, the other open stood,
Which gave such light as twinkles in a wood,
Like twilight glimpse at setting of the sun,
Or night being past, and yet not day begun;
Such light to shamefaced maidens must be shown
Where they may sport, and seem to be unknown:
Then came Corinna in a long loose gown,
Her white neck hid with tresses hanging down,
Resembling fair Semiramis going to bed,
Or Lais of a thousand wooers sped.
I snatched her gown: being thin, the harm was small,
Yet strived she to be covered therewithal;
And striving thus, as one that would be cast,
Betrayed herself, and yielded at the last.
Stark naked as she stood before mine eye,
Not one wen in her body could I spy.
What arms and shoulders did I touch and see!
How apt her breasts were to be pressed by me!

---

[1] "Dedisse nega."

How smooth a belly under her waist saw I,
How large a leg, and what a lusty thigh!
To leave the rest, all liked me passing well;
I clinged her naked¹ body, down she fell:
Judge you the rest; being tired she bade me kiss;
Jove send me more such afternoons as this!

ELEGIA VI.

Ad Janitorem, ut fores sibi aperiat.

Unworthy porter, bound in chains full sore,
On moved hooks set ope the churlish door.
Little I ask, a little entrance make,
The gate half-ope my bent side in will take.
Long love my body to such use make[s] slender,
And to get out doth like apt members render.
He shows me how unheard to pass the watch,
And guides my feet lest, stumbling, falls they catch:
But in times past I feared vain shades, and night,
Wondering if any walked without light.
Love, hearing it, laughed with his tender mother,
And smiling said, "Be thou as bold as other."
Forthwith love came; no dark night-flying sprite,
Nor hands prepared to slaughter, me affright.
Thee fear I too much: only thee I flatter:
Thy lightning can my life in pieces batter.
Why enviest me? this hostile den² unbar;
See how the gates with my tears watered are!

---

¹ Ed. A "her faire white body."
² Old eds. "dende."

233

When thou stood'st naked ready to be beat,
For thee I did thy mistress fair entreat.
But what entreats for thee sometimes[1] took place,
(O mischief!) now for me obtain small grace.
Gratis thou mayest be free; give like for like;
Night goes away: the door's bar backward strike.
Strike; so again hard chains shall bind thee never,
Nor servile water shalt thou drink for ever.
Hard-hearted porter, dost and wilt not hear?
With stiff oak propped the gate doth still appear.
Such rampired gates besieged cities aid;
In midst of peace why art of arms afraid?
Exclud'st a lover, how would'st use a foe?
Strike back the bar, night fast away doth go.
With arms or armed men I come not guarded;
I am alone, were furious love discarded.
Although I would, I cannot him cashier,
Before I be divided from my gear.
See Love with me, wine moderate in my brain,
And on my hairs a crown of flowers remain.
Who fears these arms? who will not go to meet them?
Night runs away; with open entrance greet them.
Art careless? or is't sleep forbids thee hear,
Giving the winds my words running in thine ear?
Well I remember, when I first did hire thee,
Watching till after midnight did not tire thee.
But now perchance thy wench with thee doth rest:
Ah, how thy lot is above my lot blest!

---

[1] Sometime ("quondame").

Though it be so, shut me not out therefore;
Night goes away: I pray thee ope the door.
Err we? or do the turned hinges sound,
And opening doors with creaking noise abound?
We err: a strong blast seemed the gates to ope:
Ay me, how high that gale did lift my hope!
If Boreas bears [1] Orithyia's rape in mind,
Come break these deaf doors with thy boisterous wind.
Silent the city is: night's dewy host [2]
March fast away: the bar strike from the post;
Or I more stern than fire or sword will turn,
And with my brand these gorgeous houses burn.
Night, love, and wine to all extremes persuade:
Night, shameless wine, and love are fearless made.
All have I spent: no threats or prayers move thee;
O harder than the doors thou guard'st I prove thee!
No pretty wench's keeper may'st thou be,
The careful prison is more meet for thee.
Now frosty night her flight begins to take,
And crowing cocks poor souls to work awake.
But thou, my crown, from sad hairs ta'en away,
On this hard threshold till the morning lay.
That when my mistress there beholds thee cast,
She may perceive how we the time did waste.
Whate'er thou art, farewell, be like me pained!
Careless, farewell, with my fault not distained!
And farewell, cruel posts, rough threshold's block,
And doors conjoined with an hard iron lock!

---

[1] Dyce reads, "If, Boreas, bear'st (i.e., "thou bear'st"). But
the change in the old eds. from the second to the third person is
not very harsh.
[2] A picturesque rendering of
                    "Vitreoque madentia rore
        Tempora noctis eunt."

Elegia VII.

Ad pacandam amicam, quam verberaverat.

Bind fast my hands, they have deserved chains,
While rage is absent, take some friend the pains.
For rage against my wench moved my rash arm;
My mistress weeps whom my mad hand did harm.
I might have then my parents dear misused,
Or holy gods with cruel strokes abused.
Why, Ajax, master of the seven-fold shield,
Butchered the flocks he found in spacious field.
And he who on his mother venged his ire,
Against the Destinies durst sharp [1] darts require.
Could I therefore her comely tresses tear?
Yet was she graced with her ruffled hair.
So fair she was, Atalanta she resembled,
Before whose bow th' Arcadian wild beasts trembled.
Such Ariadne was, when she bewails,
Her perjured Theseus' flying vows and sails.
So, chaste Minerva, did Cassandra fall
Deflowered except within thy temple wall.
That I was mad and barbarous all men cried:
She nothing said; pale fear her tongue had tied.
But secretly her looks with checks did trounce me,
Her tears, she silent, guilty did pronounce me.
Would of mine arms my shoulders had been scanted!
Better I could part of myself have wanted.
To mine own self have I had strength so furious,

---

[1] I should like to omit this word, to which there is nothing
to correspond in the original.

And to myself could I be so injurious?
Slaughter and mischief's instruments, no better,
Deserved chains these cursed hands shall fetter.
Punished I am, if I a Roman beat:
Over my mistress is my right more great?
Tydides left worst signs of villainy;
He first a goddess struck: another I.
Yet he harmed less; whom I professed to love
I harmed: a foe did Diomede's anger move.
Go now, thou conqueror, glorious triumphs raise,
Pay vows to Jove; engirt thy hairs with bays.
And let the troops which shall thy chariot follow,
"Io, a strong man conquered this wench," hollow.
Let the sad captive foremost, with locks spread
On her white neck, but for hurt cheeks, be led.
Meeter it were her lips were blue with kissing,
And on her neck a wanton's mark not missing.
But, though I like a swelling flood was driven,
And as a prey unto blind anger given,
Was't not enough the fearful wench to chide?
Nor thunder, in rough threatenings, haughty pride?
Nor shamefully her coat pull o'er her crown,
Which to her waist her girdle still kept down?
But cruelly her tresses having rent,
My nails to scratch her lovely cheeks I bent.
Sighing she stood, her bloodless white looks shewed,
Like marble from the Parian mountains hewed.
Her half-dead joints, and trembling limbs I saw,
Like poplar leaves blown with a stormy flaw.
Or slender ears, with gentle zephyr shaken,
Or waters' tops with the warm south-wind taken.
And down her cheeks, the trickling tears did flow,

Like water gushing from consuming snow.
Then first I did perceive I had offended;
My blood the tears were that from her descended.
Before her feet thrice prostrate down I fell,
My feared hands thrice back she did repel.
But doubt thou not (revenge doth grief appease),
With thy sharp nails upon my face to seize;
Bescratch mine eyes, spare not my locks to break
(Anger will help thy hands though ne'er so weak);
And lest the sad signs of my crime remain,
Put in their place thy kembed hairs again.

ELEGIA VIII.

Execratur lenam qukæ puellam suam meretricis arte instituebat.

There is—whoe'er will know a bawd aright,
Give ear—there is an old trot Dipsas hight.
Her name comes from the thing: she being wise,[1]
Sees not the morn on rosy horses rise,
She magic arts and Thessal charms doth know,
And makes large streams back to their fountains flow;
She knows with grass, with threads on wrung wheels
    spun,
And what with mares' rank humour may be done.
When she will, clouds the darkened heaven obscure,
When she will, day shines everywhere most pure.
If I have faith, I saw the stars drop blood,
The purple moon with sanguine visage stood;

---

[1]   "Nigri non illa parentem
    Memnonis in roseis sobria vidit equis."
  Cunningham suggests that "wise" was one of the thousand
and one euphemisms for "inebriated."

Her I suspect among night's spirits to fly,
And her old body in birds' plumes to lie.
Fame saith as I suspect; and in her eyes,
Two eyeballs shine, and double light thence flies.
Great grandsires from their ancient graves she chides,
And with long charms the solid earth divides.
She draws chaste women to incontinence.
Nor doth her tongue want harmful eloquence.
By chance I heard her talk; these words she said,
While closely hid betwixt two doors I laid.
"Mistress, thou knowest thou hast a blest youth pleased,
He stayed and on thy looks his gazes seized.
And why should'st not please? none thy face exceeds;
Ay me, thy body hath no worthy weeds!
As thou art fair, would thou wert fortunate!
Wert thou rich, poor should not be my state.
Th' opposed star of Mars hath done thee harm;
Now Mars is gone, Venus thy side doth warm,
And brings good fortune; a rich lover plants
His love on thee, and can supply thy wants.
Such is his form as may with thine compare,
Would he not buy thee, thou for him should'st care."
She blushed: "Red shame becomes white cheeks; but this
If feigned, doth well; if true, it doth amiss.
When on thy lap thine eyes thou dost deject,
Each one according to his gifts respect.
Perhaps the Sabines rude, when Tatius reigned
To yield their love to more than one disdained.
Now Mars doth rage abroad without all pity,
And Venus rules in her Æneas' city.
Fair women play; she's chaste whom none will have,
Or, but for bashfulness, herself would crave.

239

Shake off these wrinkles that thy front assault;
Wrinkles in beauty is a grievous fault.
Penelope in bows her youths' strength tried,
Of horn the bow was that approved their side.
Time flying slides hence closely, and deceives us,
And with swift horses the swift year soon leaves us.
Brass shines with use; good garments would be worn;
Houses not dwelt in, are with filth forlorn.
Beauty, not exercised, with age is spent,
Nor one or two men are sufficient.
Many to rob is more sure, and less hateful;
From dog-kept flocks come preys to wolves most grateful.
Behold, what gives the poet but new verses?
And thereof many thousand he rehearses.
The poet's god, arrayed in robes of gold,
Of his gilt harp the well-tuned strings doth hold.
Let Homer yield to such as presents bring;
(Trust me) to give, it is a witty thing.
Nor, so thou may'st obtain a wealthy prize,
The vain name of inferior slaves despise.
Nor let the arms of ancient lines beguile thee;
Poor lover, with thy grandsires I exile thee.
Who seeks, for being fair, a night to have,
What he will give, with greater instance crave.
Make a small price, while thou thy nets dost lay;
Lest they should fly; being ta'en, the tyrant play.
Dissemble so, as loved he may be thought,
And take heed lest he gets that love for nought.
Deny him oft; feign now thy head doth ache:
And Isis now will show what 'scuse to make.
Receive him soon, lest patient use he gain,
Or lest his love oft beaten back should wane.

To beggars shut, to bringers ope thy gate;
Let him within hear barred-out lovers prate.
And, as first wronged, the wronged sometimes banish;
Thy faults with his fault so repulsed will vanish.
But never give a spacious time to ire;
Anger delayed doth oft to hate retire.
And let thine eyes constrained learn to weep,
That this or that man may thy cheeks moist keep.
Nor, if thou cozenest one, dread to forswear;
Venus to mocked men lends a senseless ear.
Servants fit for thy purpose thou must hire,
To teach thy lover what thy thoughts desire.
Let them ask somewhat; many asking little,
Within a while great heaps grow of a tittle.
And sister, nurse, and mother spare him not;
By many hands great wealth is quickly got.
When causes fail thee to require a gift
By keeping of thy birth, make but a shift.
Beware lest he, unrivalled, loves secure;
Take strife away, love doth not well endure.
On all the bed men's tumbling let him view,
And thy neck with lascivious marks made blue.
Chiefly show him the gifts which others send:
If he gives nothing, let him from thee wend.
When thou hast so much as he gives no more,
Pray him to lend what thou may'st ne'er restore.
Let thy tongue flatter, while thy mind harm works;
Under sweet honey deadly poison lurks.
If this thou dost, to me by long use known,
(Nor let my words be with the winds hence blown)
Oft thou wilt say, 'live well;' thou wilt pray oft,
That my dead bones may in their grave lie soft."

As thus she spake, my shadow me betrayed;
With much ado my hands I scarcely stayed,
But her blear eyes, bald scalp's thin hoary fleeces,
And rivelled cheeks I would have pulled a-pieces.
The gods send thee no house, a poor old age,
Perpetual thirst, and winter's lasting rage.

Elegia IX.

Ad Atticum, amantem non oportere desidiosum esse, sicuti nec militem.

All lovers war, and Cupid hath his tent;
Attic, all lovers are to war far sent.
What age fits Mars, with Venus doth agree;
Tis shame for eld in war or love to be.
What years in soldiers captains do require,
Those in their lovers pretty maids desire.
Both of them watch: each on the hard earth sleeps:
His mistress' door this, that his captain's keeps.
Soldiers must travel far: the wench forth send,
Her valiant lover follows without end.
Mounts, and rain-doubled floods he passeth over,
And treads the desert snowy heaps do cover.
Going to sea, east winds he doth not chide,
Nor to hoist sail attends fit time and tide.
Who but a soldier or a lover's bold
To suffer storm-mixed snows with night's sharp cold?
One as a spy doth to his enemies go,
The other eyes his rival as his foe.
He cities great, this thresholds lies before:
This breaks town-gates, but he his mistress' door.
Oft to invade the sleeping foe 'tis good,
And armed to shed unarmed people's blood.

So the fierce troops of Thracian Rhesus fell,
And captive horses bade their lord farewell.
Sooth, lovers watch till sleep the husband charms,
Who slumbering, they rise up in swelling arms.
The keepers' hands and corps-du-gard to pass,
The soldier's, and poor lover's work e'er was.
Doubtful is war and love; the vanquished rise,
And who thou never think'st should fall, down lies.
Therefore whoe'er love slothfulness doth call,
Let him surcease: love tries wit best of all.
Achilles burned, Briseis being ta'en away;
Trojans destroy the Greek wealth, while you may.
Hector to arms went from his wife's embraces,
And on Andromache his helmet laces.
Great Agamemnon was, men say, amazed,
On Priam's loose-trest daughter when he gazed.
Mars in the deed the blacksmith's net did stable;
In heaven was never more notorious fable.
Myself was dull and faint, to sloth inclined;
Pleasure and ease had mollified my mind.
A fair maid's care expelled this sluggishness,
And to her tents willed me myself address.
Since may'st thou see me watch and night-wars move:
He that will not grow slothful, let him love.

Elegia X.

Ad puellam, ne pro amore præmia poscat.

Such as the cause was of two husband's war,
Whom Trojan ships fetch'd from Europa far,
Such as was Leda, whom the god deluded
In snow-white plumes of a false swan included.

243

Such as Amymone through the dry fields strayed,
When on her head a water pitcher laid;
Such wert thou, and I feared the bull and eagle,
And whate'er Love made Jove, should thee inveigle.
Now all fear with my mind's hot love abates:
No more this beauty mine eyes captivates.
Ask'st why I change? because thou crav'st reward;
This cause hath thee from pleasing me debarred.
While thou wert plain I loved thy mind and face:
Now inward faults thy outward form disgrace.
Love is a naked boy, his years sans stain,
And hath no clothes, but open doth remain.
Will you for gain have Cupid sell himself?
He hath no bosom where to hide base pelf.
Love and Love's son are with fierce arms at odds;
To serve for pay beseems not wanton gods.
The whore stands to be bought for each man's money,
And seeks vile wealth by selling of her coney.
Yet greedy bawd's command she curseth still,
And doth, constrained, what you do of goodwill.
Take from irrational beasts a precedent;
'Tis shame their wits should be more excellent.
The mare asks not the horse, the cow the bull,
Nor the mild ewe gifts from the ram doth pull.
Only a woman gets spoils from a man,
Farms out herself on nights for what she can;
And lets what both delight, what both desire,
Making her joy according to her hire.
The sport being such, as both alike sweet try it,
Why should one sell it and the other buy it?
Why should I lose, and thou gain by the pleasure,
Which man and woman reap in equal measure?

Knights of the post of perjuries make sale,
The unjust judge for bribes becomes a stale.
'Tis shame sold tongues the guilty should defend,
Or great wealth from a judgment-seat ascend.
'Tis shame to grow rich by bed-merchandise,
Or prostitute thy beauty for bad price.
Thanks worthily are due for things unbought;
For beds ill-hired we are indebted nought.
The hirer payeth all; his rent discharged,
From further duty he rests then enlarged.
Fair dames, forbear rewards for nights to crave:
Ill-gotten goods good end will never have.
The Sabine gauntlets were too dearly won,
That unto death did press the holy nun.
The sun slew her, that forth to meet him went,
And a rich necklace caused that punishment.
Yet think no scorn to ask a wealthy churl;
He wants no gifts into thy lap to hurl.
Take clustered grapes from an o'er-laden vine,
May bounteous love[1] Alcinous' fruit resign.
Let poor men show their service, faith and care;
All for their mistress, what they have, prepare.
In verse to praise kind wenches 'tis my part,
And whom I like eternise by mine art.
Garments do wear, jewels and gold do waste,
The fame that verse gives doth for ever last.
To give I love, but to be asked disdain;
Leave asking, and I'll give what I refrain.

---

[1] The original was "ager."

ELEGIA XI.

Napen alloquitur, ut paratas tabellas ad Corinnam perferat.

In skillful gathering ruffled hairs in order,
Nape, free-born, whose cunning hath no border.[1]
Thy service for night's scapes is known commodious,
And to give signs dull wit to thee is odious.
Corinna clips me oft by thy persuasion:
Never to harm me made thy faith evasion.
Receive these lines; them to my mistress carry;
Be sedulous; let no stay cause thee tarry,
Nor flint nor iron are in thy soft breast,
But pure simplicity in thee doth rest.
And 'tis supposed Love's bow hath wounded thee;
Defend the ensigns of thy war in me.
If what I do, she asks, say "hope for night;"
The rest my hand doth in my letters write.
Time passeth while I speak; give her my writ,
But see that forthwith she peruseth it.
I charge thee mark her eyes in front in reading:
By speechless looks we guess at things succeeding.
Straight being read, will her to write much back,
I hate fair paper should writ matter lack.
Let her make verses and some blotted letter
On the last edge to stay mine eyes the better.
What needs she tire her hand to hold the quill?
Let this word "Come," alone the tables fill.
Then with triumphant laurel will I grace them

---

[1] Bound.

And in the midst of Venus' temple place them,
Subscribing, that to her I consecrate
My faithful tables, being vile maple late.

ELEGIA XII.

Tabellas quas miserat execratur quod amica noctem negabat.

Bewail my chance: the sad book is returned,
This day denial hath my sport adjourned.
Presages are not vain; when she departed,
Nape by stumbling on the threshold, started.
Going out again, pass forth the door more wisely,
And somewhat higher bear thy foot precisely.
Hence luckless tables! funeral wood, be flying!
And thou, the wax, stuffed full with notes denying!
Which I think gathered from cold hemlock's flower,
Wherein bad honey Corsic bees did pour:
Yet as if mixed with red lead thou wert ruddy,
That colour rightly did appear so bloody.
As evil wood, thrown in the highways, lie,
Be broke with wheels of chariots passing by!
And him that hewed you out for needful uses,
I'll prove had hands impure with all abuses.
Poor wretches on the tree themselves did strangle:
There sat the hangman for men's necks to angle.
To hoarse screech-owls foul shadows it allows;
Vultures and Furies nestled in the boughs.
To these my love I foolishly committed,
And then with sweet words to my mistress fitted.
More fitly had they wrangling bonds contained
From barbarous lips of some attorney strained.
Among day-books and bills they had lain better,

In which the merchant wails his bankrupt debtor.
Your name approves you made for such-like things,
The number two no good divining brings.
Angry, I pray that rotten age you racks,
And sluttish white-mould overgrow the wax.

ELEGIA XIII.

Ad Auroram ne properet.

Now o'er the sea from her old love comes she
That draws the day from heaven's cold axletree.
Aurora, whither slid'st thou? down again!
And birds for Memnon yearly shall be slain.
Now in her tender arms I sweetly bide,
If ever, now well lies she by my side.
The air is cold, and sleep is sweetest now,
And birds send forth shrill notes from every bough.
Whither runn'st thou, that men and women love not?
Hold in thy rosy horses that they move not.
Ere thou rise, stars teach seamen where to sail,
But when thou com'st, they of their courses fail.
Poor travellers though tired, rise at thy sight,
And [1] soldiers make them ready to the fight.
The painful hind by thee to field is sent;
Slow oxen early in the yoke are pent.
Thou coz'nest boys of sleep, and dost betray them
To pedants that with cruel lashes pay them.
Thou mak'st the surety to the lawyer run,

---

[1] This line is omitted in ed. A.

That with one word hath nigh himself undone.
The lawyer and the client hate thy view,
Both whom thou raisest up to toil anew.
By thy means women of their rest are barred,
Thou set'st their labouring hands to spin and card.
All could I bear; but that the wench should rise,
Who can endure, save him with whom none lies?
How oft wished I night would not give thee place,
Nor morning stars shun thy uprising face!
How oft that either wind would break thy couch,
Or steeds might fall, forced with thick clouds' approach!
Whither go'st thou, hateful nymph? Memnon the elf
Received his coal-black colour from thyself.
Say that thy love with Cephalus were not known,
Then thinkest thou thy loose life is not shown?
Would Tithon might but talk of thee awhile!
Not one in heaven should be more base and vile.
Thou leav'st his bed, because he's faint through age,
And early mount'st thy hateful carriage:
But held'st thou in thine arms some Cephalus,
Then would'st thou cry, "Stay night, and run not thus."
Dost punish me because years make him wane?
I did not bid thee wed an aged swain.
The moon sleeps with Endymion every day;
Thou art as fair as she, then kiss and play.
Jove, that thou should'st not haste but wait his leisure,
Made two nights one to finish up his pleasure.
I chid no more; she blushed, and therefore heard me,
Yet lingered not the day, but morning scared me.

ELEGIA XIV.

Puellam consolatur cui præ nimia cura comæ deciderant.

Leave colouring thy tresses, I did cry;
Now hast thou left no hairs at all to dye.
But what had been more fair had they been kept?
Beyond thy robes thy dangling locks had swept.
Fear'dst thou to dress them being fine and thin,
Like to the silk the curious [1] Seres spin.
Or threads which spider's slender foot draws out,
Fastening her light web some old beam about?
Nor black nor golden were they to our view,
Yet although [n]either, mixed of either's hue;
Such as in hilly Ida's watery plains,
The cedar tall, spoiled of his bark, retains.
Add they were apt to curl a hundred ways,
And did to thee no cause of dolour raise.
Nor hath the needle, or the comb's teeth reft them,
The maid that kembed them ever safely left them,
Oft was she dressed before mine eyes, yet never,
Snatching the comb to beat the wench, outdrive her.
Oft in the morn, her hairs not yet digested,
Half-sleeping on a purple bed she rested;
Yet seemly like a Thracian Bacchanal,
That tired doth rashly on the green grass fall.
When they were slender and like downy moss,
Thy troubled hairs, alas, endured great loss.
How patiently hot irons they did take,
In crooked trannels [2] crispy curls to make.

---

[1] The original has "colorati Seres."
[2] Cunningham and the editor of 1826 may be right in reading "trammels" (i.e, ringlets). "Trannel" was the name for a bodkin. The original has "Ut fieret torts flexilis orbe sinus."

I cried, "'Tis sin, 'tis sin, these hairs to burn,
They well become thee, then to spare them turn.
Far off be force, no fire to them may reach,
Thy very hairs will the hot bodkin teach."
Lost are the goodly locks, which from their crown,
Phœbus and Bacchus wished were hanging down.
Such were they as Diana painted stands,
All naked holding in her wave-moist hands.
Why dost thy ill-kembed tresses' loss lament?
Why in thy glass dost look, being discontent?
Be not to see with wonted eyes inclined;
To please thyself, thyself put out of mind.
No charmed herbs of any harlot scathed thee,
No faithless witch in Thessal waters bathed thee.
No sickness harmed thee (far be that away!),
No envious tongue wrought thy thick locks' decay.
By thine own hand and fault thy hurt doth grow,
Thou mad'st thy head with compound poison flow.
Now Germany shall captive hair-tires send thee,
And vanquished people curious dressings lend thee.
Which some admiring, O thou oft wilt blush!
And say, "He likes me for my borrowed bush,
Praising for me some unknown Guelder dame;
But I remember when it was my fame."
Alas, she almost weeps, and her white cheeks,
Dyed red with shame, to hide from shame she seeks.
She holds, and views her old locks in her lap;
Ay me! rare gifts unworthy such a hap!
Cheer up thyself, thy loss thou may'st repair,
And be hereafter seen with native hair.

Elegia XV.

Ad invidos, quod fama poetarum sit perennis.

Envy, why carp'st thou my time's spent so ill?
And term'st my works fruits of an idle quill?
Or that unlike the line from whence I sprung
War's dusty honours are refused being young?
Nor that I study not the brawling laws,
Nor set my voice to sail in every cause?
Thy scope is mortal; mine, eternal fame.
That all the world may ever chant my name.
Homer shall live while Tenedos stands and Ide,
Or to the sea swift Simois shall slide.
Ascræus lives while grapes with new wine swell,
Or men with crooked sickles corn down fell.
The [1] world shall of Callimachus ever speak;
His art excelled, although his wit was weak.
For ever lasts high Sophocles' proud vein;
With sun and moon Aratus shall remain.
While bondmen cheat, fathers [be] hard,[2] bawds
      whorish,
And strumpets flatter, shall Menander flourish.
Rude Ennius, and Plautus[3] full of wit,
Are both in Fame's eternal legend writ.
What age of Varro's name shall not be told,
And Jason's Argo, and the fleece of gold?
Lofty Lucretius shall live that hour,
That nature shall dissolve this earthly bower.

---

[1] Isham copy and ed. A omit this line and the next.
[2] Old eds. "fathers hoord." ("*Durus* pater.")
[3] The poet must have read "animosi *Maccius* oris." The true reading is "animosique *Accius* oris."

Æneas' war and Tityrus shall be read,
While Rome of all the conquered world is head.
Till Cupid's bow, and fiery shafts be broken,
Thy verses, sweet Tibullus, shall be spoken.
And Gallus shall be known from East to West;
So shall Lycoris whom he loved best.
Therefore when flint and iron wear away,
Verse is immortal and shall ne'er decay.
To verse let kings give place and kingly shows,
The banks o'er which gold-bearing Tagus flows.
Let base-conceited wits admire vile things;
Fair Phœbus lead me to the Muses' springs.
About my head be quivering myrtle wound,
And in sad lovers' heads let me be found.
The living, not the dead, can envy bite,
For after death all men receive their right.
Then though death racks my bones in funeral fire,
I'll live, and as he pulls me down mount higher.

BOOK TWO

P. OVIDII NASONIS AMORUM
LIBER SECUNDUS.

ELEGIA I.
Quod pro gigantomachia amores scribere sit coactus.

I, Ovid, poet of my wantonness,
Born at Peligny, to write more address.
So Cupid wills. Far hence be the severe!
You are unapt my loser lines to hear.
Let maids whom hot desire to husbands lead,
And rude boys, touched with unknown love, me read:
That some youth hurt, as I am, with Love's bow,
His own flame's best-acquainted signs may know,
And long admiring say, "By what means learned,
Hath this same poet my sad chance discern'd?"
I durst the great celestial battles tell,
Hundred-hand Gyges, and had done it well;
With Earth's revenge, and how Olympus' top
High Ossa bore, Mount Pelion up to prop;
Jove and Jove's thunderbolts I had in hand,
Which for his heaven fell on the giants' band.
My wench her door shut, Jove's affairs I left,

Even Jove himself out of my wit was reft.
Pardon me, Jove! thy weapons aid me nought,
Her shut gates greater lightning than thine brought.
Toys, and light elegies, my darts I took,
Quickly soft words hard doors wide-open strook.
Verses reduce the horned bloody moon,
And call the sun's white horses back at noon.
Snakes leap by verse from caves of broken mountains,
And turned streams run backward to their fountains.
Verses ope doors; and locks put in the post,
Although of oak, to yield to verses boast.
What helps it me of fierce Achill to sing?
What good to me will either Ajax bring?
Or he who warred and wandered twenty year?
Or woful Hector whom wild jades did tear?
But when I praise a pretty wench's face,
She in requital doth me oft embrace.
A great reward! Heroes of famous names,
Farewell! your favour nought my mind inflames.
Wenches apply your fair looks to my verse,
Which golden Love doth unto me rehearse.

ELEGIA II.

Ad Bagoum, ut custodiam puellæ sibi commissæ laxiorem habet.

Bagous, whose care doth thy mistress bridle,
While I speak some few, yet fit words, be idle.
I saw the damsel walking yesterday,
There, where the porch doth Danaus' fact display:
She pleased me soon; I sent, and did her woo;
Her trembling hand writ back she might not do.
And asking why, this answer she redoubled,

Because thy care too much thy mistress troubled.
Keeper, if thou be wise, cease hate to cherish,
Believe me, whom we fear, we wish to perish.
Nor is her husband wise: what needs defence,
When unprotected there is no expense?
But furiously he follows his love's fire,
And thinks her chaste whom many do desire:
Stolen liberty she may by thee obtain,
Which giving her, she may give thee again:
Wilt thou her fault learn? she may make thee tremble.
Fear to be guilty, then thou may'st dissemble.
Think when she reads, her mother letters sent her:
Let him go forth known, that unknown did enter.
Let him go see her though she do not languish,
And then report her sick and full of anguish.
If long she stays, to think the time more short,
Lay down thy forehead in thy lap to snort.
Inquire not what with Isis may be done,
Nor fear lest she to the theatres run.
Knowing her scapes, thine honour shall increase;
And what less labour than to hold thy peace?
Let him please, haunt the house, be kindly used,
Enjoy the wench; let all else be refused.
Vain causes feign of him, the true to hide,
And what she likes, let both hold ratified.
When most her husband bends the brows and frowns,
His fawning wench with her desire he crowns.
But yet sometimes to chide thee let her fall
Counterfeit tears: and thee lewd hangman call
Object thou then, what she may well excuse,

To stain all faith in truth, by false crimes' use.
Of wealth and honour so shall grow thy heap:
Do this, and soon thou shalt thy freedom reap.
On tell-tales' necks thou seest the link-knit chains,
The filthy prison faithless breasts restrains.
Water in waters, and fruit, flying touch,
Tantalus seeks, his long tongue's gain is such.
While Juno's watchman Io too much eyed,
Him timeless death took, she was deified.
I saw one's legs with fetters black and blue,
By whom the husband his wife's incest knew:
More he deserved; to both great harm he framed,
The man did grieve, the woman was defamed.
Trust me all husbands for such faults are sad,
Nor make they any man that hears them glad.
If he loves not, deaf ears thou dost importune,
Or if he loves, thy tale breeds his misfortune.
Nor is it easy proved though manifest;
She safe by favour of her judge doth rest.
Though himself see, he'll credit her denial,
Condemn his eyes, and say there is no trial.
Spying his mistress' tears he will lament
And say "This blab shall suffer punishment."
Why fight'st 'gainst odds? to thee, being cast, do hap
Sharp stripes; she sitteth in the judge's lap.
To meet for poison or vile facts we crave not;
My hands an unsheathed shining weapon have not.
We seek that, through thee, safely love we may;
What can be easier than the thing we pray?

ELEGIA III.

Ad Eunuchum servantem dominam.

Ay me, an eunuch keeps my mistress chaste,
That cannot Venus' mutual pleasure taste.
Who first deprived young boys of their best part,
With self-same wounds he gave, he ought to smart.
To kind requests thou would'st more gentle prove,
If ever wench had made lukewarm thy love:
Thou wert not born to ride, or arms to bear,
Thy hands agree not with the warlike spear.
Menhandle those; all manly hopes resign,
Thy mistress' ensigns must be likewise thine.
Please her—her hate makes others thee abhor;
If she discards thee, what use serv'st thou for?
Good form there is, years apt to play together:
Unmeet is beauty without use to wither.
She may deceive thee, though thou her protect;
What two determine never wants effect.
Our prayers move thee to assist our drift,
While thou hast time yet to bestow that gift.

ELEGIA IV.

Quod amet mulieres, cujuscunque formæ sint.

I mean not to defend the scapes[1] of any,
Or justify my vices being many;
For I confess, if that might merit favour,

---

[1] "Mendosos _ _ _ mores."

Here I display my lewd and loose behaviour.
I loathe, yet after that I loathe I run:
Oh, how the burthen irks, that we should shun.
I cannot rule myself but where Love please;
Am driven like a ship upon rough seas.
No one face likes me best, all faces move,
A hundred reasons make me ever love.
If any eye me with a modest look,
I burn, and by that blushful glance am took;
And she that's coy I like, for being no clown,
Methinks she would be nimble when she's down.
Though her sour looks a Sabine's brow resemble,
I think she'll do, but deeply can dissemble.
If she be learned, then for her skill I crave her;
If not, because she's simple I would have her.
Before Callimachus one prefers me far;
Seeing she likes my books, why should we jar?
Another rails at me, and that I write,
Yet would I lie with her, if that I might:
Trips she, it likes we well; plods she, what than?
She would be nimbler lying with a man.
And when one sweetly sings, then straight I long,
To quaver on her lips even in her song;
Or if one touch the lute with art and cunning,
Who would not love those hands for their swift
      running?
And her I like that with a majesty,
Folds up her arms, and makes low courtesy.
To leave myself, that am in love with all,
Some one of these might make the chastest fall.
If she be tall, she's like an Amazon,
And therefore fills the bed she lies upon:

If short, she lies the rounder: to speak troth,
Both short and long please me, for I love both.
I think what one undecked would be, being drest;
Is she attired? then show her graces best.
A white wench thralls me, so doth golden yellow:
And nut-brown girls in doing have no fellow.
If her white neck be shadowed with black hair,
Why, so was Leda's, yet was Leda fair.
Amber-tress'd is she? then on the morn think I:
My love alludes to every history:
A young wench pleaseth, and an old is good,
Nay what is she, that any Roman loves,
This for her looks, that for her womanhood:
But my ambitious ranging mind approves?

ELEGIA V.

Ad amicam corruptam.

No love is so dear,—quivered Cupid, fly!—
That my chief wish should be so oft to die.
Minding thy fault, with death I wish to revel:
Alas! a wench is a perpetual evil.
No intercepted lines thy deeds display,
No gifts given secretly thy crime bewray.
O would my proofs as vain might be withstood!
Ay me, poor soul, why is my cause so good?
He's happy, that his love dares boldly credit;
To whom his wench can say, "I never did it."
He's cruel, and too much his grief doth favour,
That seeks the conquest by her loose behaviour.
Poor wretch, I saw when thou didst think I slumbered;
Not drunk, your faults on the spilt wine I numbered.

I saw your nodding eyebrows much to speak,
Even from your cheeks, part of a voice did break.
Not silent were thine eyes, the board with wine
Was scribbled, and thy fingers writ a line.
I knew your speech (what do not lovers see?)
And words that seemed for certain marks to be.
Now many guests were gone, the feast being done,
The youthful sort to divers pastimes run.
I saw you then unlawful kisses join;
(Such with my tongue it likes me to purloin);
None such the sister gives her brother grave,
But such kind wenches let their lovers have.
Phœbus gave not Diana such, 'tis thought,
But Venus often to her Mars such brought.
"What dost?" I cried; "transport'st thou my delight?
My lordly hands I'll throw upon my right.
Such bliss is only common to us two,
In this sweet good why hath a third to do?"
This, and what grief enforced me say, I said:
A scarlet blush her guilty face arrayed;
Even such as by Aurora hath the sky,
Or maids that their betrothed husbands spy;
Such as a rose mixed with a lily breeds,
Or when the moon travails with charmed steeds.
Or such as, lest long years should turn the dye,
Arachne[1] stains Assyrian ivory.
To these, or some of these, like was her colour:
By chance her beauty never shined fuller.

---

[1] "Mæonis Assyrium femina tinxit opus." Dyce remarks that
Marlowe "was induced to give this extraordinary version of the
line by recollecting that in the sixth book of Ovid's *Metamor-
phoses* Arachne is termed 'Mæonis,' while her father is mentioned
as a dyer."

She viewed the earth; the earth to view, beseemed her;
She looked sad; sad, comely I esteemed her.
Even kembed as they were, her locks to rend,
And scratch her fair soft cheeks I did intend.
Seeing her face, mine upreared arms descended,
With her own armour was my wench defended.
I, that erewhile was fierce, now humbly sue,
Lest with worse kisses she should me endue.
She laughed, and kissed so sweetly as might make
Wrath-kindled Jove away his thunder shake.
I grieve lest others should such good perceive,
And wish hereby them all unknown to leave.
Also much better were they than I tell,
And ever seemed as some new sweet befell.
'Tis ill they pleased so much, for in my lips
Lay her whole tongue hid, mine in hers she dips.
This grieves me not; no joined kisses spent,
Bewail I only, though I them lament.
Nowhere can they be taught but in the bed;
I know no master of so great hire sped.

Elegia VI.

In mortem psittaci.

The parrot, from East India to me sent,[1]
Is dead; all fowls her exequies frequent!
Go godly birds, striking your breast, bewail,
And with rough claws your tender cheeks assail.

---

[1] Dyce remarks that Marlowe's copy had "ales miki missus"
for "imitatrix ales."

For woful hairs let piece-torn plumes abound,
For long shril'd trumpets let your notes resound.
Why, Philomel, dost Tereus' lewdness mourn?
All-wasting years have that complaint now worn.
Thy tunes let this rare bird's sad funeral borrow;
Itys[1] a great, but ancient cause of sorrow.
All you whose pinions in the clear air soar,
But most, thou friendly turtle-dove, deplore.
Full concord all your lives was you betwixt,
And to the end your constant faith stood fixt.
What Pylades did to Orestes prove,
Such to the parrot was the turtle-dove.
But what availed this faith? her rarest hue?
Or voice that how to change the wild notes knew?
What helps it thou wert given to please my wench?
Birds' hapless glory, death thy lift doth quench.
Thou with thy quills mightst make green emeralds dark,
And pass our scarlet of red saffron's mark.
No such voice-feigning bird was on the ground,
Thou spok'st thy words so well with stammering sound.
Envy hath rapt thee, no fierce wars thou mov'dst;
Vain-babbling speech, and pleasant peace thou lov'dst.
Behold how quails among their battles live,
Which do perchance old age unto them give.
A little filled thee, and for love of talk,
Thy mouth to taste of many meats did balk.
Nuts were thy food, and poppy caused thee sleep,
Pure water's moisture thirst away did keep.

---

[1] So Dyce for "It is as great."

The ravenous vulture lives, the puttock[1] hovers
Around the air, the cadess[2] rain discovers.
And crow survives arms-bearing Pallas' hate,
Whose life nine ages scarce bring out of date.
Dead is that speaking image of man's voice,
The parrot given me, the far-world's best choice.
The greedy spirits take the best things first,
Supplying their void places with the worst.
Thersites did Protesilaus survive;
And Hector died, his brothers yet alive.
My wench's vows for thee what should I show,
Which stormy south winds into sea did blow?
The seventh day came, none following might'st thou see,
And the Fate's distaff empty stood to thee:
Yet words in thy benumbed palate rung;
"Farewell, Corinna," cried thy dying tongue.
Elysium hath a wood of holm-trees black,
Whose earth doth not perpetual green grass lack.
There good birds rest (if we believe things hidden),
Whence unclean fowls are said to be forbidden.
There harmless swans feed all abroad the river;
There lives the phœnix, one alone bird ever;
There Juno's bird displays his gorgeous feather,
And loving doves kiss eagerly together.
The parrot into wood received with these,
Turns all the godly birds to what she please.
A grave her bones hides: on her corps' great grave,
The little stones these little verses have.

---

[1] "Miluus."
[2] "Graculus."

This tomb approves I pleased my mistress well;
My mouth in speaking did all birds excel.

ELEGIA VII.

Amicæ se purgat, quod ancillam non amet.

Dost me of new crimes always guilty frame?
To overcome, so oft to fight I shame.
If on the marble theatre I look,
One among many is, to grieve thee, took.
If some fair wench me secretly behold,
Thou arguest she doth secret marks unfold.
If I praise any, thy poor hairs thou tearest;
If blame, dissembling of my fault thou fearest.
If I look well, thou think'st thou dost not move,
If ill, thou say'st I die for others' love.
Would I were culpable of some offence!
They that deserve pain, bear't with patience.
Now rash accusing, and thy vain belief,
Forbid thine anger to procure my grief.
Lo, how the miserable great-eared ass,
Dulled with much beating, slowly forth doth pass!
Behold Cypassis, wont to dress thy head,
Is charged to violate her mistress' bed!
The gods from this sin rid me of suspicion,
To like a base wench of despised condition.
With Venus' game who will a servant grace?
Or any back, made rough with stripes, embrace?
Add she was diligent thy locks to braid,
And, for her skill, to thee a grateful maid.
Should I solicit her that is so just,—
To take repulse, and cause her show my lust?

I swear by Venus, and the winged boy's bow,
Myself unguilty of this crime I know.

ELEGIA VIII.

Ad Cypassim ancillam Corinnæ

Cypassis, that a thousand ways trim'st hair,
Worthy to kemb none but a goddess fair,
Our pleasant scapes show thee no clown to be,
Apt to thy mistress, but more apt to me.
Who that our bodies were comprest bewrayed?
Whence knows Corinna that with thee I played?
Yet blushed I not, nor used I any saying,
That might be urged to witness our false playing.
What if a man with bondwomen offend,
To prove him foolish did I e'er contend?
Achilles burnt with face of captive Briseis,
Great Agamemnon loved his servant Chryseis.
Greater than these myself I not esteem:
What graced kings, in me no shame I deem.
But when on thee her angry eyes did rush,
In both thy cheeks she did perceive thee blush.
But being present, might that work the best,
By Venus deity how did I protest!
Thou goddess dost command a warm south blast,
My self oaths in Carpathian seas to cast.
For which good turn my sweet reward repay,
Let me lie with thee, brown Cypas to-day.
Ungrate, why feign'st new fears, and dost refuse?
Well may'st thou one thing for thy mistress use.
If thou deniest, fool, I'll our deeds express,
And as a traitor mine own faults confess;

Telling thy mistress where I was with thee,
How oft, and by what means, we did agree.

ELEGIA IX.

Ad Cupidinem.

O Cupid, that dost never cease my smart!
O boy, that liest so slothful in my heart!
Why me that always was thy soldier found,
Dost harm, and in thy tents why does me wound?
Why burns, thy brand, why strikes thy bow thy friends
More glory by thy vanquished foes ascends.
Did not Pelides whom his spear did grieve,
Being required, with speedy help relieve?
Hunters leave taken beasts, pursue the chase,
And than things found do ever further pace.
We people wholly given thee, feel thine arms,
Thy dull hand stays thy striving enemies' harms.
Dost joy to have thy hooked arrows shaked
In naked bones? love hath my bones left naked.
So many men and maidens without love,
Hence with great laud thou may'st a triumph move.
Rome, if her strength the huge world had not filled,
With strawy cabins now her courts should build.
The weary soldier hath the conquered fields,
His sword, laid by, safe, tho' rude places yields;[1]
The dock in harbours ships drawn from the floods,
Horses freed from service range abroad the woods.

---

[1] In some strange fashion Marlowe has mistaken the substantive "rudis" (the staff received by the gladiator on his discharge) with the adjective "rudis" (rude). The original has "Tutaque deposito poscitur ense rudis."

And time it was for me to live in quiet,
That have so oft served pretty wenches' diet.
Yet should I curse a God, if he but said,
"Live without love;" so sweet ill is a maid.
For when my loathing it of heat deprives me.
I know not whither my mind's whirlwind drives me.
Even as a headstrong course bears away
His rider, vainly striving him to stay;
Or as a sudden gale thrusts into sea
The haven-touching bark, now near the lea;
So wavering Cupid brings me back amain,
And purple Love resumes his darts again.
Strike, boy, I offer thee my naked breast,
Here thou hast strength, here thy right hand doth rest.
Here of themselves thy shafts come, as if shot;
Better than I their quiver knows them not:
Hapless is he that all the night lies quiet,
And slumbering, thinks himself much blessed by it.
Fool, what is sleep but image of cold death,
Long shalt thou rest when Fates expire thy breath.
But me let crafty damsel's words deceive,
Great joys by hope I inly shall conceive.
Now let her flatter me, now chide me hard,
Let me enjoy her oft, oft be debarred.
Cupid, by thee, Mars in great doubt doth trample,
And thy stepfather fights by thy example.
Light art thou, and more windy than thy wings;
Joys with uncertain faith thou tak'st and brings:
Yet Love, if thou with thy fair mother hear,
Within my breast no desert empire bear;
Subdue the wandering wenches to thy reign,
So of both people shalt thou homage gain.

ELEGIA X.

Ad Græcinum quod eodem tempore duas amet.

Græcinus (well I wot) thou told'st me once,
I could not be in love with two at once;
By thee deceived, by thee surprised am I,
For now I love two women equally:
Both are well favored, both rich in array,
Which is the loveliest[1] it is hard to say:
This seems the fairest, so doth that to me;
And this doth please me most, and so doth she;
Even as a boat tossed by contrary wind,
So with this love and that wavers my mind.
Venus, why doublest thou my endless smart?
Was not one wench enough to grieve my heart?
Why add'st thou stars to heaven, leaves to green woods,
And to the deep vast sea fresh water-floods?
Yet this is better far than lie alone:
Let such as be mine enemies have none;
Yea, let my foes sleep in an empty bed,
And in the midst their bodies largely spread:
But may soft[2] love rouse up my drowsy eyes,
And from my mistress' bosom let me rise!
Let one wench cloy me with sweet love's delight,
If one can do't; if not, two every night.
Though I am slender, I have store of pith,
Nor want I strength, but weight, to press her with:
Pleasure adds fuel to my lustful fire,

---

1 "Artibus in dubio est haec sit an illa prior." Dyce suggests
that Marlowe read "Artubus."
2 The original has "sævus," for which Marlowe seems to have
read "suavis."

I pay them home with that they most desire:
Oft have I spent the night in wantonness,
And in the morn been lively ne'ertheless.
He's happy who Love's mutual skirmish slays;
And to the gods for that death Ovid prays.
Let soldiers chase their enemies amain,
And with their blood eternal honour gain,
Let merchants seek wealth and with perjured lips,
Being wrecked, carouse the sea tired by their ships;
But when I die, would I might droop with doing,
And in the midst thereof, set my soul going,
That at my funeral some may weeping cry,
"Even as he led his life, so did he die."

ELEGIA XI.

Ad amicam navigantem.

The lofty pine, from high Mount Pelion raught,
Ill ways by rough seas wondering waves first taught;
Which rashly 'twixt the sharp rocks in the deep,
Carried the famous golden-fleeced sheep.
O would that no oars might in seas have sunk!
The Argo wrecked had deadly waters drunk.
Lo, country gods and know[n] bed to forsake
Corinna means, and dangerous ways to take.
For thee the East and West winds make me pale,
With icy Boreas, and the Southern gale.
Thou shalt admire no woods or cities there,
The unjust seas all bluish do appear.
The ocean hath no painted stones or shells,
The sucking shore with their abundance swells.
Maids on the shore, with marble-white feet tread,

So far 'tis safe; but to go farther, dread.
Let others tell how winds fierce battles wage,
How Scylla's and Charybdis' waters rage;
And with what rock[s] the feared Ceraunia threat;
In what gulf either Syrtes have their seat.
Let others tell this, and what each one speaks
Believe; no tempest the believer wreaks.[1]
Too late you look back, when with anchors weighed,
The crooked bark hath her swift sails displayed.
The careful shipman now fears angry gusts,
And with the water sees death near him thrusts.
But if that Triton toss the troubled flood,
In all thy face will be no crimson blood.
Then wilt thou Leda's noble twin-stars pray,
And, he is happy whom the earth holds, say.
It is more safe to sleep, to read a book,
The Thracian harp with cunning to have strook.
But if my words with winged storm hence slip,
Yet, Galatea, favor thou her ship.
The loss of such a wench much blame will gather,
Both to the sea-nymphs and the sea-nymphs' father.
Go, minding to return with prosperous wind,
Whose blast may hither strongly be inclined.
Let Nereus bend the waves unto this shore,
Hither the winds blow, here the spring-tide roar.
Request mild Zephyr's help for thy avail,
And with thy hand assist thy swelling sail.
I from the shore thy known ship first will see,

---

[1] Dyce was doubtless right in supposing "wreaks" to be used
metri causa for "wrecks." Cunningham wanted to give the
meaning "recks;" but that meaning does not suit the context.
The original has "credenti nulla procella nocet."

And say it brings her that preserveth me.
I'll clip and kiss thee with all contentation;
For thy return shall fall the vowed oblation;
And in the form of beds we'll strew soft sand;
Each little hill shall for a table stand:
There, wine being filled, thou many things shalt tell,
How, almost wrecked, thy ship in main seas fell.
And hasting to me, neither darksome night,
Nor violent south-winds did thee aught affright,
I'll think all true, though it be feigned matter!
Mine own desires why should myself not flatter?
Let the bright day-star cause in heaven this day be,
To bring that happy time so soon as may be.

ELEGIA XII.

Exultat, quod amica potitus sit.

About my temples go, triumphant bays!
Conquered Corinna in my bosom lays.
She whom her husband, guard, and gate, as foes,
Lest art should win her, firmly did enclose:
That victory doth chiefly triumph merit,
Which without bloodshed doth the prey inherit.
No little ditched towns, no lowly walls,
But to my share a captive damsel falls.
When Troy by ten years' battle tumbled down,
With the Atrides many gained renown:
But I no partner of my glory brook,
Nor can another say his help I took.
I, guide and soldier, won the field and wear her,
I was both horseman, footman, standard-bearer.
Nor in my act hath fortune mingled chance:

275

O care-got triumph hitherwards advance!
Nor is my war's cause new; but for a queen,
Europe and Asia in firm peace had been;
The Lapiths and the Centaurs, for a woman,
To cruel arms their drunken selves did summon;
A woman forced the Trojans new to enter
Wars, just Latinus, in thy kingdom's centre;
A woman against late-built Rome did send
The Sabine fathers, who sharp wars intend.
I saw how bulls for a white heifer strive,
She looking on them did more courage give.
And me with many, but me without murther,
Cupid commands to move his ensigns further.

ELEGIA XIII.

Ad Isidem, ut parientem Corinnam servet.

While rashly her womb's burden she casts out,
Weary Corinna hath her life in doubt.
She, secretly from me, such harm attempted,
Angry I was, but fear my wrath exempted.
But she conceived of me; or I am sure
I oft have done what might as much procure.
Thou that frequentst Canopus' pleasant fields,
Memphis, and Pharos that sweet date-trees yields,
And where swift Nile in his large channel skipping,
By seven huge mouths into the sea is slipping.
By feared Anubis' visage I thee pray,—
So in thy temples shall Osiris stay,
And the dull snake about thy offerings creep,
And in thy pomp horned Apis with thee keep,—
Turn thy looks hither, and in one spare twain:

Thou givest my mistress life, she mine again.
She oft hath served thee upon certain days,
Where the French[1] rout engirt themselves with bays.
On laboring women thou dost pity take,
Whose bodies with their heavy burdens ache;
My wench, Lucina, I entreat thee favor;
Worthy she is, thou should'st in mercy save her.
In white, with incense, I'll thine altars greet,
Myself will bring vowed gifts before thy feet,
Subscribing *Naso with Corinna saved*:
Do but deserve gifts with this title graved.
But, if in so great fear I may advise thee,
To have this skirmish fought let it suffice thee.

ELEGIA XIV.

In amicam, quod abortivum ipsa fecerit.

What helps it woman to be free from war,
Nor, being armed, fierce troops to follow far,
If without battle self wrought wounds annoy them,
And their own privy-weaponed hands destroy them.
Who unborn infants first to slay invented,
Deserved thereby with death to be tormented.
Because thy belly should rough wrinkles lack,
Wilt thou thy womb-inclosed offspring wrack?
Had ancient mothers this vile custom cherished,
All human kind by their default had perished;
Or stones, our stock's original should be hurled,

---

[1] "Gallica turma" (i.e., the company of *Galli*, the priests of
Isis).

Again, by some, in this unpeopled world.
Who should have Priam's wealthy substance won,
If watery Thetis had her child fordone?
In swelling womb her twins had Ilia killed,
He had not been that conquering Rome did build.
Had Venus spoiled her belly's Trojan fruit,
The earth of Cæsars had been destitute.
Thou also that wert born fair, had'st decayed,
If such a work thy mother had assayed.
Myself, that better die with loving may,
Had seen, my mother killing me, no day.
Why tak'st increasing grapes from vinetrees full?
With cruel hand why dost green apples pull?
Fruits ripe will fall; let springing things increase;
Life is no light price of a small surcease.
Why with hid irons are your bowels torn?
And why dire poison give you babes unborn?
At Colchis, stained with children's blood, men rail,
And mother-murdered Itys they bewail.
Both unkind parents; but, for causes sad,
Their wedlocks' pledges venged their husbands bad.
What Tereus, what Iason you provokes,
To plague your bodies with such harmful strokes?
Armenian tigers never did so ill,
Nor dares the lioness her young whelps kill.
But tender damsels do it, though with pain;
Oft dies she that her paunch-wrapt child hath slain:
She dies, and with loose hairs to grave is sent,
And whoe'er see her, worthily[1] lament.

---

[1] Marlowe has given a meaning the very opposite of the
original—"Et clamant 'merito' qui modo cumque vident."

But in the air let these words come to naught,
And my presages of no weight be thought.
Forgive her, gracious gods, this one delict,
And on the next fault punishment inflict.

ELEGIA XV.

Ad annulum, quem dono amicæ dedit.

Thou ring that shalt my fair girl's finger bind,
Wherein is seen the giver's loving mind:
Be welcome to her, gladly let her take thee,
And, her small joints encircling, round hoop make thee.
Fit her so well, as she is fit for me,
And of just compass for her knuckles be.
Blest ring, thou in my mistress' hand shall lie,
Myself, poor wretch, mine own gifts now envy.
O would that suddenly into my gift,
I could myself by secret magic shift!
Then would I wish thee touch my mistress' pap,
And hide thy left hand underneath her lap,
I would get off, though strait and sticking fast,
And in her bosom strangely fall at last.
Then I, that I may seal her privy leaves,
Lest to the wax the hold-fast dry gem cleaves,
Would first my beautous wench's moist lips touch;
Only I'll sign naught that may grieve me much.
I would not out, might I in one place hit:
But in less compass her small fingers knit.
My life! that I will shame thee never fear,
Or be a load thou should'st refuse to bear.
Wear me, when warmest showers thy members wash,
And through the gem let thy lost waters pash,

But seeing thee, I think my thing will swell,
And even the ring perform a man's part well.
Vain things why wish I? go, small gift, from hand;
Let her my faith, with thee given, understand.

ELEGIA XVI.

Ad amicam, ut ad rura sua veniat.

Sulmo, Peligny's third part, me contains,
A small, but wholesome soil with watery veins,
Although the sun to rive the earth incline,
And the Icarian froward dog-star shine;
Pelignian fields with liquid rivers flow,
And on the soft ground fertile green grass grow;
With corn the earth abounds, with vines much more,
And some few pastures Pallas' olives bore;
And by the rising herbs, where clear spring slide,
A grassy turf the moistened earth doth hide.
But absent is my fire; lies I'll tell none,
My heat is here, what moves my heat is gone.
Pollux and Castor, might I stand betwixt,
In heaven without thee would I not be fixt.
Upon the cold earth pensive let them lay,
That mean to travel some long irksome way.
Or else will maidens young men's mates to go,
If they determine to persevere so.
Then on the rough Alps should I tread aloft,
My hard way with my mistress would seem soft.
With her I durst the Libyan Syrts break through,
And raging seas in boisterous south-winds plough.

No barking dogs, that Scylla's entrails bear,
Nor thy gulfs, crook'd Malea, would I fear.
No flowing waves with drowned ships forth-poured
By cloyed Charybdis, and again devoured.
But if stern Neptune's windy power prevail,
And waters' force helping Gods to fail,
With thy white arms upon my shoulders seize;
So sweet a burden I will bear with ease.
The youth oft swimming to his Hero kind,
Had then swum over, but the way was blind.
But without thee, although vine-planted ground
Contains me; though the streams the fields surround;
Though hinds in brooks the running waters bring,
And cool gales shake the tall trees' leafy spring;
Healthful Peligny, I esteem naught worth,
Nor do I like the country of my birth.
Scythia, Cilicia, Britain are as good,
And rocks dyed crimson with Prometheus' blood.
Elms love the vines; the vines with elms abide,
Why doth my mistress from me oft divide?
Thou swear'dst, division should not twixt us rise,
By me, and by my stars, thy radiant eyes;
Maids' words more vain and light than falling leaves,
Which, as it seems, hence wind and sea bereaves.
If any godly care of me thou hast,
Add deeds unto thy promises at last.
And with swift nags drawing thy little coach
(Their reins let loose), right soon my house approach.
But when she comes, you swelling mounts, sink down,
And falling valleys be the smooth ways' crown.

Elegia XVII.

Quod Corinnæ soli sit serviturus

To serve a wench if any think it shame,
He being judge, I am convinced of blame.
Let me be slandered, while my fire she hides,
That Paphos, and flood-beat Cythera guides.
Would I had been my mistress' gentle prey,
Since some fair one I should of force obey.
Beauty gives heart; Corinna's looks excel;
Ay me, why is it known to her so well?
But by her glass disdainful pride she learns,
Nor she herself, but first trimmed up, discerns.
Not though thy face in all things make thee reign,
(O face, most cunning mine eyes to detain!)
Thou ought'st therefore to scorn me for thy mate,
Small things with greater may be copulate.
Love-snared Calypso is supposed to pray
A mortal nymph's[1] refusing lord to stay.
Who doubts, with Peleus Thetis did consort?
Egeria with just Numa had good sport.
Venus with Vulcan, though, smith's tools laid by,
With his stump foot he halts ill-favouredly.
This kind of verse is not alike; yet fit,
With shorter numbers the heroic sit.
And thou, my light, accept me howsoever;
Lay in the mid bed, there be my lawgiver.
My stay no crime, my flight no joy shall breed,

---

[1] Marlowe read "nymphæ" for "nymphe."

Nor of our love, to be ashamed we need.
For great revenues I good verses have,
And many by me to get glory crave.
I know a wench reports herself Corinne;
What would not she give that fair name to win?
But sundry floods in one bank never go,
Eurotas cold, and poplar-bearing Po;
Nor in my books shall one but thou be writ,
Thou dost alone give matter to my wit.

ELEGIA XVIII.

Ad Macrum, quod de amoribus scribat.

To tragic verse while thou Achilles train'st,
And new sworn soldiers' maiden arms retain'st,
We, Macer, sit in Venus' slothful shade,
And tender love hath great things hateful made.
Often at length, my wench depart I bid,
She in my lap sits still as erst she did.
I said, "It irks me:" half to weeping framed,
"Ay me!" she cries, "to love why art ashamed?"
Then wreathes about my neck her winding arms,
And thousand kisses gives, that work my harms:
I yield, and back my wit from battles bring,
Domestic acts, and mine own wars to sing.
Yet tragedies, and sceptres fill'd my lines,
But though I apt were for such high designs,
Love laughed at my cloak, and buskins painted,
And rule so, soon with private hands acquainted.
My mistress' deity also drew me fro it,
And love triumphed o'er his buskined poet.
What lawful is, or we profess love's art:

(Alas, my precepts turn myself to smart!)
We write, or what Penelope sends Ulysses,
Oh Phillis' tears that her Demophoon misses;
What thankless Jason, Macareus, and Paris,
Phedra, and Hippolyte may read, my care is;
And what poor Dido, with her drawn sword sharp,
Doth say, with her that loved the Aonian harp.
As soon as from strange lands Sabinus came,
And writings did from divers places frame,
White-cheeked Penelope knew Ulysses' sign,
The step-dame read Hippolytus' lustless line.
Æneas to Elisa answer gives,
And Phillis hath to read, if now she lives;
Jason's sad letter doth Hypsipyle greet;
Sappho her vowed harp lays at Phœbus' feet.
Nor of thee, Macer, that resound'st forth arms,
Is golden love hid in Mars' mid alarms.
There Paris is, and Helen's crime's record,
With Laodamia, mate to her dead lord,
Unless I err to these thou more incline,
Than wars, and from thy tents will come to mine.

Elegia XIX.

Ad rivalem cui uxor curæ non erat.

Fool, if to keep thy wife thou hast no need,
Keep her from me, my more desire to breed;
We scorn things lawful; stolen sweets we affect;
Cruel is he that loves whom none protect.
Let us, both lovers, hope and fear alike,
And may repulse place for our wishes strike.
What should I do with fortune that ne'er fails me?

Nothing I love that at all times avails me.
Wily Corinna saw this blemish in me,
And craftily knows by what means to win me.
Ah, often, that her hale head ached, she lying,
Willed me, whose slow feet sought delay, by flying!
Ah, oft, how much she might, she feigned offence;
And, doing wrong, made show of innocence.
So, having vexed, she nourished my warm fire,
And was again most apt to my desire.
To please me, what fair terms and sweet words has she!
Great gods! what kisses, and how many ga' she!
Thou also that late took'st mine eyes away,
Oft cozen [1] me, oft, being wooed, say nay;
And on thy threshold let me lie dispread,
Suff'ring much cold by hoary night's frost bred.
So shall my love continue many years;
This doth delight me, this my courage cheers.
Fat love, and too much fulsome, me annoys,
Even as sweet meat a glutted stomach cloys.
In brazen tower had not Danae dwelt,
A mother's joy by Jove she had not felt.
While Juno Io keeps, when horns she wore,
Jove liked her better than he did before.
Who covets lawful things takes leaves from woods,
And drinks stolen waters in surrounding floods.
Her lover let her mock that long will reign:
Ay me, let not my warnings cause my pain!
Whatever haps, by sufferance harm is done,

---

[1] The reading of the original is "Saepe time insidias."

What flies I follow, what follows me I shun.
But thou, of thy fair damsel too secure,
Begin to shut thy house at evening sure.
Search at the door who knocks oft in the dark,
In night's deep silence why the ban-dogs[1] bark.
Whither the subtle maid lines brings and carries,
Why she alone in empty bed oft tarries.
Let this care sometimes bite thee to the quick,
That to deceits it may me forward prick.
To steal sands from the shore he loves a-life[2]
That can affect a foolish wittol's wife.
Now I forwarn, unless to keep her stronger
Thou dost begin, she shall be mine no longer.
Long have I borne much, hoping time would beat thee
To guard her well, that well I might entreat thee.
Thou suffer'st what no husband can endure,
But of my love it will an end procure.
Shall I, poor soul, be never interdicted?
Nor never with night's sharp revenge afflicted.
In sleeping shall I fearless draw my breath?
Wilt nothing do, why I should wish thy death?
Can I but loathe a husband grown a bawd?
By thy default thou dost our joys defraud.
Some other seek that may in patience strive with thee,
To pleasure me, forbid me to corrive with thee.

---

[1] Dogs tied up on account of their fierceness.
[2] As dearly as life.

BOOK THREE

P. OVIDII NASONIS AMORUM

LIBER TERTIUS.

ELEGIA I.

Deliberatio poetæ, utrum elegos pergat scribere an potius tragœdias.

An old wood stands, uncut of long year's space,
'Tis credible some god head haunts the place.
In midst thereof a stone-paved sacred spring,
Where round about small birds most sweetly sing.
Here while I walk, hid close in shady grove,
To find what work my muse might move, I strove.
Elegia came with hairs perfumed sweet,
And one, I think, was longer, of her feet:
A decent form, thin robe, a lover's look,
By her foot's blemish greater grace she took.
Then with huge steps came violent Tragedy,
Stern was her front, her cloak on ground did lie:
Her left hand held abroad a regal sceptre,
The Lydian buskin [in] fit paces kept her.
And first she [1] said, "When will thy love be spent,

---

[1] Old eds. "he."

O poet careless of thy argument?
Wine-bibbing banquets tell thy naughtiness,
Each cross-way's corner doth as much express.
Oft some points at the prophet passing by,
And, 'This is he whom fierce love burns,' they cry.
A laughing-stock thou art to all the city;
While without shame thou sing'st thy lewdness' ditty.
'Tis time to move great things in lofty style,
Long hast thou loitered; greater works compile.
The subject hides thy wit; men's acts resound;
This thou wilt say to be a worthy ground.
Thy muse hath played what may mild girls content,
And by those numbers is thy first youth spent.
Now give the Roman Tragedy a name,
To fill my laws thy wanton spirit frame."
This said, she moved her buskins gaily varnished,
And seven times shook her head with thick locks
          garnished.
The other smiled (I wot), with wanton eyes:
Err I, or myrtle in her right hand lies?
"With lofty words, stout Tragedy," she said,
"Why tread'st me down?   art thou aye gravely play'd?
Thou deign'st unequal lines should thee rehearse;
Thou fight'st against me using mine own verse.
Thy lofty style with mine I not compare,
Small doors unfitting for large houses are.
Light am I, and with me, my care, light Love;
Not stronger am I, than the thing I move.
Venus without me should be rustical:
This goddess' company doth to me befall.
What gate thy stately words cannot unlock,
My flattering speeches soon wide open knock.

And I deserve more than thou canst in verity,
By suffering much not borne by thy severity.
By me Corinna learns, cozening her guard,
To get the door with little noise unbarred;
And slipped from bed, clothed in a loose nightgown,
To move her feet unheard in setting down.
Ah, how oft on hard doors I engraved,
From no man's reading fearing to be saved!
But, till the keeper went forth, I forgot not,
The maid to hide me in her bosom let not.
What gift with me was on her birthday sent,
But cruelly by her was drowned and rent.
First of thy mind the happy seeds I knew;
Thou hast my gift, which she would from thee sue."
She left; I said, "You both I must beseech,
To empty air may go my fearful speech.
With sceptres and high buskins th' one would dress me,
So through the world should bright renown express me.
The other gives my love a conquering name;
Come, therefore, and to long verse shorter frame.
Grant, Tragedy, thy poet time's least tittle:
Thy labour ever lasts; she asks but little."
She gave me leave; soft loves, in time make haste;
Some greater work will urge me on at last.

Elegia II.

Ad amicam cursum equorum spectantem.

I sit not here the noble horse to see;
Yet whom thou favour'st, pray may conqueror be.
To sit and talk with thee I hither came,
That thou may'st know with love thou mak'st me flame.

Thou view'st the course; I thee: let either heed
What please them, and their eyes let either feed.
What horse-driver thou favour'st most is best,
Because on him thy care doth hap to rest.
Such chance let me have: I would bravely run,
On swift steeds mounted till the race were done.
Now would I slack the reigns, now lash their hide,
With wheels bent inward now the ring-turn ride.
In running if I see thee, I shall stay,
And from my hands the reins will slip away.
Ah, Pelops from his coach was almost felled,
Hippodamia's looks while he beheld!
Yet he attained, by her support, to have her:
Let us all conquer by our mistress' favour.
In vain, why fly'st back? force conjoins us now:
The place's laws this benefit allow.
But spare my wench, thou at her right hand seated;
By thy sides touching ill she is entreated.
And sit thou rounder, that behind us see;
For shame press not her back with thy hard knee.
But on the ground thy clothes too loosely lie:
Gather them up, or lift them, lo, will I.
Envious garment, so good legs to hide!
The more thou look'st, the more the gown's envied.
Swift Atalanta's flying legs, like these,
Wish in his hands grasped did Hippomenes.
Coat-tucked Diana's legs are painted like them,
When strong wild beasts, she stronger, hunts to strike
        them.
Ere these were seen, I burnt: what will these do?
Flames into flame, floods thou pour'st seas into.
By these I judge; delight me may the rest,

Which lie hid, under her thin veil supprest.
Yet in the meantime wilt small winds bestow,
That from thy fan, moved by my hand, may blow?
Or is my heat of mind, not of the sky?
Is't women's love my captive breast doth fry?
While thus I speak, black dust her white robes ray;[1]
Foul dust, from her fair body go away!
Now comes the pomp; themselves let all men cheer;[2]
The shout is nigh; the golden pomp comes here.
First, Victory is brought with large-spread wing:
Goddess, come here; make my love conquering.
Applaud you Neptune, that dare trust his wave,
The sea I use not: me my earth must have.
Soldier applaud thy Mars, no wars we move,
Peace pleaseth me, and in mid peace is love.
With augurs Phœbe with hunters stands;
To thee Minerva turn the craftsmen's hands.
Ceres and Bacchus countrymen adore,
Champions please Pollux, Castor loves horsemen more.
Thee, gentle Venus, and the boy that flies,
We praise: great goddess aid my enterprise.
Let my new mistress grant to be beloved;
She becked, and prosperous signs gave as she moved.
What Venus promised, promise thou we pray
Greater than her, by her leave, thou'rt, I'll say.
The gods, and their rich pomp witness with me,
For evermore thou shalt my mistress be.
Thy legs hang down, thou may'st, if that be best,

---

[1] Defile.
[2] A strange rendering of "linguis animisque favete."

Awhile thy tiptoes on the footstool[1] rest.
Now greater spectacles the Prætor sends,
Four chariot-horses from the lists' even ends.
I see whom thou affect'st: he shall subdue;
The horses seem as thy desire they knew.
Alas, he runs too far about the ring;
What dost? thy waggon in less compass bring.
What dost, unhappy? her good wishes fade:
Let with strong hand the reign to bend be made.
One slow we favour, Romans, him revoke:
And each give signs by casting up his cloak.
They call him back; lest their gowns toss thy hair,
To hide thee in my bosom straight repair.
But now again the barriers open lie,
And forth the gay troops on swift horses fly.
At least now conquer, and outrun the rest:
My mistress' wish confirm with my request.
My mistress hath her wish; my wish remain:
He holds the palm: my palm is yet to gain.
She smiled, and with quick eyes behight some grace:
Pay it not here, but in another place.

ELEGIA III

De amica quæ perjuraverat.

What, are there gods? herself she hath forswore,
And yet remains the face she had before.
How long her locks were ere her oath she took,

---

[1] "Cancellis" (i. e., the rails).

So long they be since she her faith forsook.
Fair white with rose-red was before commixt;
Now shine her looks pure white and red betwixt.
Her foot was small: her foot's form is most fit:
Comely tall was she, comely tall she's yet.
Sharp eyes she had: radiant like stars they be,
By which she, perjured oft, hath lied to me.
In sooth, th' eternal powers grant maids society
Falsely to swear; their beauty hath some deity.
By her eyes, I remember, late she swore,
And by mine eyes, and mine were pained sore.
Say gods: if she unpunished you deceive,
For other's faults why do I loss receive.
But did you not so envy Cepheus' daughter,
For her ill-beauteous mother judged to slaughter.
'Tis not enough, she shakes your record off,
And, unrevenged, mocked gods with me doth scoff.
But by my pain to purge her perjuries,
Cozened, I am the cozener's sacrifice.
God is a name, no substance, feared in vain,
And doth the world in fond belief detain.
Or if there be a God, he loves fine wenches,
And all things too much in their sole power drenches.
Mars girts his deadly sword on for my harm;
Pallas' lance strikes me with unconquered arm;
At me Apollo bends his pliant bow;
At me Jove's right hand lightning hath to throw.
The wronged gods dread fair ones to offend,
And fear those, that to fear them least intend.
Who now will care the altars to perfume?
Tut, men should not their courage so consume.
Jove throws down woods and castles with his fire,

But bids his darts from perjured girls retire.
Poor Semele among so many burned,
Her own request to her own torment turned.
But when her lover came, had she drawn back,
The father's thigh should unborn Bacchus lack.
Why grieve I? and of heaven reproaches pen?
The gods have eyes, and breasts as well as men.
Were I a god, I should give women leave,
With lying lips my godhead to deceive.
Myself would swear the wenches true did swear,
And I would be none of the gods severe.
But yet their gift more moderately use,
Or in mine eyes, good wench, no pain transfuse.

Elegia IV.

Ad virum servantem conjugem.

Rude man, 'tis vain thy damsel to commend
To keeper's trust: their wits should them defend.
Who, without fear, is chaste, is chaste in sooth:
Who, because means want, doeth not, she doth.
Though thou her body guard, her mind is stained;
Nor, 'less she will, can any be restrained.
Nor can'st by watching keep her mind from sin,
All being shut out, the adulterer is within.
Who may offend, sins least; power to do ill
The fainting seeds of naughtiness doth kill.
Forbear to kindle vice by prohibition;
Sooner shall kindness gain thy will's fruition.
I saw a horse against the bit stiff-necked,
Like lightning go, his struggling mouth being checked:
When he perceived the reins let slack, he stayed,

And on his loose mane the loose bridle laid.
How to attain what is denied we think,
Even as the sick desire forbidden drink.
Argus had either way an hundred eyes,
Yet by deceit Love did them all surprise.
In stone and iron walls Danae shut,
Came forth a mother, though a maid there put.
Penelope, though no watch looked unto her,
Was not defiled by any gallant wooer.
What's kept, we covet more: the care makes theft,
Few love what others have unguarded left.
Nor doth her face please, but her husband's love:
I know not what men think should thee so move
She is not chaste that's kept, but a dear whore: [1]
Thy fear is than her body valued more.
Although thou chafe, stolen pleasure is sweet play;
She pleaseth best, "I fear," if any say.
A free-born wench, no right 'tis up to lock,
So use we women of strange nations' stock.
Because the keeper may come say, "I did it,"
She must be honest to thy servant's credit.
He is too clownish whom a lewd wife grieves,
And this town's well-known custom not believes;
Where Mars his sons not without fault did breed,
Remus and Romulus, Ilia's twin-born seed.
Cannot a fair one, if not chaste, please thee?
Never can these by any means agree.
Kindly thy mistress use, if thou be wise;

---

[1] Dyce calls this line an "erroneous version of 'Non proba vir servat, sed adultera; cara est.'" But Merkel's reading is "Non proba fit quam vir servat, sed adultera cara"—which is accurately rendered by Marlowe.

Look gently, and rough husbands' laws despise.
Honour what friends thy wife gives, she'll give many,
Least labour so shall win great grace of any.
So shalt thou go with youths to feast together,
And see at home much that thou ne'er brought'st thither.

ELEGIA V AND VI.

Ad amnem dum iter faceret ad amicam.

Flood with reed-grown slime banks, till I be past
Thy waters stay: I to my mistress haste.
Thou hast no bridge, nor boat with ropes to throw,
That may transport me, without oars to row.
Thee I have passed, and knew thy stream none such,
When thy wave's brim did scarce my ankles touch.
With snow thawed from the next hill now thou gushest,
And in thy foul deep waters thick thou rushest.
What helps my haste? what to have ta'en small rest?
What day and night to travel in her quest?
If standing here I can by no means get
My foot upon the further bank to set.
Now wish I those wings noble Perseus had,
Bearing the head with dreadful adders clad;
Now wish the chariot, whence corn-fields were found,
First to be thrown upon the untilled ground:
I speak old poets' wonderful inventions,
Ne'er was, nor [e'er] shall be, what my verse mentions.
Rather, thou large bank-overflowing river,
Slide in thy bounds; so shalt thou run for ever.
Trust me, land-stream, thou shalt no envy lack,
If I a lover be by thee held back.
Great floods ought to assist young men in love,

Great floods the force of it do often prove.
In mid Bithynia, 'tis said, Inachus
Grew pale, and, in cold fords, hot lecherous.
Troy had not yet been ten years' siege outstander,
When nymph Neæra rapt thy looks, Scamander.
What, not Alpheus in strange lands to run,
The Arcadian virgin's constant love hath won?
And Creusa unto Xanthus first affied,
They say Peneus near Phthia's town did hide.
What should I name Asop, that Thebe loved,
Thebe who mother of five daughters proved,
If, Achelous, I ask where thy horns stand,
Thou say'st, broke with Alcides' angry hand.
Not Calydon, nor Ætolia did please;
One Deianira was more worth than these.
Rich Nile by seven mouths to the vast sea flowing,
Who so well keeps his water's head from knowing,
Is by Evadne thought to take such flame,
As his deep whirlpools could not quench the same.
Dry Enipeus, Tyro to embrace,
Fly back his stream charged; the stream charged, gave
    place.
Nor pass I thee, who hollow rocks down tumbling,
In Tibur's field with watery foam art rumbling.
Whom Ilia pleased, though in her looks grief revelled,
Her cheeks were scratched, her goodly hairs dishevelled.
She, wailing Mar's sin and her uncle's crime,
Strayed barefoot through sole places on a time.
Her, from his swift waves, the bold flood perceived,
And from the mid ford his hoarse voice upheaved,
Saying, "Why sadly tread'st my banks upon,
Ilia sprung from Idæan Laomedon?

Where's thy attire? why wanderest here alone?
To stay thy tresses white veil hast thou none?
Why weep'st and spoil'st with tears thy watery eyes?
And fiercely knock'st thy breast that open lies?
His heart consists of flint and hardest steel,
That seeing thy tears can any joy then feel.
Fear not: to thee our court stands open wide,
There shalt be loved: Ilia, lay fear aside.
Thou o'er a hundred nymphs or more shalt reign,
For five score nymphs or more our floods contain.
Nor, Roman stock, scorn me so much, I crave;
Gifts than my promise greater thou shalt have."
This said he: she her modest eyes held down;
Her woful bosom a warm shower did drown.
Thrice she prepared to fly, thrice she did stay,
By fear deprived of strength to run away.
Yet rending with enraged thumb her tresses,
Her trembling mouth these unmeet sounds expresses:
"O would in my forefather's tomb deep laid,
My bones had been while yet I was a maid:
Why being a vestal am I wooed to wed,
Deflowered and stained in unlawful bed?
Why stay I? men point at me for a whore:
Shame, that should make me blush, I have no more."
This said; her coat hoodwinked her fearful eyes,
And into water desperately she flies.
'Tis said the slippery stream held up her breast,
And kindly gave her what she liked best.
And I believe some wench thou hast affected,
But woods and groves keep your faults undetected.
While thus I speak the waters more abounded,
And from the channel all abroad surrounded.

Mad stream, why dost our mutual joys defer?
Clown, from my journey why dost me deter?
How would'st thou flow wert thou a noble flood?
If thy great fame in every region stood?
Thou hast no name, but com'st from snowy mountains;
No certain house thou hast, nor any fountains;
Thy springs are nought but rain and melted snow,
Which wealth cold winter doth on thee bestow.
Either thou art muddy in mid-winter tide,
Or full of dust dost on the dry earth slide.
What thirsty traveller ever drunk of thee?
Who said with grateful voice, "Perpetual be!"
Harmful to beasts, and to the fields thou proves,
Perchance these others, me mine own loss moves.
To this I fondly loves of floods told plainly,
I shame so great names to have used so vainly.
I know not what expecting, I erewhile,
Named Ochelous, Inachus, and Nile.
But for thy merits I wish thee, white stream,
Dry winters aye, and suns in heat extreme.

ELEGIA VII.

Quod ab amica receptus, cum ea coire non potuit conqueritur.

Either she was foul, or her attire was bad,
Or she was not the wench I wished to have had.
Idly I lay with her, as if I loved not,
And like a burden grieved the bed that moved not.
Though both of us performed our true intent,
Yet could I not cast anchor where I meant.
She on my neck her ivory arms did throw,

Her arms far whiter than the Scythian snow.
And eagerly she kissed me with her tongue,
And under mine her wanton thigh she flung,
Yea, and she soothed me up, and called me "Sir,"
And used all speech that might provoke and stir.
Yet like as if cold hemlock I had drunk,
It mocked me, hung down the head and sunk.
Like a dull cipher, or rude block I lay,
Or shade, or body was I, who can say?
What will my age do, age I cannot shun,
Seeing in my prime my force is spent and done?
I blush, that being youthful, hot, and lusty,
I prove neither youth nor man, but old and rusty.
Pure rose she, like a nun to sacrifice,
Or one that with her tender brother lies.
Yet boarded I the golden Chie twice,
And Libas, and the white-cheeked Pitho thrice.
Corinna craved it in a summer's night,
And nine sweet bouts had we before daylight.
What, waste my limbs through some Thessalian charms?
May spells and drugs do silly souls such harms?
With virgin wax hath some imbast[1] my joints?
And pierced my liver with sharp needle-points?
Charms change corn to grass and make it die:
By charms are running springs and fountains dry.
By charms mast drops from oaks, from vines grapes fall,
And fruit from trees when there's no wind at all.
Why might not then my sinews be enchanted?

---

[1] The verb "embace" or "imbase" is frequently found in the
sense of "abase." Here the meaning seems to be "weakened,
enfeebled." (Ovid's words are "Sagave pœnicea defixit nomina
cera.")

And I grow faint as with some spirit haunted?
To this, add shame: shame to perform it quailed me,
And was the second cause why vigor failed me.
My idle thoughts delighted her no more,
Than did the robe or garment which she wore.
Yet might her touch make youthful Pylius fire
And Tithon livelier than his years require.
Even her I had, and she had me in vain,
What might I crave more, if I ask again?
I think the great gods grieved they had bestowed,
This benefit: which lewdly I foreslowed.[1]
I wished to be received in, in I get me.
To kiss, I kiss; to lie with her, she let me.
Why was I blest? why made king to refuse it?
Chuff-like had I not gold and could not use it?
So in a spring thrives he that told so much,
And looks upon the fruits he cannot touch.
Hath any rose so from a fresh young maid,
As she might straight have gone to church and prayed?
Well, I believe, she kissed not as she should,
Nor used the sleight and cunning which she could.
Huge oaks, hard adamants might she have moved,
And with sweet words caus[ed] deaf rocks to have loved.
Worthy she was to move both gods and men,
But neither was I man nor lived then.
Can deaf ears take delight when Phæmius sings?
Or Thamyris in curious painted things?
What sweet thought is there but I had the same?

---

[1] Neglected.

And one gave place still as another came.
Yet notwithstanding, like one dead it lay,
Drooping more than a rose pulled yesterday.
Now, when he should not jet, he bolts upright,
And craves his task, and seeks to be at fight.
Lie down with shame and see thou stir no more.
Seeing thou would'st deceive me as before.
Thou cozenest me: by thee surprised am I,
And bide sore loss with endless infamy.
Nay more, the wench did not disdain a whit
To take it in her hand, and play with it.
But when she saw it would by no means stand,
But still drooped down, regarding not her hand,
"Why mock'st thou me," she cried, "or being ill,
Who bade thee lie down here against thy will?
Either thou are witched with blood of frogs new dead,
Or jaded cam'st thou from some other's bed."
With that, her loose gown on, from me she cast her;
In skipping out her naked feet much graced her.
And lest her maid should know of this disgrace,
To cover it, spilt water in the place.

Elegia VIII.

Quod ab amica non recipiatur, dolet.

What man will now take liberal arts in hand,
Or think soft verses in any stead to stand?
Wit was sometimes more precious than gold;
Now poverty great barbarism we hold
When our books did my mistress fair content
I might not go whither my papers went.
She praised me, yet the gate shut fast upon her,

I here and there go, witty with dishonour.
See a rich chuff, whose wounds great wealth inferred,
For bloodshed knighted, before me preferred.
Fool, can'st thou him in thy white arms embrace?
Fool, can'st thou lie in his enfolding space?
Know'st not this head a helm was wont to bear?
This side that serves thee, a sharp sword did wear.
His left hand, whereon gold doth ill alight,
A target bore: blood-sprinkled was his right.
Can'st touch that hand wherewith some one lies dead?
Ah, whither is thy breast's soft nature fled?
Behold the signs of ancient fight, his scars!
Whate'er he hath, his body gained in wars.
Perhaps he'll tell how oft he slew a man,
Confessing this, why dost thou touch him then?
I, the pure priest of Phœbus and the Muses,
At thy deaf doors in verse sing my abuses.
Not what we slothful know, let wise men learn,
But follow trembling camps and battles stern,
And for a good verse draw the first dart forth:
Homer without this shall be nothing worth.
Jove, being admonished gold had sovereign power,
To win the maid came in a golden shower.
Till then, rough was her father, she severe,
The posts of brass, the walls of iron were.
But when in gifts the wise adulterer came,
She held her lap ope to receive the same.
Yet when old Saturn heaven's rule possest,
All gain in darkness the deep earth supprest.
Gold, silver, iron's heavy weight, and brass,
In hell were harboured; here was found no mass.
But better things it gave, corn without ploughs,

Apples, and honey in oaks' hollow boughs.
With strong ploughshares no man the earth did cleave,
The ditcher no marks on the ground did leave.
Nor hanging oars the troubled seas did sweep,
Men kept the shore and sailed not into deep.
Against thyself, man's nature, thou wert cunning,
And to thine own loss was thy wit swift running.
Why gird'st thy cities with a towered wall,
Why let'st discordant hands to armour fall?
What dost with seas? with th' earth thou wert content;
Why seek'st not heaven, the third realm, to frequent?
Heaven thou affects: with Romulus, temples brave,
Bacchus, Alcides, and now Cæsar have.
Gold from the earth instead of fruits we pluck;
Soldiers by blood to be enriched have luck.
Courts shut the poor out; wealth gives estimation.
Thence grows the judge, and knight of reputation.
All,[1] they possess: they govern fields and laws,
They manage peace and raw war's bloody jaws.
Only our loves let not such rich churls gain:
'Tis well if some wench for the poor remain.
Now, Sabine-like, though chaste she seems to live,
One her commands, who many things can give.
For me, she doth keeper and husband fear,
If I should give, both would the house forbear.
If of scorned lovers God be venger just,
O let him change goods so ill-got to dust.

---

[1] A very loose rendering of Ovid's couplet—
"Omnia possideant; illis Campusque Forumque
Serviat; hi pacem crudaque bella gerant."

ELEGIA IX.

Tibulli mortem deflet.

If Thetis and the Morn their sons did wail,
And envious Fates great goddesses assail;
Sad Elegy, thy woful hairs unbind:
Ah, now a name too true thou hast I find.
Tibullus, thy work's poet, and thy fame,
Burns his dead body in the funeral flame.
Lo, Cupid brings his quiver spoiled quite,
His broken bow, his firebrand without light!
How piteously with drooping wings he stands,
And knocks his bare breast with self-angry hands.
The locks spread on his neck receive his tears,
And shaking sobs his mouth for speeches bears.
So at Æneas' burial, men report,
Fair-faced Iulus, he went forth thy court.
And Venus grieves, Tibullus' life being spent,
As when the wild boar Adon's groin had rent.
The gods' care we are called, and men of piety,
And some there be that think we have a deity.
Outrageous death profanes all holy things,
And on all creatures obscure darkness brings.
To Thracian Orpheus what did parents good?
Or songs amazing wild beasts of the wood?
Where[1] Linus by his father Phœbus laid,
To sing with his unequalled harp is said.
See Homer from whose fountain ever filled

---

[1] The original has—
　　　"Aelison in silvis idem pater, aelinon, altis
　　　　　Dicitur invita concinuisse lyra."
In Marlowe's copy the couplet must have been very different.

Pierian dew to poets is distilled:
Him the last day in black Avern hath drowned:
Verses alone are with continuance crowned.
The work of poets lasts: Troy's labour's fame,
And that slow web night's falsehood did unframe.
So Nemesis, so Delia famous are,
The one his first love, th' other his new care.
What profit to us hath our pure life bred?
What to have lain alone in empty bed?
When bad Fates take good men, I am forbod
By secret thoughts to think there is a God.
Live godly, thou shalt die; though honour heaven,
Yet shall thy life be forcibly bereaven.
Trust in good verse, Tibullus feels death's pains,
Scarce rests of all what a small urn contains.
Thee, sacred poet, could sad flames destroy?
Nor feared they thy body to annoy?
The holy god's gilt temples they might fire,
That durst to so great wickedness aspire.
Eryx' bright empress turned her looks aside,
And some, that she refrained tears, have denied.
Yet better is't, than if Corcyra's Isle,
Had thee unknown interred in ground most vile.
Thy dying eyes here did thy mother close,
Nor did thy ashes her last offerings lose.
Part of her sorrow here thy sister bearing,
Comes forth, her unkembed locks asunder tearing.
Nemesis and thy first wench join their kisses
With thine, nor this last fire their presence misses.
Delia departing, "Happier loved," she saith,
"Was I: thou liv'dst, while thou esteem'dst my faith."
Nemesis answers, "What's my loss to thee?

His fainting hand in death engrasped me."
If aught remains of us but name and spirit,
Tibullus doth Elysium's joy inherit.
Their youthful brows with ivy girt to meet him,
With Calvus learned Catullus comes, and greet him;
And thou, if falsely charged to wrong thy friend,
Gallus, that car'dst not blood and life to spend.
With these thy soul walks: souls if death release,
The godly sweet Tibullus doth increase.
Thy bones, I pray, may in the urn safe rest,
And may th' earth's weight thy ashes naught molest.

ELEGIA X.

Ad Cererem, conquerens quod ejus sacris cum amica concumbere
non permittatur.

Come were the times of Ceres' sacrifice;
In empty bed alone my mistress lies.
Golden-haired Ceres crowned with ears of corn,
Why are our pleasures by thy means forborne?
Thee, goddess, bountiful all nations judge,
Nor less at man's prosperity any grudge.
Rude husbandmen baked not their corn before,
Nor on the earth was known the name of floor.[1]
On mast of oaks, first oracles, men fed;
This was their meat, the soft grass was their bed.
First Ceres taught the seed in fields to swell,
And ripe-eared corn with sharp-edged scythes to fell.

---

[1] Threshing-floor ("area").

She first constrained bulls' necks to bear the yoke,
And untilled ground with crooked ploughshares broke.
Who thinks her to be glad at lovers' smart,
And worshipped by their pain and lying apart?
Nor is she, though she loves the fertile fields,
A clown, nor no love from her warm breast yields:
Be witness Crete (nor Crete doth all things feign),
Crete proud that Jove her nursery maintain.
There he who rules the world's star-spangled towers,
A little boy, drunk teat-distilling showers.
Faith to the witness Jove's praise doth apply;
Ceres, I think, no known fault will deny.
The goddess saw Iasion on Candian Ide,
With strong hand striking wild beasts' bristled hide.
She saw, and as her marrow took the flame,
Was divers ways distract with love and shame.
Love conquered shame, the furrows dry were burned,
And corn with least part of itself returned.
When well-tossed mattocks did the ground prepare,
Being fit-broken with the crooked share,
And seeds were equally in large fields cast,
The ploughman's hopes were frustrate at the last.
The grain-rich goddess in high woods did stray,
Her long hair's ear-wrought garland fell away.
Only was Crete fruitful that plenteous year;
Where Ceres went, each place was harvest there.
Ida, the seat of groves, did sing with corn,
Which by the wild boar in the woods was shorn.
Law-giving Minos did such years desire,
And wished the goddess long might feel love's fire.
Ceres, what sports to thee so grievous were,
As in thy sacrifice we them forbear?

Why am I sad, when Proserpine is found,
And Juno-like with Dis reigns under ground?
Festival days ask Venus, songs, and wine,
These gifts are meet to please the powers divine.

ELEGIA XI.

Ad amicam a cujus amore discedere non potest.

Long have I borne much, mad thy faults me make;
Dishonest love, my wearied breast forsake!
Now have I freed myself, and fled the chain,
And what I have borne, shame to bear again.
We vanquish, and tread tamed love under feet,
Victorious wreaths at length my temples greet.
Suffer, and harden: good grows by this grief,
Oft bitter juice brings to the sick relief.
I have sustained, so oft thrust from the door,
To lay my body on the hard moist floor.
I know not whom thou lewdly didst embrace,
When I to watch supplied a servant's place.
I saw when forth a tired lover went,
His side past service, and his courage spent,
Yet this is less than if he had seen me;
May that shame fall mine enemies' chance to be.
When have not I, fixed to thy side, close laid?
I have thy husband, guard, and fellow played.
The people by my company she pleased;
My love was cause that more men's love she seized.
What, should I tell her vain tongue's filthy lies,
And, to my loss, god-wronging perjuries?

What secret becks in banquets with her youths,
With privy signs, and talk dissembling truths?
Hearing her to be sick, I thither ran,
But with my rival sick she was not than.
These hardened me, with what I keep obscure:
Some other seek, who will these things endure.
Now my ship in the wished haven crowned,
With joy hears Neptune's swelling waters sound.
Leave thy once-powerful words, and flatteries,
I am not as I was before, unwise.
Now love and hate my light breast each way move,
But victory, I think, will hap to love.
I'll hate, if I can; if not, love 'gainst my will,
Bulls hate the yoke, yet what they hate have still.
I fly her lust, but follow beauty's creature,
I loathe her manners, love her body's feature.
Nor with thee, nor without thee can I live,
And doubt to which desire the palm to give.
Or less fair, or less lewd would thou might'st be:
Beauty with lewdness doth right ill agree.
Her deeds gain hate, her face entreateth love;
Ah, she doth more worth than her vices prove!
Spare me, oh, by our fellow bed, by all
The gods, who by thee, to be perjured fall.
And by thy face to me a power divine,
And by thine eyes, whose radiance burns out mine!
Whate'er thou art, mine art thou: choose this course,—
Wilt have me willing, or to love by force?
Rather I'll hoist up sail, and use the wind,
That I may love yet, though against my mind.

ELEGIA XII.

Dolet amicam suam ita suis carminibus innotuisse ut rivales multos
sibi pararit.

What day was that, which all sad haps to bring,
White birds to lovers did not always sing?
Or is I think my wish against the stars?
Or shall I plain some god against me wars?
Who mine was called, whom I loved more than any,
I fear with me is common now to many.
Err I? or by my books is she so known?
'Tis so: by my wit her abuse is grown.
And justly: for her praise why did I tell?
The wench by my fault is set forth to sell.
The bawd I play, lovers to her I guide:
Her gate by my hand is set open wide.
'Tis doubtful whether verse avail or harm,
Against my good they were an envious charm.
When Thebes, when Troy, when Cæsar should be writ,
Alone Corinna moves my wanton wit.
With Muse opposed, would I my lines had done,
And Phœbus had forsook my work begun!
Nor, as use will not poets' record hear,
Would I my words would any credit bear.
Scylla by us her father's rich hair steals,
And Scylla's womb mad raging dogs conceals.
We cause feet fly, we mingle hares with snakes,
Victorious Perseus a winged steed's back takes.
Our verse great Tityus a huge space outspreads,
And gives the viper-curled dog three heads.
We make Enceladus use a thousand arms,
And men enthralled by mermaid's singing charms.

The east winds in Ulysses' bags we shut,
And blabbing Tantalus in mid-waters put.
Niobe flint, Callist we make a bear,
Bird-changed Progne doth her Itys tear.
Jove turns himself into a swan, or gold,
Or his bull's horns Europa's hand doth hold.
Proteus what should I name? teeth, Thebes' first seed?
Oxen in whose mouths burning flames did breed?
Heaven-star, Electra, that bewailed her sisters?
The ships, whose godhead in the sea now glisters?
The sun turned back from Atreus' cursed table?
And sweet-touched harp that to move stones was able?
Poets' large power is boundless and immense,
Nor have their words true history's pretence.
And my wench ought to have seemed falsely praised,
Nor your credulity harm to me hath raised.

ELEGIA XIII.

De Junonis festo.

When fruit-filled Tuscia should a wife give me,
We touched the walls, Camillus, won by thee.
The priests to Juno did prepare chaste feasts,
With famous pageants, and their home-bred beasts.
To know their rites well recompensed my stay,
Though thither leads a rough steep hilly way.
There stands an old wood with thick trees dark-clouded:
Who sees it grants some deity there is shrouded.
An altar takes men's incense and oblation,
An altar made after the ancient fashion.
Here, when the pipe with solemn tunes doth sound,
The annual pomp goes on the covered ground.

White heifers by glad people forth are led,
Which with the grass of Tuscan fields are fed,
And calves from whose feared front no threatening flies,
And little pigs base hogsties' sacrifice,
And rams with horns their hard heads wreathed back;
Only the goddess-hated goat did lack,
By whom disclosed, she in the high woods took,
Is said to have attempted flight forsook.
Now is the goat brought through the boys with darts,
And give[n] to him that the first wound imparts.
Where Juno comes, each youth and pretty maid,
Show large ways, with their garments there displayed.
Jewels and gold their virgin tresses crown,
And stately robes to their gilt feet hang down.
As is the use, the nuns in white veils clad,
Upon their heads the holy mysteries had.
When the chief pomp comes, loud the people hollow;
And she her vestal virgin priests doth follow.
Such was the Greek pomp, Agamemnon dead;
Which fact and country wealth Halesus fled;
And having wandered now through sea and land,
Built walls high towered with a prosperous hand.
He to th' Hetrurians Juno's feast commended:
Let me and them by it be aye befriended.

Elegia XIV.

Ad amicam, si peccatura est, ut occulte peccet.

Seeing thou art fair, I bar not thy false playing,
But let not me, poor soul, know of thy straying.
Nor do I give thee counsel to live chaste,
But that thou would'st dissemble, when 'tis past.

She hath not trod awry, that doth deny it.
Such as confess have lost their good names by it.
And hidden secrets openly to bewray?
The strumpet with the stranger will not do,
Before the room be clear and door put-to.
Will you make shipwreck of your honest name,
And let the world be witness of the same?
Be more advised, walk as a puritan,
And I shall think you chaste, do what you can.
Slip still, only deny it when 'tis done,
And, before folk, immodest speeches shun.
The bed is for lascivious toyings meet,
There use all tricks, and tread shame under feet.
When you are up and dressed, be sage and grave,
And in the bed hide all the faults you have.
Be not ashamed to strip you, being there,
And mingle thighs, yours ever mine to bear.
There in your rosy lips my tongue entomb,
Practise a thousand sports when there you come.
Forbear no wanton words you there would speak,
And with your pastime let the bedstead creak;
But with your robes put on an honest face,
And blush, and seem as you were full of grace.
Deceive all; let me err; and think I'm right,
And like a wittol think thee void of slight.
Why see I lines so oft received and given?
This bed and that by tumbling made uneven?
Like one start up your hair tost and displaced,
And with a wanton's tooth your neck new-rased.
Grant this, that what you do I may not see;
If you weigh not ill speeches, yet weigh me.
My soul fleets when I think what you have done,

And through every vein doth cold blood run.
Then thee whom I must love, I hate in vain,
And would be dead, but dead with thee remain.
I'll not sift much, but hold thee soon excused.
Say but thou wert injuriously accused.
Though while the deed be doing you be took,
And I see when you ope the two-leaved book,
Swear I was blind; deny if you be wise,
And I will trust your words more than mine eyes.
From him that yields, the palm is quickly got,
Teach but your tongue to say, "I did it not,"
And being justified by two words, think
The cause acquits you not, but I that wink.

ELEGIA XV.

Ad Venerem, quod elegis finem inponat.

Tender Loves' mother a new poet get,
This last end to my Elegies is set.
Which I, Peligny's foster-child, have framed,
Nor am I by such wanton toys defamed.
Heir of an ancient house, if help that can,
Not only by war's rage made gentleman.
In Virgil Mantua joys: in Catull Verone;
Of me Peligny's nation boasts alone;
Whom liberty to honest arms compelled,
When careful Rome in doubt their prowess held.
And some guest viewing watery Sulmo's walls,
Where little ground to be enclosed befalls,
"How such a poet could you bring forth?" says:
"How small soe'er, I'll you for greatest praise."

Both loves, to whom my heart long time did yield,
Your golden ensigns pluck out of my field.
Horned Bacchus graver fury doth distil,
A greater ground with great horse is to till.
Weak Elegies, delightful Muse, farewell;
A work that, after my death, here shall dwell.

THE END.